POLICE AND YOUTH

This book brings the knowledge gained from the Teen And Police Service Academy (TAPS), which has been implemented internationally to create partnerships with at-risk teens and police, proactively addressing some of the most pressing conditions in their communities.

Readers will learn about the nuances of both youth culture and police culture and will better understand the conflict stemming from race and social class. Straightforward solutions stemming from the President's Task Force on 21st Century Policing are demonstrated to provide useful strategies for communities struggling with police–youth relations. This book is especially germane to Texas schools and law enforcement, which must comply with Community Safety Education Act of Texas. It mandates instruction for all peace officers, high school seniors, those applying for their driver's license, and those required to take corrective driver instruction.

Police and YOUth is ideal as a primer for students, instructors, police officers, and citizens who stand to benefit from improving police–youth relations. It provides the tools needed to educate all parties and ultimately improve relations between police and the communities they serve.

Everette B. Penn, Ph.D. is the Director of the Teen And Police Service Academy and Professor of Criminology at the University of Houston–Clear Lake. This "academic-practitioner" applies theory to practice through programming, research, teaching and training to reduce the social distance between the most at-risk/at-promise youth and police in the United States and abroad. He is the author of over 75 scholarly works, a former Volunteer In Service to America (VISTA), Fulbright Scholar and U.S. Army Officer. He is a certified Master Police Trainer, and the recipient of dozens of awards from governmental agencies, academic and civic organizations. More about Dr. Penn and TAPS Academy can be found at: www.tapsacademy.org.

Shannon A. Davenport, ABD, is a doctoral candidate of Juvenile Justice at Prairie View A&M University. Her research interest includes police and youth relations, police legitimacy, emotional regulation, and at-risk youth. Combining research, teaching, and service, she volunteers with the Teen And Police Service Academy collecting and analyzing data. She is the author of several publications on topics including the "Me Too Movement" and "Social Distance Between Minority Youth and Police."

Routledge Series on Practical and Evidence-Based Policing

Police and YOUth
Everette B. Penn and Shannon A. Davenport

POLICE AND YOUTH

Everette B. Penn and Shannon A. Davenport

Routledge
Taylor & Francis Group

NEW YORK AND LONDON

First published 2022
by Routledge
605 Third Avenue, New York, NY 10158

and by Routledge
2 Park Square, Milton Park, Abingdon, Oxon, OX14 4RN

Routledge is an imprint of the Taylor & Francis Group, an informa business

© 2022 Taylor & Francis

Library of Congress Cataloging-in-Publication Data
Names: Penn, Everette B. (Everette Burdette) author. | Davenport,
Shannon A., author.
Title: Police and youth / Everette B. Penn & Shannon A. Davenport.
Description: 1 Edition. | New York : Routledge, 2021. | Series:
Practical and evidence based policing | Includes bibliographical
references and index.
Identifiers: LCCN 2020049271 (print) | LCCN 2020049272 (ebook) |
ISBN 9781138388581 (hardback) | ISBN 9781138388604 (paperback) |
ISBN 9780429424519 (ebook)
Subjects: LCSH: Police services for juveniles—United States. |
Police-community relations—United States. | Minority youth—
United States.
Classification: LCC HV8079.25 .P46 2021 (print) | LCC HV8079.25
(ebook) | DDC 363.2/30835—dc23
LC record available at https://lccn.loc.gov/2020049271
LC ebook record available at https://lccn.loc.gov/2020049272

ISBN: 978-1-138-38858-1 (hbk)
ISBN: 978-1-138-38860-4 (pbk)
ISBN: 978-0-429-42451-9 (ebk)

DOI: 10.4324/9780429424519

Typeset in Bembo
by codeMantra

Dedicated to my son Regis, an African-American youth who is turning into a Black man! Stay rooted in justice through active-listening, and lead the voice and fairness for people most in-need as you traverse this turbulent American journey.

Everette B. Penn, Ph.D.
Director, Teen And Police Service Academy

CONTENTS

INTRODUCTION

This chapter elaborates on the relationship and interaction between police and youth while understanding the principles and practices of mutual understanding, procedural justice, active listening, and voice. *Police and YOUth* focuses on the interaction between youth 10–24 years of age while also providing a lens for citizens to see themselves and their interaction with law enforcement. The chapter provides six "You's" geared toward readers' demographic that could greatly benefit from reading *Police and YOUth*:

1) You are a police official or criminal justice policymaker.
2) You are a Criminology/Criminal Justice student.
3) You are assigned a task of "doing something about youth."
4) You need to implement a program to respond to a need based on evidence-based resources.
5) You are a parent who needs to understand the issues in the headlines.
6) You are a youth.

Although our focus is the interaction between police and youth, we know the principals of mutual understanding, procedural justice, voice, and active listening are good solid practices for all to use as police interact with youth and adults. In fact, the principals in this book applied to policing just may be able to improve our daily lives as we interact with each other.

There are six **"Yous"** we would like to highlight reading *Police and YOUth*:

1) *You are a police official or criminal justice policy maker.* As a police leader, director, or elected official, you are a policy maker. You determine the actions of many by your decisions. What you say becomes the training and practice

DOI: 10.4324/9780429424519-1

for others. This book helps you understand the realness of this subject by introducing to some (and enlightening for others), the challenges that come from the interaction between law enforcement and youth. This book provides the evidence-based data and research necessary to support your decisions. It enables you to present information on the topic of police and youth confidently in front of constituents, citizens, collaborators, and even cynics knowing that you rely on research, not trends or whims, to better policing, and the relationship to youth and your community.

2) *You are a student of Criminology/Criminal Justice.* Perhaps you are in college or have an interest in developing a sub-field of Youth and Police Studies. Over a 15-week semester, you will learn the history and practices of policing, as well as the persona of being a youth today and how both intersect to create the complex theory, research, and practice in Criminology/Criminal Justice. Just as Juvenile Justice developed to become its own sub-discipline of Criminology/Criminal Justice, so too could Youth and Police Studies advance to become a sub-discipline studying the intersection, conflict, and cohesiveness of youth and police in our society.

3) *You have been assigned the task of "doing something about youth."* We imagine that you received an email from your lieutenant, sergeant, captain, or chief asking you to respond to the following questions so that the chief may brief the public: What programs do you have for our youth? What are you doing to help the youth? How can we stop the youth gang, drug, truancy, crime, alcohol, fill-in-the-blank problem? For you, this book will arm you with the facts to implement a research-oriented program that directly responds to the public's call for more and better interaction between youth and police.

4) *You need to implement a program quickly to respond to a need.* The truth is that emergency situations will arise. Perhaps they do not rise to the point of a Ferguson or Baltimore scenario, but the emergency is real in your jurisdiction, and you need to respond quickly. This book provides you with the resources about evidence-based programming, contact information for further research, and help preparing briefings for decision-makers to implement. We need you to consider how to implement the most appropriate program for your jurisdiction rather than start from square one devising a program, the method, and evaluation.

5) *You are a parent, and you need to understand the issues that make headlines.* Why are youth being shot by police? Why are police shot by youth? Do Black Lives, Brown Lives, Blue Lives, or, for that matter, any lives matter? This book will allow you to appreciate police and youth cultures, to see the contrast and comparisons of the two to understand the tension that exists, and, more importantly, to know that upon completion of the book that there is hope. There are tools that bring the two to mutual understanding and defuse tension to make each contact an example of mutual respect and justice for all.

6) *You are a youth.* Your birth certificate may say you are a teenager or young adult, but your mind races with curiosity and maturity beyond that of your parents when they were your age. For questions that took them hours to answer' you have the information in seconds with just a few clicks on your Smartphone. You are coming of age in a world of instant information, the coronavirus, and the greatest divide between the rich and the poor. You demand to know why youth are disrespected by police and others in authority. For you, respect is earned not given. You desire to be heard by so-called adults, but if they don't hear you, you have your own means of being heard—Instagram, Snapchat, Tick Tok, Twitter, and even Facebook allow you to share your voice. Through your music, style, clothing, and expressions, your story is *your* story. Just because you wear your pants sagging, oversized clothes, and a hoodie does not mean someone has the right to follow you and shoot you down. You know you have the right to go to stores, parks, and neighborhoods no matter your age or skin color, and you want everyone to know you know your rights!

As a criminologist, and consultant to dozens of criminal justice agencies who have trained, taught, managed, and most importantly, listened to youth for over 30 years, the subject of improving the relationship between police and the community is a passion that for lead author Everette Penn combines academic and real-world experiences in order to create solutions for the reader. *Police and YOUth* focuses on the interaction between youth aged 10–24 years of age and law enforcement; but through a wider lens, all citizens can see themselves and their interaction with law enforcement. You–aged 15, 35, or 85–should see yourself in this book as the bridge between community and law enforcement. We call it reducing the social distance, which we define as bridging the gap between police and youth. By better understanding each other, we reduce or even eliminate biases, stereotypes, and differences that come from seeing a person by race, gender, or social class. We strive to see people for the sum of their character and their individual characteristics.

The above is a lot to accomplish in a short book such as this, so it is important for you to feel as if the persons writing the book know what they are saying and know you as the reader. By describing the types of readers, you can see we know who will use this book. Finally, you need to feel confident that the authors are knowledgeable about the subject of policing and youth. Meet your authors:

Everette B. Penn is a Professor of Criminology and former Chair of the Social and Cultural Sciences Department in the College of Human Sciences and Humanities at the University of Houston–Clear Lake. He chaired an interdisciplinary department for programs in Anthropology, Criminology, Cross-Cultural Studies, Geography, Political Science, Public Service Leadership, and Sociology. Before that, he was a founding faculty member of the School of Juvenile Justice and Psychology at Prairie View A&M University. At the turn of the century, he taught in the Ph.D. in Juvenile Justice program (Race and Juvenile Justice) and directed the Masters of Juvenile Justice program. His dissertation for his Ph.D. program was in residential treatment programs for juveniles in Pennsylvania. A graduate of the Ph.D. program in Criminology at Indiana University of Pennsylvania, he has over 75 publications in juvenile delinquency, international education, and crime prevention. His works are found in outlets such as the *Journal of Criminal Justice Education, Criminal Justice Studies, Criminal Justice Policy Review, Police Chief, Houston Chronicle, Chicago Sun-Times, El Paso Times,* and with publishers Carolina Academic Press, Sage, and Routledge.

A strong supporter of international education and exchange, he received a Fulbright to Egypt in 2005 and served on the Fulbright Association Board as the Chair of the Diversity Task Force. He was also a Fulbright Ambassador for the State Department. His belief in reducing social distance stemmed from living in Cairo, Egypt, shortly after the attacks on the United States on September 11, 2001. Dr. Penn has served in leadership positions in both the American Society of Criminology and the Academy of Criminal Justice Sciences, including Chair of the People of Color and Crime. As an academic-practitioner he has been working with youth for over 35 years in various capacities: an academic tutor, U.S. Army Officer, VISTA volunteer (Volunteer in Service to America), criminal investigator, camp counselor, school teacher, juvenile caseworker, camp director, church youth director, mentor, and a college professor teaching juvenile delinquency, race and crime, youth, law, and society. Dr. Penn was raised in Washington, DC, in the 1980s, when the nation's capital was known as the "Murder Capital of the World." He attended college at Rutgers University and had many interactions with New Jersey and Maryland law enforcement as he and classmates traveled along Interstate 95 between New Jersey and Washington, DC. These interactions provided the impetus for his intensity, interest, and research to find solutions to ease the tension between minority youth and law enforcement. After graduating with a BA in Political Science from Rutgers University he would go on to receive degrees and training from the University of Central Texas (now Texas A&M); Leadership Institute for Non-Profit Executives, Rice University; Poverty Research, University of Michigan; and Nonprofit Management, Case Western Reserve University.

Believing there should be a synergy created by the university and the community it serves, Dr. Penn co-founded and leads the Teen And Police Service (TAPS) Academy (www.tapsacademy.org). This 2011 Department of Justice-funded program reduces the social distance between at-risk teens and police internationally. By moving both teens and police through a Texas Education Agency-approved curriculum covering topics such as conflict resolution, police interaction, active shooter, gang involvement, date violence, drug usage, and many other pressing subjects, both groups develop a mutual understanding. TAPS has been externally evaluated and found to be effective to improve understanding and respect among law enforcement, youth, and their communities nationally and internationally. The TAPS curriculum in the form of TEEN POL is approved to grant one high school credit to students in the state of Texas upon completion.

Dr. Penn trains thousands of police officials annually. He has been recognized as a vital source of policy development and training for numerous police departments globally including Houston, Texas; Columbus, Ohio; New York City; St. Kitts; Trinidad and Tobago in the West Indies; and Johannesburg, South Africa to name just a few.

Dr. Penn is the recipient of dozens of recognitions and awards from various organizations including the U.S. Department of State, Fulbright Association, Rice University, Prairie View A&M University, University of Houston–Clear Lake, City of Houston, American Society of Criminology, Academy of Criminal Justice Sciences, National Association of Blacks in Criminal Justice, and Texas Young Lawyers Association.

My co-author is Shannon Davenport. The future Dr. Davenport is 20 years younger than me but brings a great perspective from her experience and up-bringing. She is no stranger to exposure to policing, having come from the city of New Orleans, known as the "Big Easy" because of the partying and excessive drinking that occurs during different events. The behavior can result in a heavy police presence to assure both tourists and locals that their safety is a top priority. With heavy policing, excessive policing can be the outcome. Let us get to know Shannon Davenport. She says:

> Growing up in New Orleans, I have seen the worst and best of policing because of my environment and the exposure to New Orleans culture. I was one of those individuals who did not like the police, and I know some can relate. There was no specific reason why I had a dislike of the police, even though I never really had any interaction with them. I had family members and friends who had negative encounters with police officers, and I guess it was something that I vicariously learned. I always felt that police officers, in general, were given too much authority and used that to their advantage. I would often hear people make the comment, "you're afraid to go after the real criminals because you know they won't back down; instead you want to mess with us and hand out tickets when you should do your job and fight crime." Because of the stories of corruption in the New Orleans Police Department (NOPD), I lacked respect for police officers because I thought they were all crooked. I thought to myself, "how can they enforce the law when they're the ones breaking the law." The NOPD has had a history of corruption over the past 30 years. According to "Frontline: Law and Disorder," an article published by PBS, there was an incident in March 1990 in which a young man who had escaped from a work-release program had a standoff with an NOPD officer and shot and killed him. Once word got back to the other

officers, they were enraged and wanted the young man to pay for his crime. The young man was shot in the arm and eventually apprehended. While being driven to the hospital, officers lined the street, threatening to kill him. He was taken to the First District police station, where the officer who was shot and killed worked. The young man was transported to the hospital after getting into a "scuffle" while at the police station, and X-rays were taken but subsequently lost. The young man was also injected with iodine, to which he was allergic, and he died 13 hours later.

The coroner ruled his death to be consistent with a bad fall, while other autopsies indicated that he was beaten to death. The family of the young man was awarded $333,000 from NOPD in damages after the investigation, one-third of the money going to the officer's family for wrongful death. Civil rights attorney (who is only identified by the last name) Howell describes this incident as "the beginning of the end for this police department, the fact that this could happen in broad daylight, openly." This incident and others received national attention. The *New York Times Magazine* published an article on NOPD describing them as "The Thinnest Blue Line" (Keegan, 1996). The *New York Times* attributed corruption at that time to the moonlighting culture and private security details due to the low salaries. In 1993, new police officers were making only $20,000 per year.

In 2005, Hurricane Katrina hit New Orleans. It was a natural disaster causing damage that the city was unprepared for. The devastation of Hurricane Katrina impacted my life and my family, but this disaster impacted nearly everyone in the city of New Orleans. My family and I hesitated to evacuate when the city was under a mandatory evacuation. We figured we could ride the storm out, and everything would be okay. Little did we know, this storm would change the city of New Orleans forever. My family and I decided at the very last minute to evacuate. I remember it like it was yesterday because I would never have imagined my life would suddenly change. In high school, my older brother gifted me his 1997 Maxima, and that was the car that we decided to take because it was in better condition than the other cars. The trip to Houston, which would typically take five hours, took us 22 hours as we sat in bumper-to-bumper traffic. It was dreadful. It felt like we were never going to make it to our destination. We eventually made it and had to room with 12 other family members in an apartment. I thought it would only be temporary, so at the time, it was not a big deal. We all tried to make the best of the situation, but when we were able to see the aftermath and destruction of the storm, we all knew we would be longer in this predicament. Usually, devastating times bring the family together, where we lean on one another to get through the tough times. Unfortunately, this time divided the family even more because of the egos and pride involved, which prevented unity. I remember an old saying: "We can't achieve anything with the crab in a barrel mentality." That's exactly how I felt when I witnessed the friction among the family, especially since we all had just endured being displaced by Hurricane Katrina. According to the National Geographic, Hurricane Katrina was the second-costliest hurricane to hit the United States behind Hurricane Rita. The hurricane's effects forced many citizens of New Orleans to evacuate, leaving behind cherished memories and family for safety and shelter. Many citizens were forced to relocate temporarily and permanently due to the storm's aftermath because there was nothing left to return to in the city. The aftermath of Hurricane Katrina resulted in more than 1,300 fatalities including an estimated $40 to $50 billion in damages (Amadeo, 2018). Houston became a home for many of the evacuees and myself and my family. During this time, it was a lot to process having to adjust to a new city that was so culturally diverse than what I was accustomed to.

During this time, I had just finished high school and was enrolled at the University of New Orleans. I was ready to begin my college life, and suddenly, it all changed in a matter of days due to the storm. This infuriated me because, like many other young adults going through my developmental process, I thought because you are a certain age, it makes you so-called "grown." However, that was not the case for me and as for many others. In time, my age exposed how immature I was and how much my brain was not fully developed and capable of making rational decisions. Because I lacked the mental capacity to process the severity of the devastation, I was unprepared to deal with the storm's aftermath. At the time, I was incapable of communicating effectively, which led to me not being able to express myself and my emotions effectively either.

I grew up in a household where we did not express emotions and did not have effective communication. Instead of talking out our problems the correct way, we would express ourselves by saying whatever came to mind to convey how we felt at that very moment. The problem with this is that in order to express to someone how you feel, you need time to process what you are feeling and explain it. This mentality only continued to get worse as I got older. I developed bad habits that were not conducive to interacting with others, especially when interacting with any authority figure. This type of behavior hindered me a lot because it caused many people to get the wrong impression of me that sometimes was a lasting impression. The bad habits and behaviors that I learned growing up were not acceptable anymore, and it was something that would continue to hinder me if I did not change it. I realized at the time that when people were giving me constructive criticism, it was not because they were trying to find fault or disrespect me. It was because these people had been where I was and were only trying to help change my trajectory in life to help me become better. This process was one of the most challenging and rewarding at the same time. In retrospect, I was going through the normal developmental process that challenges many of us to make decisions in life that can have an impact on our future. I am just fortunate enough that the right people crossed my path to guide me through this process. Eventually, through a lot of self-reflecting and prayer, I made the necessary adjustments and changes I needed to be productive to make "grown" decisions in my life that delivered positive results needed for me to have this opportunity.

I graduated from the University of Houston-Downtown and received my Bachelor of Science degree in Psychology with a minor in Communication. I continued to pursue my education and received my master's degree in Criminology at the University of Houston–Clear Lake. In 2013, I graduated and began volunteering with TAPS Academy to gain some experience in the field. While working with TAPS Academy, I found my true calling and purpose. I never thought I would be the one to work with police officers because of my dislike and disdain for them, stemming from the stories I had heard about the police growing up. However, working with the police officers in the program helped me to gain a better perspective of the daily challenges they face. It allowed me to appreciate the work they do and their bravery in risking their lives for the lives of others. Working with the program, I gained a sense of family and unity, which is necessary to give back to those in need of the program's services. Helping to spread awareness and provide the necessary information to bridge the gap between citizens and police officers is vital, especially with what is going on today.

I took some time off from school and continued working with the program and decided that in August of 2017, I would enroll in Prairie View A&M University to obtain my Ph.D. in Juvenile Justice. I am currently in the program to receive my Ph.D. in 2021 as I am currently ABD (all but dissertation). I am also the Educational Consultant for TAPS Academy and an adjunct professor at Prairie View A&M University.

The purpose of telling my personal story is to let you know that I am no different from you. Like many, going through the developmental process and the challenges life present allow us to add experiences and memories to our individual growth and development. However, the journey that we all have in common is navigating this thing called "life." Being a co-author of this book will allow me to provide insight that can be relatable when social media is the dominant way of communicating and receiving national news. It will also allow me to provide vital information on how "millennials" are adjusting to the changes that are occurring and what needs to be done to bridge the gap between youth and police.

After reading this book, you will understand:

1. The current state of youth and police relations.
2. The history of policing as related to issues of race and use of force.
3. The youth culture and its challenges with traditional society.
4. The 21st Century Task Force on Policing, its purpose, and its recommendations.
5. The Teen And Police Service (TAPS) Academy, its purpose, and findings to improve relations between youth and police.
6. Policing by TOTALS.
7. That the Community Safety Education Act of Texas is a model for the United States to improve police and citizens relations.
8. Why the authors call for a discipline of Youth and Police Studies.

This book responds to the historic time in American policing from 2012–2020. This is a time when questions about the trust of law enforcement raged from the streets of urban America to the mouth of the President of the United States. This is a time when policing moved from President Obama's policing and community focus to return to a law-and-order approach under President Trump. We hope that this book provides answers and solutions to reduce the social distance between youth, the community, and the police of the United States of America.

1

THE WORLD IS VERY DIFFERENT NOW

2012–2017

During his 1961 inaugural address, President John F. Kennedy stated: "The world is very different now. For man holds in his mortal hands the power to abolish all forms of human poverty, and all forms of human life" (Kennedy, 1961). These words were not excitable hyperbole but stood as a warning to a country with nuclear weapons and the financial resources to eradicate both. As this chapter reflects on the years 2012 through 2017 in American policing, the United States was at a powerful time of change. This was a time when policing looked deep within itself to examine the relationship it had with citizens, especially African-American and Latino men. The questions that still exist today are: How deep did we look? Did we look in the right places? What were the conclusions we reached?

There are times when change comes without warning, and an issue touches the United States unlike any other, which is the relationship between citizens and law enforcement. However, years earlier, in 1991, there was Rodney King. King was the African-American taxi driver who was the victim of the March 3, 1991, beating by Los Angeles police officers. This beating, which was filmed by a nearby stranger, eventually led to the 1992 Los Angeles riots over the acquittal of three of the officers and failure of the jury to decide on the fourth. In the six days of rioting, 63 people lost their lives, and $775 million of insurance claims were filed, making it the costliest civil unrest in the history of the United States (Mulligan, 1992). The federal government prosecuted the officers on civil charges. Two were found guilty, and the city of Los Angeles eventually awarded Mr. King $3.8 million in damages (Mydans, 1994). Mr. King, author of the book *The Riot Within, My Journey from Rebellion to Redemption* (King & Spagnola, 2012) drowned in his swimming pool at the age of 47 on June 17,

DOI: 10.4324/9780429424519-2

2012. As an activist, Rodney King is known for his brief but pertinent question: "Can we all just get along?"

The question of getting along is deeply rooted in feelings of connectedness with each other. Sociologist Emory Bogardus developed the "social distance scale" in the 1920s. It was a tool used to measure attitudes, feelings of warmth, hostility, indifference, or intimacy that one racial group had toward other racial groups (Bogardus, 1925). A significant finding was that as contact and familiarity increase, social distance decreased. Our initial ability to get along with others different from ourselves because of race, ethnicity, religion, age, geographic location, or sexual orientation is hampered by our fight-or-flight response for self-protectionism (Penn, 2013). Our desire to protect ourselves is triggered by our own biases, stereotypes, and damaging preconceived notions we hold about a group and specific persons we interact with from that group.

As this book is being written, COVID-19, caused by a coronavirus called SARS-CoV-2, has resulted in more than 124 million cases worldwide and more than 2.7 million deaths internationally (Worldometer, n.d.), of which more than a half-million occurred in the United States (CDC COVID Data Tracker, n.d.), and the term "social distancing" is being used very differently than when it was formulated in the work of Bogardus (1925). As defined by US government agencies in the coronavirus context, social distancing involves "remaining out of congregate settings, avoiding mass gatherings, and maintaining distance" whenever possible to limit the ability of the coronavirus to spread (Bates, 2020). It should be noted that a more accurate term for removing people from close contact is "physical distancing." In the way Bogardus (1925) and Penn (2013) have used the term, it is more relevant to understanding social distance as the interweaving of psychological beliefs and social constructs created about a racial or ethnic group that causes people to reduce contact with that group purposely. An example of understanding the term "social distance" can be understood through Penn's commercial flight travels. He said,

> I fly often because of speaking engagements and other business related to the subject of police and citizen relations. One airline (you know, the one where you line up in "A" group, "B" group, and the dreaded "C" group) brings the concept of social distancing to life. Now I must admit I am a big Black guy, 6 feet 2, 300 lbs., so it could be my size that deters people from sitting next to me when only middle seats are available. When I am an "A" lister, I choose an open row and take the aisle seat. I purposely look friendly, make eye contact, and allow the middle space to look inviting by not placing anything on the seat. Yet, more often than not, people will go by my seat and sit next to someone from their own race or gender. Often, I end up sitting next to a middle-aged African-American man, interestingly having the same characteristics as myself. The few times a

White man or woman does sit next to me for the short plane ride, there is a constant questioning from my new travel partner: What is your line of work? What book are you reading? Tell me about your family. Are you going home? Is the trip business or pleasure? I answer politely and engage in conversation, but I cannot help but ask myself if this person is asking these questions to separate me from the stereotypes he or she may hold about African-American men. Are the questions and my calming responses a way to counter the fight-or-flight feeling they have? Since we are on a plane, there is no flight (departure) or fight (this would cause unnecessary delay and also the risk of arrest).

(Penn, personal memo)

In October of 2018, this social distance tension was captured on a cell-phone camera as Delsie Gayle, an elderly Black woman, was called "an ugly Black bastard" and "a stupid cow" during a two-minute profanity-filled insult by 77-year-old passenger David Mesher on a flight to London Stansted. In the video crew members could be seen assisting with moving Gayle to another seat, and Mesher was allowed to stay in his seat. Ironically, there was a seat in between them. After Gayle was removed to another seat, the video shows that Mesher calmly stated: "he is all right." Mesher did an interview with ITV's *Good Morning Britain* where he explained how he "probably lost his temper" as Gayle did not get up when he asked her to move. He stated that he is not a racist and asked to be forgiven by Gayle. Gayle also did an interview and vowed never to fly with that airline again and said that what she went through was "awful." Gayle also expressed her disappointment with the incident by saying "I just can't believe in this day and age, this is still going on." See the video: "Ryanair racist who called woman 'black b★★★★★d' says he just lost his temper as he appears on GMB to APOLOGISE for vile rant" (Christodoulou, 2018).

Another example of social distance occurred on the morning of May 23, 2020, in Central Park, New York City. Amy Cooper, a White woman, was walking her dog without a leash. Christian Cooper, a Black man who was birdwatching at the time, asked Ms. Amy Cooper to place her dog on a leash. Christian Cooper started to film the incident. Frantically, Amy Cooper stated: "I'm taking a picture and calling the cops, I'm going to tell them an African-American man is threatening my life" (Ly, Vera, & Ries, 2020).

In the *White Man and the Colored Man: Lectures on the Origin and Variety of the Human Races* (1871), Lombroso (often referred to as the Father of Criminology) states:

Blacks represent the lowest and most primitive race… Even if he (the Negro) is dressed in the European way and has accepted the customs of modern culture, all too often, there remains in him a lack of respect for life of his fellow men, the disregard for life which all wild people have in common… The mentality is furthered in the Negro by his scorn of his white fellow-citizens, and by bestial sexual impulse" (Carroll, 1900).

A litany of works such as *The Negro a Beast: Or, In the Image of God*, 1900 (Carroll, 1900); and other celebrated works of post-slavery United States (1870s–early 1900s) presented the newly freed Black as having "unstable character," "like a baby," and being non-human, more "akin to apes."

Gabbidon (2020), building upon the work of "Negrophobia" (Lawrence, 1987; Armour, 1997), describes this concept as the exaggerated fear of being criminally victimized by Black Americans. Because of the fear, there may be pre-emptive action such as shooting to ward off the attack, as Gabbidon (2020) states, "in a situation where a white person shoots a black person who he or she *thought* [emphasis in original] was a perceived robber, based on statistics and stereotypes that feed into 'Negrophobia'" (p. 133). The thought goes further with the rationale that the courts and perhaps the entire criminal justice system accepts this claim because Blacks lead in two of the eight Uniform Crime Report (UCR) categories: robbery and murder. Implicit bias becomes a norm of thinking to allow the shooting and even killing of a Black man because he can potentially be a robber or murderer. Gabbidon (2020) states the problem with this premise is that "in the socially constructed minds of many whites and some racial minorities, all blacks and Latinos look like potential robbers" and "… crime becomes racialized or, put another way, crime becomes associated with particular racial/ethnic groups" (p. 134).

Unfortunately, the intersection of social distance, race, and policing made for two more cases of national attention with the deaths of Breonna Taylor on March 13, 2020, and George Floyd on May 25, 2020. Breonna Taylor was an emergency room technician and according to the *New York Times* (Oppel, Taylor, & Bogel-Burroughs, 2021), was shot and killed by Louisville police officers during a botched raid. This event became a national exhibit of the racial injustice that occurs with policing in Black communities. The Louisville police had been investigating two men selling drugs in close proximity to Breonna Taylor's home. A warrant was signed on the basis that one of the men used her apartment to receive packages. On the night of the raid, the police broke the door off the hinges, and Breonna Taylor's boyfriend, Kenneth Walker, fired his gun, striking Sgt. Jonathan Mattingly in his thigh, thinking he was an intruder. Brett Hanikson responded by firing several shots blindly into the apartment, striking Breonna Taylor five times. According to *The Courier Journal*, the dispatch log cited that Breonna Taylor did not receive attention for more than 20 minutes after being struck (Duvall & Costello, 2021).

A grand jury in September 2020 indicted one of the former Louisville detectives involved; Brett Hankison pleaded not guilty for wanton endangerment of the neighbors whose apartment was shot into when he fired without a clear sight, hitting the window and glass patio door of Breonna Taylor's apartment.

No charges were announced against the other officers involved, who also fired shots. Four of the detectives received termination letters. However, no one was charged for the death of Breonna Taylor.

George Floyd's murder resulted in protest and riots, creating international attention to the plight of unarmed Black men dying in police custody. According to *The New York Times*, on May 25, George Floyd was arrested after a convenience store clerk called the police to report Floyd had used a counterfeit $20 bill to buy cigarettes. The combined videos from the bystanders and security cameras reconstructed by *The New York Times* show officers violating department policies with actions that turned fatal. George Floyd was pinned down by three officers, unconscious and unable to breathe, which resulted in his death. The day after George Floyd's death, the Minneapolis Police Department fired all four officers involved in the incident. On May 29, third-degree and second-degree manslaughter charges were filed against Derek Chauvin, the officer seen on video pinning George Floyd to the ground. On June 3, prosecutors added a second-degree murder charge against Derek Chauvin and charged the other three officers with aiding and abetting second-degree murder. Derek Chauvin kept his knee on George Floyd's neck for about nine minutes and 29 seconds. There have been some discrepancies with the actual duration of the time that George Floyd was pinned down. This became a national symbol for protectors and a cry for help among the Black community regarding unfair and unequal treatment with law enforcement and Black community members. This incident has resulted in uniting an international community of people, organizations, and corporations demanding fair and equal treatment for all when in police custody (Hill et al., 2021).

The death of Ahmaud Arbery in February 2020 is another example of the effect of social distance and how Blacks are perceived as a threat. Ahmaud Arbery was a 25-year-old Black man gunned down by White residents while jogging in his South Georgia neighborhood. A video went viral of Arbery walking into a house under construction in the neighborhood and running out of it, alarming residents because thefts had occurred in the previous days. Another video was released, which also went viral, revealing the incident that occurred with Gregory McMichael and his son Travis McMichael confronting Arbery because he looked suspicious and out of place, which ultimately led to Arbery's murder. A third White man was involved and was responsible for recording the incident, which implicated him as an accomplice to the murder. The killing of Ahmaud Arbery sparked an outcry from protesters who voiced their frustration about the arrest of the men involved in his murder. They went as far as protesting on the McMichael family's lawn with signs, and some even had weapons. Arrests were delayed because of Georgia's citizen arrest and self-defense statutes, which contributed to a nationwide protest for Ahmaud Arbery (Fausset, 2021). The men were eventually arrested months later.

Social distance causes stereotyping to occur, thus allowing for unfavorable labels, terms, and remarks to be placed on a group of people. We researched,

TABLE 1.1 Street Names for Police and Race

Police	Blacks	Whites	Latinos	Native Americans	Asians
Pig	Coon	Cracker	Spic	Alcoholic	Eggroll
Bacon	Feebleminded	Red Neck	Wetback	Red N★★ger	Yellow
"12," twelves	Ape	Casper	Pepper belly	Red Skin	Tiny-eyed
Hog	Beggar	Dandruff	River N★★ger	Cherry N★★ger	Ching-Chong
"Ls"	Convict	Trailer-trash	Border N★★ger	Blanket A★★	Ninja
Co★★sucker	N★★ger	Privileged	Taco N★★ger	Cowboy Killer	Rice N★★ger
Po-po	Baboon	Bird-Sh★t	Chile Shi★ter	Prairie N★★ger	Yolk
One-time	Colored	Cowf★ck	Orange Picker	Salmon N★★ger	Winky
D★ck	Ghetto	Dried Sh★t	Boarder Hopper	Savage	Seaweed-Sucker

Source: http://rsdb.org/race/blacks; https://newstaco.com/2011/03/29/top-latino-racial-slurs/.

listened, and even asked people what are some of the negative terms used to describe people from other races and ethnicities. See Table 1.1.

The list above is just the start. Penn remembers teaching at a police academy in the United States and arriving before his class to see a board from a previous class for police officers. At the top of the board, the words "What Police Label Residents." The list, in order from one to 10 was: "Turds," "Crackheads," "Babymommas," "CITs (Crisis Intervention Team)," "Hoes," "Bitches and Hoes," "Ma'am/Sir," "Gang-Bangers," "Bums," and "Johns." Perhaps the board at the police academy was part of an exercise in which officers identified their social distancing from the community they serve with the intent to reduce it for better policing in the future. What would the list look like for youth?

When the concept of social distance is understood, used correctly, and ultimately reduced, we learn to see the characteristics of the person rather than the negative images of that group to which a person belongs. We learn to appreciate the similarities we all share rather than to focus on differences. In both airplane examples above, the passengers all shared a common goal: trying to travel from one point to another. Although there may be an uncomfortable feeling sitting next to someone from whom you may feel there is a great social distance, travelers are bound together in an effort to get to a destination by air travel. Thus, Penn's desire to travel from Houston to Dallas is greater than the fight-or-flight feeling that may exist because someone from a different group is sitting next to him. Penn rationalized his thoughts like this: we have a common goal; the flight is just for one hour, let us enjoy the experience. By sitting next to the person and conversing with him or her, we may find we have commonalities in family, business, personal interests, people, vacations, food, or recreational activities.

This book is based on the hypothesis that social distance is why the tension between youth and law enforcement exists, and that tension is exacerbated if the social distance is not reduced between the two groups. Responding to or even overcoming social distance requires positive contact with members from other groups, avoiding people, images, shows, and literature that promote stereotypical beliefs and differences, and a constant focus on the characteristics of the individual rather than sweeping stereotypical views of a group.

Perhaps it is social distance that provides the background for police-to-citizen and citizen-to-police shootings during the timeframe of 2012 to 2017. The unlawful use of force by police officers has been a common complaint from citizens in some of the poorest and most disenfranchised neighborhoods in the United States (Cobbina, 2019; Barlow & Barlow, 2018; Bryant-Davis et al., 2017; Rios & Vigil, 2017; Alexander, 2016; Alexander, 2012; Unnever & Gabbidon, 2011; Penn, Greene, & Gabbidon, 2006). Few, if any, garnered the attention of the United States and the world like the Rodney King case up until 2012 through 2017. Maybe the difference is technology and social media? Today the commonness of people having camera phones and technology allowing images, thoughts, and beliefs to travel virtually anywhere in the world makes events that were hearsay, talk, or legend 15 years ago become an international storyline in a matter of hours. Let us look at just some of these tragic cases demonstrating the social distance between citizens (especially African Americans and Latinos) and law enforcement during this significant period of 2012–2017. By no means are all cases presented here; sadly, each name below represents a tragic loss of life. The authors can only imagine the pain in the hearts of family members and loved ones even years later. We extend our condolences as we hope our text will help to eliminate loss of life in the future.

Trayvon Martin

A new volume of American policing began on February 26, 2012, when 14-year-old Trayvon Martin was killed by a security guard who was instructed by local police not to pursue the "suspicious" looking boy he reported in his 911 call. Yet, the security guard followed, stated he was losing in a fight with Martin and felt his life was in danger. He then used a gun to kill the unarmed Trayvon Martin. He was found not guilty of murder. Although no footage of the event was captured, people swarmed social media in a storm of Facebook postings, tweets, blogs, and other forms of 21st-century technology to start the Black Lives Matter movement. As an organization, the Black Lives Matter movement works internationally to reduce the systematic loss of Black lives.

They affirm Black contributions to society, their humanity, and resilience in the face of deadly oppression. Thus, the organization puts its sweat, equity, and love for Black people into creating a political project—taking the hashtag off social media and into the streets. According to BlackLivesMatter.com, the call for Black lives to matter is a rallying cry for ALL Blacks striving for liberation (About Black Lives Matter, 2020).

Andy Lopez

In October 2013, Sonoma County, California, sheriff's deputies Erick Gelhaus and Michael Schemmel were on patrol in their vehicle. On October 22, 2013, in Santa Rosa, California, 13-year-old Andy Lopez walked through a vacant lot carrying an Airsoft pellet gun that was designed to resemble an AK-47 assault rifle. Gelhaus opened fire on Lopez, presumably mistaking the Airsoft gun for a real firearm. The shooting prompted many protests in Santa Rosa and throughout California (Colton, 2013).

Eric Garner

On July 17, 2014, New York City police officers approached Eric Garner in Staten Island, New York City, who was selling single cigarettes without the tax stamp. He stated he was tired of being harassed and that he was not selling cigarettes. The officers tried to arrest Garner. Garner resisted. Officer Daniel Pantaleo then put his arm around Garner's neck, applying an illegal chokehold for 15–19 seconds while arresting him. Pantaleo denied applying a chokehold, but video on the scene as well a New York City Medical Examiner's Office report stated the cause of death was compression of the neck, compression of the chest, and prone positioning during physical restraint by police. New York Police Department policy prohibits the use of chokeholds. Garner laid on the sidewalk after the chokehold was applied, stating "I can't breathe" 11 times. Contributing conditions included acute and chronic bronchial asthma, obesity, and hypertensive cardiovascular disease. On July 13, 2015, an out-of-court settlement by the City of New York paid the Garner family $5.9 million for the death of Eric Garner (Snyder et al., 2017).

John Crawford III

On August 5, 2014, 911-caller Ronald Ritchie told police a man was in Beavercreek, Ohio, Walmart, pointing a rifle at shoppers inside the store. Police arrived in the toy aisle to find 22-year-old John Crawford III holding what they believed to be a weapon and talking on his cell phone. When asked to do so, Crawford failed to drop the "weapon," and Beavercreek police officer, Sean Williams, shot Crawford dead as he talked to his mother on his cell phone.

The perceived deadly weapon was an air pistol. A grand jury did not indict the officers involved (Lawson, 2015).

Michael Brown

On August 9, 2014, 18-year-old Michael Brown was killed by a Ferguson, Missouri, police officer. No footage of the actual event between the officer and Brown was captured, but the image of his lifeless body was transmitted internationally through technology and social media platforms, reminding viewers of the horrid images of Emmett Till in Money, Mississippi, 59 years earlier. Till's death became an important Civil Rights Movement image, as his mother, Mamie Till, stated she wanted an open casket for her son, "so the whole world could see what they had done to my baby." The concern in the Brown case was the misuse of force by law enforcement. Both a St. Louis County jury and the US Department of Justice concluded the officer shot and killed Brown in self-defense. Yet, protests became nights of riots as the story traveled abroad, and protesters responded to law enforcement with "Hands Up; Don't Shoot!" (Lawson, 2015).

Tamir Rice

On November 22, 2014, two Cleveland, Ohio, police officers, Timothy Loehmann and Frank Garmback, responded to a 911 call stating a Black male "keeps pulling a gun out of his pants and pointing it at people." The caller states, "it is probably a fake pistol." The caller also states, "he is probably a juvenile." This information was not relayed to Loehmann or Garmback, who reported that they both continuously yelled "show me your hands" through the open patrol car window upon their arrival. Loehmann further claimed that instead of showing his hands, it appeared as if Rice was trying to draw: "I knew it was a gun, and I knew it was coming out." In response, the officer shot twice, hitting Rice once in the torso. He died on the following day. The item in Rice's hand was later found to be a toy gun. The prosecution presented evidence to a grand jury. There was no indictment of the officers on the basis that Rice was drawing what appeared to be an actual firearm from his waist as the police arrived. A lawsuit brought against the city of Cleveland by Rice's family was subsequently settled for $6 million (Adamson, 2017).

Officers Rafael Ramos and Wenjian Liu

Five months later, on December 20, 2014, New York City police officers Rafael Ramos and Wenjian Liu sat in their patrol car when Ismaaiyl Brinsley approached the car, took a shooter's stance, and shot and killed both officers through the open window. Later, Brinsley was found dead in a subway station from a self-inflicted gunshot wound. On his Instagram account, Brinsley stated the motive for the killings was to avenge the deaths of Eric Garner and Michael Brown. He stated: "I'm putting Wings on Pigs Today … They Take 1 of Ours … Let's Take 2 of Theirs."

The Michael Brown shooting and other incidents from that year caused international news writers to declare that police officers killing unarmed Blacks was the top news story of 2014 (Jauregui, 2021). Also, in 2014 according to the Officer Down Memorial Webpage, 157 officers lost their lives; 48 by gunfire, 52 by an auto accident, and 57 by other means (Blinder, 2021).

Walter Scott

On April 4, 2015, Walter Scott was pulled over in North Charleston, South Carolina, for a faulty taillight. Although Scott was not a youth, his story has to be told because of the irony and clarity of the case. One retired police chief simply called it "a lynching" (personal communication). The story told by the officer was that a scuffle took place, the officer feared for his life and fired his weapon, killing the 50-year-old Scott. Just a few years ago, this case would have been disposed of as fact because of the officer's sworn testimony. Yet, this case is different because cell-phone video was available. It shows Scott running from the officer for approximately 17 feet and the officer shooting eight times. Scott then falls to his death. Officer testimony made before the video was made public stated that CPR was performed. However, the video shows no CPR being performed on Scott after he was shot. The officer was dismissed from the police force and charged with murder.

In 1985, the Supreme Court of the United States ruled that deadly force can be used only when there is probable cause that the suspect poses a significant threat of death or serious injury to the officer or others (*Tennessee v. Garner,* 1985). In December 2016, a mistrial was the result of the wrongful death of Walter Scott. The result was reached after the jury deliberated for days and failed to reach a verdict. The jury foreman, the only Black on the jury, sent a note to the judge while in deliberation, stating, "It's just one juror that has the issue." Another juror sent a note stating: "I cannot in good conscience consider a guilty verdict" (Alcindor, 2015). A retrial was scheduled in 2017, two years after the incident. Former officer Michael Slager pleaded guilty and received a 20-year sentence. Because technology provided the evidence proving a violation of the fleeing felon doctrine (a law that permits the use of force against an individual who is suspected of a felony and is in flight from apprehension) the City of North Charleston settled the case in October 2015 with a $6.5 million settlement to the Scott family (Alcindor, 2015).

Sandra Bland

In July 2015, Sandra Bland was ordered to get out of her car when she was stopped by a Texas State Trooper outside Prairie View A&M University.

Tensions were high between the officer and Bland from the start. Dash camera video and audio from the trooper's car show how the encounter unfolded. The Department of Public Safety Officer told Bland to put out her cigarette. As it is lawful to smoke during a traffic stop in Texas, she refused. After being asked to get out of the car, the trooper grabbed her and pulled her out of the car. She later died in a Waller County, Texas, jail. According to the police investigation, the death was ruled a suicide. This incident refueled the Black Lives Matter movement as her video captured national and international attention. The incident illustrated the escalating tension between community members during the very stressful experience of police contact. This case, along with other incidents above, provided the impetus for the Community Safety Education Act discussed later in the book (Klein, 2018).

Mario Woods

Mario Woods was shot and killed by five San Francisco police officers in December 2015. According to *The San Francisco Chronicle*, the interaction stemmed from Woods slashing a man in the upper arm. Woods allegedly reached into the car where a man and a female companion were sitting and slashed the man across his left shoulder with a knife. The injured man went to San Francisco General Hospital, where two officers responded to the initial crime scene. The police radioed for back up in search of the assailant. Two officers spotted Woods, who matched the suspect's description. According to one of the officers involved in the incident, when they got out of the car, "the man began to back-pedal." The officers claimed that Woods grabbed a knife out of his jeans pocket while saying, "you're not taking me today." Police shot several beanbag rounds at Woods, but Woods still held on to the knife. When Woods headed toward a bystander who was observing the incident, the officers fired their weapons, resulting in the fatal shooting of Woods (Matier & Ross, 2016). The Department of Police Accountability found that the five officers used unnecessary force, but ultimately concluded the officers had followed policy protocol. This resulted in the officers receiving no discipline because they did not deviate from department policies. The deadly force the officers used could be found in the policy that existed at the time of the incident (Mark, 2020).

Alton Sterling

On July 5, 2016, Alton Sterling, a 37-year-old Black man, was shot dead at close range by two White Baton Rouge Police Department officers in Baton Rouge, Louisiana. Sterling was known as "CD Man." The officers were called to the scene because of a 911 call reporting that a man in a red shirt was selling CDs and was using a gun to threaten people outside the Triple S. Food Mart. The officers tased Sterling after he resisted. He was forced to the ground where two officers got on top of him, attempting to control his arms. One yelled that he was reaching for a gun in his pocket. He was shot six times. Multiple bystanders recorded the shooting. The officers retrieved a loaded .38-caliber revolver from Sterling's front pants pocket (Gay, 2016).

Philando Castile

On July 6, 2016, Philando Castile, a 32-year-old Black American, was in a car with his girlfriend Diamond Reynolds and her four-year-old daughter. Castile was pulled over while driving in Falcon Heights, Minnesota. It was around 9 PM when St. Anthony, Minnesota, police officer Jeronimo Yanez and his partner stopped the car and asked for Castile's license and registration. Castile told Officer Yanez he had a firearm, to which Yanez replied, "Don't reach for it then." Castile said, "I'm, I, I was reaching for... " Yanez said, "Don't pull it out." Castile replied, "I'm not pulling it out." Reynolds said, "He's not... " Yanez repeated, "Don't pull it out," and then shot Castile seven times, while his girlfriend sat in the passenger seat and her daughter was in the back. After the shooting, Reynolds videoed the dying Castile and later posted it on Facebook. On November 16, the Ramsey County prosecutor announced Yanez was charged with three felonies, including second-degree manslaughter. Yanez was acquitted of all charges, claiming on June 16, 2017, that he feared for his own life. Yanez was fired on the same day. The paramedics on the scene of Castile's death did find a gun in his pocket (Erkkinen, 2017).

Officers Lorne Ahrens, Michael Krol, Michael Smith, Brent Thompson, and Patricio Zamarripa

Shortly after the Alton Sterling and Philando Castile deaths, a peaceful protest march occurred on July 7, 2016, in Dallas, Texas. Toward the march's conclusion, Micah Johnson ambushed and fired upon a group of police officers, killing five and injuring nine others. The five officers who died were Lorne Ahrens, Michael Krol, Michael Smith, Brent Thompson, and Patricio Zamarripa. Reports indicate that Johnson was angry over police shootings of Black men and he stated that he wanted to kill White people, especially White police officers. Johnson fled inside a building on the campus of El Centro College, where police sent in a bomb attached to a remote-control robot. This was the first time United States law enforcement used a robot to kill a suspect (Adegbile, 2016).

Deputy Brad Garafola and Officers Matthew Gerald and Montrell Jackson

On July 17, 2016, Gavin Eugene Long shot six police officers in Baton Rouge, Louisiana, in the wake of the shooting of Alton Sterling 12 days earlier. The three officers who died were Deputy Brad Garafola of the East Baton Rouge Parish Sheriff's Office and Officers Matthew Gerald and Montrell Jackson of the Baton Rouge Police Department. Long, an African-American male, was a military veteran who committed the shooting on his 29th birthday (Fox 8, 2020).

Jordan Edwards

On April 29, 2017, police responded to a call in Balch Springs, Texas, around 11 PM that reported several underage kids were walking around drunk. Upon the officers' arrival, they allegedly heard gunshots and became engaged in an "unknown altercation with a vehicle backing down the street towards the officers in an aggressive manner." One of the officers fired multiple shots, striking and killing 15-year-old Jordan Edwards. The Dallas County Medical Examiner's Officer ruled his death a homicide due to a rifle wound to the head. Dallas County District Attorney Faith Johnson released a statement expressing how the honor student's death could have been avoided. The police later admitted the vehicle was not moving toward the officers, but rather away from them. On August 28, Officer Roy Oliver was found guilty of murder (Sullivan et al., 2017).

As noted earlier in the chapter, the Black Lives Matter movement was created to remind individuals of the importance of having the right to live (this includes all lives, especially, Black lives). Alicia Garza, Patrisse Cullors, and Opal Tometi founded the movement on July 13, 2013, in response to cases, some listed above, in which individuals had lost their lives at the hands of law enforcement as a result of social injustice.

Brown Lives Matter was founded based on circumstances similar to the development of Black Lives Matter. Killings of Latino men were going unnoticed, and that needed to be remedied. On February 10, 2015, an unarmed 35-year-old Latino man named Antonio Zambrano-Montes was killed by Pasco, Washington, police in an execution-style shooting. He was unarmed and did not understand English; he was shot dead after allegedly throwing rocks at the police officers (Helsel, 2015). It has been suggested that support for Brown Lives Matter may come from this incident and others not receiving as much attention due to the Black Lives Matter movement (Love, 2015).

Blue Lives Matter was a countermovement created to support the contention that those who are prosecuted and convicted of killing law enforcement should be considered perpetrators of a hate crime. According to *The Washington Post*, Louisiana became the first state in May 2016 to amend hate crime provisions to include law enforcement and firefighters (Guariglia, 2017).

The five-year period of 2012 to 2017 moved the tension between police and citizens to the forefront of news, political campaigns, policy, late-night television, academic research, training, and law-making. With such a focus, the question is: Why did these events occur and capture national and international attention in this period, but by late 2018, few, if any, shootings received national attention? The answer stems from a focus on race at a national level, and common use of available technology.

Issues of race in the United States became a national discourse when Barack Obama became the 44th President of the United States on January 20, 2009 (The Inauguration of President Barack Obama, 2009). African Americans considered it a proud day when a nation bleached with Atlantic Slave Trade, a slavery economy, and segregation overcame its past to elect a Black man as President. Lead author Penn and his family were among the hundreds of thousands braving the cold of January 2009 to witness the historic inauguration. In contrast to the excitement experienced by Penn and his family, a colleague related to Penn what took place on election night in 2008 as she exercised in her suburban Houston gym. As televisions in the gym projected Obama to be President-elect, a White, middle-aged man yelled out, "How the hell did we let this happen?" The authors wonder: Was he referring to the win of a Democrat or the win of a Black man as president of the United States? Throughout Obama's presidency, the United States moved the subject of race relations to the forefront of the national discussion.

The second element adding to the national and international focus on these incidents was the availability of technology. Today most people have access to smartphones with camera and video readily available. Smartphones allow images to be taken and posted internationally in minutes by even the most amateur photographer or witness. In response, police departments have issued body-worn cameras. These cameras are usually designed for hand-held use and are worn on the uniform of an officer recording the events in and around their area while performing law enforcement duties. On December 2, 2014, President Obama proposed that the federal government reimburse localities half the cost of implementing body-worn camera programs. On September 21, 2015, Attorney General Loretta Lynch announced that the United States Department of Justice had disbursed $23.2 million in grants "to expand the use of body-worn cameras and explore their impact" (Gimbel, 2015). The grants were given to 73 local agencies in 32 states. According to *The Washington Post*, "Only a few dozen departments, most of them small" had implemented body-worn camera programs before 2014. In the aftermath of the shootings in Ferguson, Washington, DC, New York, and Los Angeles, pilot programs for body camera implementation commenced nationwide (Hermann & Weiner, 2014).

A 2014 report titled "Police Officer Body-Worn Cameras" by Michael D. White (2014) stated the benefits of body cameras are many because they: (1) increase transparency; (2) increase police legitimacy; (3) deter police from abusive behavior; (4) deter citizens from resisting police initiatives; (5) provide evidentiary support for arrest and prosecution; and (6) become an opportunity to increase police training. For all the benefits of a body camera, the report encourages police departments and states to work with researchers to resolve privacy, officer safety, and health concerns, and increased costs for training and the need to develop policy.

According to the Pew Research Center, around seven in 10 Americans use social media. Social media trends have heavily shaped the ability to connect with others and share news and is used as a platform for entertainment. Since 2011, 69% of all Americans use some platform of social media. Young adults were among the earliest adopters of social media, and the levels continue to increase among older adults. Using social media is almost a daily routine; three-quarters of Facebook users, and around six in ten Instagram users log in daily.

The elements of strain between communities and police officers and the ability to document these incidents through smartphone cameras and proliferate the information through social media have brought a wave of protest in response. Super Bowl Champion quarterback Colin Kaepernick did not stand during the national anthem playing in 2016 during the third preseason game of the San Francisco 49ers. According to an article by Steve Wyche (2016), when Kaepernick was asked about his actions after the game, he stated: "I am not going to stand up to show pride in a flag for a country that oppresses Black people and people of color...."

Later he would change his method of protest to kneeling as a way of being more respectful to former and current United States military members while still maintaining his stance on supporting Black people and fighting against social inequality. Other players joined in during the 2016 season. The act was polarizing, with enough fans opting to boycott games to cause NFL ratings to decline. Kaepernick opted out of the final year of his contract with the 49ers and has not played NFL football since. According to the *New York Daily News*, President Donald Trump "tweeted in," subliminally expressing his disappointment with Kaepernick's method of protesting while directly stating to other NFL players who kneeled during the national anthem "Get that son of a b---- off the field right now. Out, you're fired!" (Slattery & Chia, 2018).

Now deceased Houston Texans owner Bob McNair chimed in on the incident regarding the NFL players protesting by stating, "NFL can't have inmates running the prison." This comment came during a meeting where NFL players were not present; however, an NFL executive and former player Troy Vincent was present and was extremely offended by the comment. Vincent said that in all his years of playing in the NFL—during which, he said, he had been called every name in the book, including the N-word—he never felt like an "inmate" (Stites, 2017).

According to *The Guardian*, in 2018, Colin Kaepernick was honored by Amnesty International for peaceful protest with the Ambassador of Conscience Award for standing up to racial inequality. In response to the player demonstrations, the NFL agreed to commit $90 million over the following seven years to social justice causes (*The Guardian,* 2018). According to CBS News, Kaepernick discussed in a 2015 interview that the shooting of Mario Woods in San Francisco was what inspired him to take a stand against police brutality and social injustices. He created a camp for youth, called Know Your Rights Camp, shortly after the incident with Mario Woods to give back to minority youth by providing knowledge on how to interact with police when coming in contact with them. While Kaepernick has not been selected by any NFL team, with the May 2020 death of George Floyd, sports teams honored the Black Lives Movement with ceremonies, kneeling, and symbols on uniforms in stadiums. The NBA even placed the words "Black Lives Matter" on its basketball courts.

Summary

Social distancing, as used by Bogardus and Penn, provides the foundation for understanding the social constructs of race, gender, social class, and policing in the United States. Although the term is currently being used differently to refer to the distance a person should maintain between them and another person in light of COVID-19, social distance allows us to understand the comfort level we feel toward another group. Social distance is truly the desired distance we have toward others. Most people are comfortable being with people who share common thoughts, values, beliefs, and experiences. Being exposed to others creates feelings of uncertainty and fear. Such fear can create a desire to demonize the unknown and consider the other lesser than or evil. This chapter provided a brief history of some cases that brought the tension between police and youth to the forefront of the national debate between 2012 and 2017. Evidence was brought to us through advancements in technology and social media communication. These cases created an us-versus-them, warlike mentality that promoted the Black Lives Matter movement as a response, to promote the life of a Black person as being as valuable in comparison with persons in other racial and ethnic groups. This chapter summarized the concepts of social distance and race to explain the divide between youth—specifically Black and Brown youth—and the police.

2

AMERICAN POLICING

Yesterday, Today, and Tomorrow

Two weeks after the 2016 presidential election, lead author Everette Penn was on a radio show called *Houston Matters* in Houston, Texas, as part of a six-member panel consisting of the Sheriff-elect Ed Gonzalez; the leader of the Black Lives Matter movement in Houston, Ashton Woods; the executive director and co-founder of the Center for the Healing of Racism, Cherry Steinwender; the Executive Assistant Police Chief of Houston, Michael Dirden; and a local activist, Dr. Assata Richards. The host of the show asked the question: "Since Houston was the fourth largest city in the United States and viewed as the most diverse city in the United States, why has our city not experienced the same racial tension as seen in New York, Los Angeles, or Chicago?" The answers were as diverse as the city itself, but Richards gave the one that stood out for Penn. She explained that people who live in the South are sheltered, and a lot occurs that is unreported. On reflection, we believe the answer is much more substantive. Indeed crime does go unreported, and perhaps because of the history of slavery and segregation, there may be a more docile frame of mind by some citizens toward authority. However, there is a uniqueness in Houston policing that is essential to understanding why police and youth relations have not erupted to the confrontations viewed in so many cities around the United States and the world. The root and foundation are found in the work of Dr. Lee P. Brown, sometimes known as the "Father of Community Policing" (Brown, 2012).

For three decades, from the 1970s through the 2000s, Lee P. Brown served at all levels of law enforcement, including as a beat officer in San Jose, California; Sheriff in Multnomah County, Oregon; Public Safety Commissioner in Atlanta, Georgia; Police Chief of Houston, Texas; Police Commissioner of New York City; the first Director of the White House Office of National

DOI: 10.4324/9780429424519-3

Drug Control Policy; and three terms as mayor of Houston, Texas—all with a Ph.D. in Criminology he earned in 1970 from the University of California at Berkeley. The author challenges readers to find a criminology professional with as much local and federal experience armed with the tools of research coming from a doctoral education. He accurately states in his 2012 book, *Policing in the 21st Century: Community Policing*:

> ...community policing is a concept and not a program. Community policing goes beyond a public affairs unit or specialized officers dedicated to being the law enforcement agencies' face and voice. Community policing is a full-fledged way of conducting business for a department.
>
> *(Brown, 2012, p. 2).*

This spirit of community policing as a practice implemented in the entire police department is a philosophy that still resonates in the Houston Police Department today, decades after Dr. Brown served as mayor and police chief. As a criminologist working with the Houston Police Department for 10 years, Penn has observed that keeping a philosophy of community policing as part of the everyday activities of a large urban police department is not easy. Houston is not without its faults when it comes to the use of force, questionable shootings, and strained police–citizen interactions, as will be discussed later in the text, yet it does present a model of entrenched community policing that has provided dividends for improved police–citizen relations. Let us look at the history of policing to understand these challenges and the legacy of policing in the United States.

History of American Policing

The history of American policing can be divided into six stages: the Early Policing Era (before the 1900s); the Political Era (late 1800s to 1930); the Professionalism Era (1930s to the early 1980s); the Get-Tough Policing Era (mid-1980s through 1994); the Community Policing Era (1995 through 2015); and the 21st-Century Policing Era (2015 to the present). A book could be written on any one of these stages, and many books go more extensively into the history of policing. Instead, we will take just a few pages to provide an overview of each, leaving the last stage—21st-Century Policing—for the latter part of this text.

The Early Policing Era: Before the 1900s

American policing has its origins in England. The early practice of policing started with tithing, in which 10 families would band together for protection and then work to maintain order. Through self-policing and protection, they established rules to maintain civility (Tilly et al., 1975).

This system would lead to the Home Rule practice in 1066 in which 55 military districts would band together, forming shires. One officer was charged with keeping order; thus, the term "shire-reeve" or sheriff (Uchida, 1993). The practice continued with freemen pledging loyalty to the king, which was called the Frankpledge (Morris, 1910). These freemen were obligated to participate in the watch system, in which shifts were established to watch over a specific area. If the person on watch saw an offense take place, he would let out the "hue and cry" to which all were to respond. Soon the practice led to people paying others to take their watch shift. Finally, this practice gave way to both a night and day watch system by paid staff, eventually leading to what we see today as a paid police force protecting an entire city night and day (Miller, Hess, & Orthmann, 2013).

Students of policing in the United States know that Sir Robert Peel of England provided the basis for what we call police administration today. As Home Secretary, Peel introduced the Metropolitan Police Act in 1829, which created the London Metropolitan Police, which is identified as the first modern police department by many historians and scholars (Uchida, 1997; Miller, Hess, & Orthmann, 2013). Peel believed that policing should involve crime prevention and social assistance (Lentz & Chaires, 2007). Due to individual authority, each police officer established local standards for the formal control used when interacting with citizens. For example, according to Uchida (1997), police intervention relied on institutional legitimacy, whereas informal control of policing consisted of personal discretion that helped develop legitimacy among the citizens. This resulted in different policing in different neighborhoods. Uchida (1997) explains how police officers in New York were free to act as they wished, as long as it met the public's expectations. If citizens disagreed with certain actions, it could have resulted in a lack of legitimacy. Early policing wrestled with the same issues that contemporary policing battles today: legitimacy, infringement of individual rights, power of the officers, and use of force. The brave officers of early law enforcement were viewed as semiskilled labor, and to their chagrin, they were often ignored or insulted. Acknowledging the trepidation the public had toward policing, Peel felt that police would succeed only if they had the public's approval, and that would be achieved through a better-quality officer. With his guidance, the London Metropolitan Police established *Peel's Principles*. They are found below and can be viewed as the commandments of policing.

1. The mission of the police is to prevent crime and disorder.
2. The police's ability to perform their duties depends on the public's approval of their existence, actions, and behavior as well as earning the public's respect.
3. Earning the public's respect and approval includes gaining their cooperation in observing all laws.

4. High levels of public cooperation result in low levels of physical force by police.
5. Police strive for and sustain public favor not by catering to public opinion but by constantly demonstrating absolute impartial service to the law and to all members of the public, regardless of social standing.
6. Physical force should only be used when persuasion, advice, and warning have failed to induce compliance or restore order; only the minimum amount of force necessary should be used to achieve the police objective.
7. At all times, police should maintain a relationship with the public that honors the historical tradition that the police are the public and the public are the police, the police being only members of the public who are paid to give full-time attention to duties which are incumbent on every citizen in the interests of community welfare and existence.
8. Police should strictly adhere to their function and never appear to usurp the judiciary's powers to avenge individuals or the State, judge guilt, and impose punishment.
9. The test of police efficiency is the absence of crime and disorder, not the police action in dealing with it.

Other points by Peel included:

- The police must be stable, efficient, and militarily organized under government control.
- The absence of crime will best prove the efficiency of the police.
- Crime news must be widely distributed.
- Territorial distribution of the force by hours and shifts must be accomplished.
- No quality is more indispensable to an officer than a perfect command of his temper; a quiet, determined action has more effect than violent action.
- Good appearance commands respect.
- Proper securing and training of personnel lie at the root of police efficiency.
- Public safety requires that a policeman be given a number.
- Police headquarters should be centrally located and easily accessible to all people.
- Policemen should be appointed on a probationary basis.
- Police records are necessary for the correct distribution of police strength.
- The best way to select men is to size them up and then find out what their neighbors think of them.

While reading Peel's words as they applied to London in the early 1800s, the importance of these guiding principles resonates today. Almost 200 years ago the relationship between police and the public was paramount. Peel instructs that "the ability of the police to perform their duties depends on the public's approval...." He also states, "that there should be a use of physical force only when persuasion, advice, and warning have failed...." This is sage advice for policing today.

Original policing in England gave life to the development of policing agencies in the United States, with Philadelphia starting in 1837, Houston also in 1837, Boston in 1838, and New York City in 1844. These early police force members often had no uniform or badge as they tried to follow Peel's Principles. To truly understand early policing in the United States, we must move the calendar back to 1720 to appreciate the coming together of race and policing in the United States. Over 100 years before policing would begin in large cities, the earliest policing in the United States had its very foundation in the control of African Americans.

The first Africans were brought to the United States as slaves in 1619. Roughly, 12 million people were taken and sold into slavery; however, half did not survive the journey. For those Africans who survived the Middle Passage, a six-week horrific journey chained together in the hulls of slave ships after being taken from their homelands in western Africa, these human beings were considered the property of their White slave owners. The conditions of the voyage were unbelievable. The slaves were branded with hot irons, and 300 to 400 individuals were often confined to an area of less than five feet of headroom, with no ventilation; with no space for a bucket for human waste, diseases were at an all-time high, resulting in the death of many slaves (American History USA, n.d.).

Thus, when one of the slaves attempted to achieve freedom from slavery by running away from captivity, he or she was considered stolen property in deed and in law. The financial loss for the White slave owner was great. A male slave was estimated to cost $20,000 in 2011 dollars, with a cook being worth 20% more, a carpenter 45% more, and a blacksmith 55% more. Thus, a runaway slave was considered $30,000 or more of stolen property (Williamson & Cain, 2011). The White slave owners needed a force to capture and return their highly valued property. The response was the first modern police force in the United States: the slave patrols of South Carolina in 1704 (Walker & Katz, 2012, p. 32). Hadden (2001) documents that privately paid slave catchers were initially employed even earlier in the 1640s. In 1686 a South Carolina statute authorized any White person to apprehend and send home any slave who did not have permission to travel. Apprehending and returning slaves became a duty, punishable by fine if the White person did not comply. In 1712 "An Act for the Better Ordering and Governing of Negroes and Slaves" stated that the children of all slaves, to include "negroes, mulatoes, mustizoes, or Indians" would be slaves. It was punishable by whipping any slave leaving their plantation without a written pass. This law required every slave owner to have their slave quarters searched every 14 days for "future and runaway slaves, guns, swords, clubs, and any other mischievous weapons," as well as possible stolen goods (Barlow & Barlow, 2018; Rothenberg, 2007; Websdale, 2001). This law became the model for slave codes and control of African slaves throughout the South (Rothenberg, 2007). By 1750 every Southern city had a form of slave patrol to return the stolen property (or, more accurately, a human being fleeing the horrific conditions of slavery) (Foner, 1975).

Thus, the origin of policing in the United States had its very essence in race as police agents were used to capture and bring back to slavery Black men, women, and children running to freedom.

The Political Era: Late 1800s to 1930

As police departments began to appear in urban areas of the United States in the mid-1800s, a period of political dominance developed as winners of political office often had spoils to share with those who had assisted in their election and rise to office. During this time of the Industrial Revolution, immigrants from Europe, as well as migrants from the South (mainly Blacks leaving the agrarian, Jim Crow South), made their way to cities such as New York, Philadelphia, Boston, and Chicago. The movement of these immigrants and migrants in search of a better life promoted the study of the city and criminal activity. Through his Atlanta School work in the 1890s, W.E.B. Du Bois was one of the first American social scientists to look to sociological factors (age, social class, poverty, education level, discrimination, and environment) to explain criminality (Du Bois, 1899/1966). He followed the work of Quetelet from France who produced some of the first scientific work on crime. This marked a shift in believing that biological traits such as race were causal factors of crime (Beirne, 1987).

W.E.B. Du Bois's work is found in his seminal *The Philadelphia Negro: A Social Study* (Du Bois, 1899/1966). Although most credit for the study of urban crime and environmental factors is given to the Chicago School theorists, it must be noted that Du Bois's work was published decades before pivotal pieces such as *Introduction to the Science of Sociology* by Park and Burgess (1924); "The Growth of the City" by Burgess (1925); *Social Factors in Juvenile Delinquency* by Shaw and McKay (1931); and *Juvenile Delinquency in Urban Areas* by Shaw and McKay (1942). The focus of these pieces was to build the scientific study of crime using sociology. Using official data such as crime reports, and other government documents, geographical layouts indicating social ills such as high crime, truancy, and poverty were found (Williams & McShane, 2018). In addition, life histories and case studies were developed to learn more about the lives of the poor, racial groups, less educated, delinquents, criminals, and addicts through scientific observation and participation (Williams & McShane, 2018).

A key element to grasp when looking at crime in urban areas is social disorganization. Park, Burgess, and McKenzie (1925) and Shaw and McKay (1942) looked at major cities such as Philadelphia and Chicago and created concentric zones radiating from the center of the city and outward. The first zone in the middle part of the city was the central business district. It was here where the factories and businesses that attracted the immigrants and migrants to the city were found. Few people lived in Zone 1, otherwise known as the Loop or central business district (Park & Burgess, 1925).

The worker lived in the primary location of study for the Atlanta and Chicago Schools: Zone 2, known as the Zone of Transition. Here places to live were cheap and close to the factories, two desirable characteristics for the worker. Within Zone 2 they found a characteristic of social disorganization as described by Shaw and McKay (1942). They based the concept of social disorganization on primary relationships and being loyal to an area. If residents had strong family ties, social networks, and a sense of ownership or care for the neighborhood, then the area was considered a socially organized community. Without these characteristics, an area was viewed as socially disorganized. These areas consisted of characteristics including (1) low economic status, (2) a mixture of different ethnic groups, (3) highly mobile residents moving in and out of the area, and (4) disrupted families and broken homes. They found that socially disorganized areas consistently had higher crime rates than socially organized areas. Conflict, decay, high mobility, disease, addictions, prostitution, gambling, and other "ills of the city" made urban life in the early 1900s undesirable for most, yet it was required for many as they came to the cities to improve their financial status and followed a trend that would continue for decades: moving out of Zone 2 as soon as their income and resources allowed.

Whether it was John from London, England, or LeRoy from Durant, Mississippi, the reality was the same; during this period newcomers to the industrialized cities of the United States worked long hours with little protection, and what protection the worker did have often had its origins in a patronage system based on corruption inside and outside of the police department (Reiss, 1992).

The Professionalism Era: 1930s to the Early 1980s

August Vollmer is known as the "father of American policing" for his work in raising the level of professionalism in police work. In the 1930s, policing moved away from a political system of rewards and spoils to incorporate trained professionals, such as the Federal Bureau of Investigation (FBI), founded on July 26, 1908, which enforced federal law and coordinated judicial policy. The federal government used the FBI as a tool to investigate criminals who evaded arrest and prosecution by crossing state lines. During this time, the Uniform Crime Report (UCR) system began.

Standards of operation, procedures, and protection of legal rights dominated this time period, as courts provided protection of due process. The concern was the fairness of policing to all people regardless of factors such as race, ethnicity, gender, age, or social or economic status.

It was the social-historical events of the 1940s through the 1980s that created the issues of urban decay, African-American and minority settlement in cities, and a continued timeline of differential treatment of African Americans, resulting in the tension faced by modern policing. A paramilitary style was introduced by military veterans entering policing and gaining positions of leadership. What these leaders learned in World War II, Korea, and Vietnam were tactics that reflected an us-versus-them approach. Local police enforced vagrancy, poll taxes, convict leasing of prisoners, and the targeting of particular groups of people. According to Vitale (2018), from 1962 to 1974 the United States operated international police training emphasizing counterinsurgency and the use of espionage, bomb-making, and interrogation techniques. Many of the trainers and techniques were employed in the Drug Enforcement Agency (DEA) and FBI, and in local police practices, bringing international Cold War practices to be used against citizens in the United States.

First, the importance of World War II on modern policing must be appreciated. Not only did service members apply their military training to policing in order to create a paramilitary organization, but veterans coming home earned benefits from the G.I. Bill, which transformed American cities and the suburbs that surrounded the socially disorganized areas with the highest crime rates.

The G.I. Bill gave service members returning home from World War II (1941–1945) medical care, as well as educational and housing loan benefits for having served. Those who wished to continue their education could do so tuition-free while also receiving a cost-of-living stipend (Serow, 2004). This opened the door for veterans to receive government loans to purchase a home, business, or farm. These loans enabled veterans and their families to leave the crime-prone Zone 2 city life and move to the suburbs. In 1947 almost 49% of college admissions were veterans using their G.I. Bill benefits (Serow, 2004). The power of the millions of veterans using their new benefits reshaped the United States. College and trade school admissions rose dramatically, and the birth of the suburbs began, as "cookie-cutter" communities developed in Zones 3, 4, 5, and 6 to accommodate the newly educated, trained, and financially backed veteran. Thus, it spawned the great prosperity of America of the 1950s. Here the "greatest generation" (Brokaw, 1998) enjoyed economic growth, as reflected by shows such as *Leave it to Beaver, Father Knows Best,* and *Make Room for Daddy* that depicted male-earning households in which the women stayed home tending to the house and children (Blakemore 2019). Former President Donald Trump refers to this time in his statement: "Make America Great Again!"

Although the G.I. Bill extended benefits to all veterans, it helped White male veterans prosper and accumulate wealth in the post-war years far more than veterans of color, as will be shown later in the book. In fact, the wide disparity in the bill's implementation ended up helping drive growing gaps in wealth, education, and civil rights between White and Black Americans.

As employment, college attendance, and wealth surged for Whites, disparities with their Black counterparts not only continued but widened. There was, writes historian Ira Katznelson, "no greater instrument for widening an already huge racial gap in post-war America than the GI Bill." (Blakemore, 2019).

When lawmakers began drafting the G.I. Bill in 1944, some Southern Democrats feared that returning Black veterans would use public sympathy for veterans to advocate against Jim Crow laws. To make sure the G.I. Bill largely benefited White people, the lawmakers drew on tactics they had previously used to ensure that the New Deal helped as few Black people as possible. Mississippi Congressman John Rankin served as the Chair of the House Veterans Committee. Rankin was known for his virulent racism: he defended segregation and opposed interracial marriage; during World War II he proposed legislation to confine, then deport, every person with Japanese heritage, and even proposed (unsuccessfully) a provision to exclude Blacks from receiving the unemployment entitlements in the G.I. Bill. As the congressmember leading the G.I. Bill through the US Congress, he insisted that the program be administered by individual states instead of the federal government. This provided for fewer controls making way for tactics including intimidation, misinformation, lack of information, physical attacks, lynching, and even the refusal to mail the proper forms to Black veterans (Blakemore, 2019).

While the G.I. Bill's language did not specifically exclude Black veterans from its benefits, it was structured in a way that ultimately shut doors for the millions of Black veterans who had bravely served their country. The post-war housing boom provides an example, as it almost entirely excluded Black Americans, as Whites moved to the suburbs, Blacks remained in cities that received less and less investment from businesses and banks. Instead of being administered by the federal government, the G.I. Bill, which granted low-interest mortgages, was set up so White-run financial institutions issued the loans, often refusing to make loans to Black people. For example, in 1947, only two of the more than 3,200 home loans guaranteed by the Department of Veterans Affairs (VA) in 13 Mississippi cities went to Black borrowers. "These impediments were not confined to the South," noted Katznelson. "In New York and the northern New Jersey suburbs, fewer than 100 of the 67,000 mortgages insured by the GI bill supported home purchases by non-whites" (Blakemore, 2019).

For those Blacks who received loans, redlining was the next obstacle. This decades-old practice of marking maps by race to characterize the risks of lending money and providing insurance made purchasing a home even more difficult for Black veterans. Lenders froze out more impoverished neighborhoods, ensuring that loan assistance and insurance would be denied. Neighborhoods were also free to write racist restrictions to deny people from purchasing homes. A 1939 covenant in Houston Texas, stated: "None of the lots in said addition shall ever be sold, conveyed, leased, or devised to any person or persons other than of the Caucasian race" (Werner, 1984). This was legal until the Fair

Housing Act of 1968, which prohibited unlawful discrimination in housing based on race, color, sex, national origin, or religion.

Black veterans in search of the education they had been guaranteed via the G.I. Bill fared no better. Many Blacks returning home from the war did not even try to take advantage of the Bill's educational benefits. Because of lower wages and fewer economic opportunities, they could not afford to spend time in school. Those desiring to go to college soon learned their segregated public-school education provided poor preparation.

Additionally, those with the economic and educational footing to apply for a college education faced another obstacle. Northern universities dragged their feet when it came to admitting Black students, and Southern colleges barred Black students entirely. James Meredith needed a Presidential decree and National Guard Troops to attend the University of Mississippi as the first Black student in 1962. Autherine Lucy was expelled from the University of Alabama in response to the riots of Whites when she entered in 1956. Rice University, one of the most prestigious universities of the South, did not admit its first Black student until 1965. The VA itself encouraged Black veterans to apply for vocational training instead of university admission, and arbitrarily denied educational benefits to some students. Thus, the Historically Black Colleges and Universities (HBCUs) of the South were the paths taken by most of the Black veterans in the 1940s, 1950s, and 1960s. A full 95% of Black veterans were sent to Black colleges—institutions underfunded and overwhelmed by the influx of new students. Most of the colleges were unaccredited, and thousands of Black veterans were turned away (Blakemore, 2019). Historian Hilary Herbold writes: "Though Congress granted all soldiers the same benefits theoretically, the segregationist principles of almost every institution of higher learning effectively disbarred a huge proportion of Black veterans from earning a college degree." As employment, college attendance, and wealth surged for Whites, disparities among their Black counterparts not only continued but widened. Today the generations of benefits stemming from the application of the G.I. Bill leaves gaps in income: the median income for White households in 2017 was $68,145, according to the United States Census; for Black households, it was $40,258 (Blakemore, 2019).

Poverty and living in socially disorganized areas provide a well-tested theoretical foundation for crime (Shaw & McKay, 1942; Elliott & Merrill, 1934; Burgess, 1925; Du Bois, 1899/1996). As described above, Blacks were restricted from moving to suburban neighborhoods and were forced to remain in the city as Whites fled to the suburbs. Social disorganization (Shaw & McKay, 1942) is the major premise that allows us to understand crime in urban areas. Although concentric zones are not as pronounced today as in the early 1900s, socially disorganized areas today are often called "hot spots," and they have the same characteristics of (a) fluctuating or transient populations; (b) significant number of families on welfare; (c) families renting; (d) several ethnic groups in one area; (e) high truancy rates; (f) high infant mortality rates; (g) high rates of unemployment; (h) large number of condemned buildings; and (i) a higher percentage of foreign-born and African-American heads of families; as well as single female-headed households. These ills of the city combined to make for the social unrest of the 1960s, as conflict between those with means to leave Zone 2 developed between those stuck, blocked, or without opportunity to leave the zone.

It was a time when thousands of Americans experienced a series of social injustices, and the social unrest resulted in riots. The riots were a result of the underlying issues of discrimination and government intimidation that plagued the country around this time. Some riots, such as those in Detroit in 1967, were among the most violent and destructive in the United States history. From 1964 to 1971, there were approximately 750 riots that resulted in 228 killings and 12,741 people injured (Postrel, 2004). Americans were concerned about their civil liberties, giving rise to the civil rights movement, which organized protests against the police and government. Dr. Martin Luther King Jr. was one of the civil rights movement leaders during this time and was assassinated due to his involvement in the fight against social injustice and segregation. King's initiative helped to influence the Civil Rights Acts of 1964 signed by President Lyndon B. Johnson and the Voting Rights Act of 1965, which was memorable because it signified a major victory against racial inequality and social injustice. President Johnson also created the Commission on Law Enforcement and Administration of Justice in 1966, a group of 19 individuals appointed to study the criminal justice system. This spearheaded the "war on crime" because of the tumultuous period of the 1960s. A final report, "The Challenge of Crime in a Free Society," was created from the efforts of the Crime Commission, which was comprised of hundreds of advisors and consultants using data to address the needs and the necessary changes in policing, the courts, and corrections (President's Commission on Law Enforcement and Administration of Justice, 1967).

William Julius Wilson captured the strain on the urban areas in the 1970s and 1980s in his 1987 work, *Truly Disadvantaged* (Wilson, 1987). Wilson moves the social understanding further by explaining how Whites and other ethnic groups quickly moved out of Zone 2 conditions and how they built up the suburbs while African Americans did not leave the urban cities as fluidly. Discrimination, opportunity, resources, and income explain the different patterns of exiting and explains why many African-American families were trapped in Zone 2 conditions. Those that could move did. With them left the "social buffers" of conformity, increased economic stability, and examples of manhood and family; what was left were voids in the lives of children, youth, and young people without a "village," an African proverb concept that strongly encourages the collectiveness of an entire community to be hands-on when raising children, youth, and young people (African Proverbs, 2019). Within the African-American population, heterogeneous characteristics were developed that made for more division, less social control, and greater divides in income and resources. Since factories and other providers of job-to-career opportunities left Zone 2 because of social unrest, the income opportunities were limited to service economy jobs in fast food and retail stores and manual labor. The poor became poorer.

"Warrior policing" became the practice in the socially disorganized economic ghettos of the major urban areas of the United States. Warrior policing stems from the paramilitary policing style that developed in America soon after World War II. As veterans filled the ranks of police departments, they brought policing tactics and a frame of mind synonymous with war. Significant developments occurred in the 1950s and 1960s to professionalize policing, but what also developed were practices of stop and frisk, zero tolerance, and saturated patrols. Police used a wide net in hot spots and often caught "dolphins" as they searched for "tuna," as average citizens were questioned and arrested along with career criminals. Indiscriminate suppression of criminal activity and alienation of the local residents caught up in these crackdowns began to undermine police authority, credibility, and respect. Such methods caused a questioning of police legitimacy. This occurred in urban areas filled with the African-American poor trapped in socially disadvantaged areas that became hot spots of crime. William Julius Wilson (1987) called them the "truly disadvantaged."

People who could escape from these areas fled to new suburban neighborhoods, taking with them a wariness of police. Those leaving for greener pastures would be replaced by a new generation, plagued by crime and distrustful of the police. The law-abiding people of these urban communities tried to mind their own business, staying away from criminals and police alike. Criminal activity flourished, unrestrained by social convention or police activity. In the absence of citizen input, the police found no reason to abandon their tried-and-true warrior police methods (Penn & King, 2016).

Compounding the already dismal economic conditions faced by Blacks in the urban cities of the United States, post-World War I through the 1980s, was the single female-headed Black households that continued to rise, from 18% in the 1950s to 40% in the 1980s.

Damaske, Bratter, and Frech (2017) conclude that single female-headed households face higher unemployment and low educational and work experience levels. Cohen (1955) describes the outcome for youth who are frustrated by their status of being poor and living in socially disorganized areas. Unable to meet the "middle-class measuring rod/values" of ambition, individual responsibility, educational achievement, deferred gratification, rationality, manners, courtesy, personality, avoidance of aggression and violence, the pursuit of hobbies, and respect for property, they establish their own values, often looking to delinquency and crime to achieve status.

A new economy developed to support the lack of legitimate income in households. Young Black adults were not working consistently enough to earn

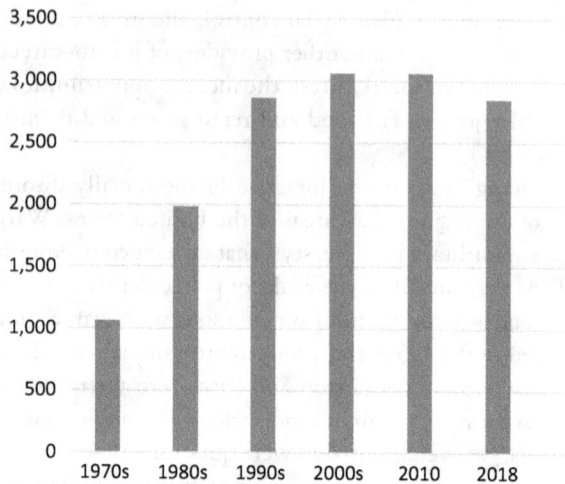

FIGURE 2.1 BLACK FEMALE-HEADED HOUSEHOLDS (NUMBERS IN 1,000S)

Source: United States Census Bureau (2020). Poverty Rate for People in Female-Householder Families Lowest on Record. The United States Census Bureau. Retrieved December 2, 2020, from https://www.census.gov/library/stories/2019/09/poverty-rate-for-people-in-female-householder-families-lowest-on-record.html.

a decent living to provide for the family. The street drug market at the time was an easy if risky way to provide for the family. It provided incentives to continue involvement in this lifestyle rather than returning to legitimate work. The drug market offers highly profitable opportunities that would not be afforded to certain individuals otherwise, resulting in engagement in illegitimate activities, such as selling drugs, for stability (Hagedorn, 1994).

The Get-Tough Policing Era: Mid-1980s through 1994

The get-tough era period of United States policing resonates with Penn because during these years he was a teenager growing up in Washington, DC. He was attending an American Legion Boy's Nation summer camp just outside Washington, DC, in June of 1986 when the news came that University of Maryland basketball star, Len Bias, the second pick in the NBA draft, died two days after being drafted by the Boston Celtics. The cause of death was a crack/cocaine overdose. Bias is considered by many to be the greatest basketball player not to play at professional level. His death brought to the attention of the nation the harms of cocaine and its less expensive, easily dispensed form, crack.

In the 1980s there was an increase in the use and sale of crack cocaine in the United States. Crack was affordable and was in high demand and had a lasting impact on the African-American community. According to Kenneth

B. Nunn (2002), African-American males were targeted, and as a result, the African-American male was removed from the home and community. Incarcerations of African Americans were at an all-time high in comparison to those of other races. The result: In 2000, the rate for African-American incarceration was 3,457 per 100,000 compared to their White counterparts at 449 per 100,000 (Nunn, 2002).

The relocation of manufacturing industries away from the city widened the gap in America's inner cities. Selling crack cocaine was a lucrative business for both the small- and big-time drug dealers in the community. On average, a small-time drug dealer who sold crack earned a median net income of $2,000 per month (Nunn, 2002). The demand for the drug increased, causing competition with drug dealers within the same community, which increased violent crime.

President Ronald Reagan initiated the "war on drugs," which combated drug trafficking that aimed to end the epidemic of crack cocaine. The war on drugs used deterrence theory to ground and implement harsher punishment to discourage the use of and involvement with drugs. There was a 100-to-1 ratio between the penalties for selling and possession of crack cocaine versus powdered cocaine, respectively, which guided the minimal mandatory punishment. The results of the "war on drugs" movement led to an immense increase in the prison population and an increase of poor, young Black males from the inner city being locked up. According to Nunn (2002), millions of African Americans were imprisoned due to the war on drugs and unfairly treated by the criminal justice system. By 2002, the prison population grew to an astounding 1.3 million (Nunn, 2002). The percentage of African Americans arrested for drug offenses doubled from 22% to 44%, and during that period, African-American arrests accounted for over 80% of total arrests.

In 1986, First Lady Nancy Reagan launched the "Just Say No" campaign to raise awareness of drug abuse. She is known for her infamous line, "Say yes to your life. Furthermore, when it comes to drugs and alcohol, just say no." Her intentions and approach were thoughtful, but the execution of it did not work. DARE (Drug Abuse Resistance Education) was one of the programs developed from the "Just Say No" campaign to help educate children on the dangers of drugs and encourage them not to participate in drug use. The DARE program was based on the premise of law enforcement and children coming together in a classroom setting once a week to learn how to handle peer pressure that could contribute to drug involvement. DARE and other youth and policing programs are further discussed in Chapter 5.

Dr. Lee Brown, then Director of the Office of National Drug Control Policy at the White House, delivered a keynote address on drugs and crime on May 21, 1994, at Harvard Law School. He listed "Eight Myths about Drugs" that drug experts recommended to help resolve the county's crisis at the time. The data may have changed over the years, but the myth remains the same.

Eight Myths About Drugs

Myth #1: "Everything is getting worse, and nothing is getting better..." However, according to the data, there was a substantial decline is drug use over the past decade. The data showed in 1979, more than 23 million Americans were using illegal drugs, and by 1992, it declined to 11.4 million.

Myth #2: "Current drug policy is making things worse, and the drug policy does not address the real problems of violence and HIV transmission." In fact, violence and the transmission of HIV were the results of drug use. Degeneration of the community, breakdown of the family structure because of drug addiction, and loss of productivity were the direct result of drug use. Addressing the illegal drug problem, in return, will help address the direct implications of other underline issues the communities face.

Myth #3: "Enforcement just adds to the problem. Drug enforcement and the application of criminal justice should be given up in favor of harm reduction approaches." Effective enforcement helps to reduce drug use and drug supply. Development of programs are effective methods to enforcement to help with drug control, and in return, trickle over to the criminal justice system by addressing the overcrowding of the prisons and jails.

Myth #4: "There is massive support for policy change by social thinkers, policy officials, and the public. This includes support for legalization or the decriminalization of drug use." Data collected at that time showed otherwise. "A 1990 Gallup Poll showed that 80% of the public thought that legalizing drugs was a bad idea. Only 14% thought it was a good idea. Among American 12 graders surveyed in the 1992–93 school year, 84% said that their friends would disapprove of their smoking marijuana regularly, and 94% said their friends would disapprove of occasionally taking cocaine" (Brown, 1994). There was no substantial support for policy change regarding legalization and decriminalization of drug use according to the myth.

Myth #5: Legalizing drugs, or decriminalizing drug use, will eliminate the illegal drug markets and the violence in our streets. There is no argument that drugs generate violence; however, prevention methods are a way to address the problem associated with the drug market. As Dr. Brown stated, "Legalization advocates just don't get it. Many drugs are illegal because they are addictive. They are mind-altering and causing a catastrophic outcome."

Myth #6: "Legalizing drugs will be free of cost." As this myth goes, there is *nothing to suggest* that legalizing drugs will increase drug use or its consequences." The Prohibition is a clear indication of what would happen; drug laws and drug enforcement were eliminated. The idea of drug legalization will not increase drug use is indeed a myth. According to alcohol use data from the 1930s, the repeal of the Volstead Act resulted in higher alcohol levels prior to Prohibition.

Myth #7: "There are excellent foreign models to show that decriminalization works: the Netherlands and the United Kingdom are two."[1] However, according to the international press, this is another myth based on the dire consequences of the unforced drug laws. The Dutch have remained unscathed by their citizens' use, but that cannot be said for the thousands of foreign visitors that visit to buy drugs, steal, or panhandle to maintain the addiction.

Myth #8: "Drug use is a personal matter, and it affects no one other than the user." Indeed, anyone familiar with alcohol addiction, similarly with drug use, can attest that the user's family members and friends are usually affected. Therefore, so much emphasis has been placed on the drug policy to correct the problem with illegal drug use.

Source: http://www.ndsn.org/july94/czar.html

Brown (1994) concluded his argument stating:

These are not the only myths about drug legalization. The one point that legalization proponents always seem to overlook is what effect drug legalization would have on our youth. Already, the nation is reeling from a wave of youth violence that is particularly devastating to young African-American males, who are both victims and perpetrators. African American males have the highest violent crime victimization rate and are half of all homicide victims. Nine of every 10 African American homicide victims were killed by other African Americans. *To introduce legalized drugs into this mix would be the moral equivalent of genocide.* [emphasis in original]

Brown also expressed his concerns with legalization and how the drug policy needed a radical change. He believed the focus in addressing illegal drugs should be thoughtful and effective. He stated, "such pressures lead to desperately conceived notions that will ultimately be more devasting than the current crisis" (Brown, 1994). Helping to address the current crisis of illegal drugs created different initiatives such as community policing, empowerment zones, national service, health care reform, and welfare reform to offer a powerful combination of hope and opportunity in communities where drugs and violence were heavily concentrated.

At this time, tension ran high between individuals from these concentrated areas and law enforcement. As noted earlier, in March 1991, Rodney King, an African-American male, was subjected to a beating by four White police officers for allegedly speeding at the rate of 110 mph. This incident gained national attention because a widely publicized film showed the extent of the beating. Three of the officers were acquitted, and the jury failed to reach a verdict concerning the fourth officer. The verdict sparked outrage among the African-American population, which led to rioting for six days in Los Angeles. Sixty-three people were killed, and 2,373 were injured, with the riot ending only with the assistance of the National Guard, the United States Army, and the United States Marine Corps. On April 16, 1993, two of the officers were found guilty and sentenced to prison, while the other two officers were acquitted of charges after the federal government prosecuted the case. The city of Los Angeles awarded Rodney King $3.8 million in damages. King went on to write an autobiography discussing his childhood growing up with an abusive father. He discusses his addiction to alcohol and other drugs and his run-ins with law enforcement. He was found dead in 2012 at the bottom of his pool. Without visible signs of foul play, his death was ruled as accidental (Maurantonio, 2014).

The Get-Tough Era ended with the largest crime bill that had been passed to date: HR 3355, the Violent Crime Control and Law Enforcement Act of 1994, which provided funding for 100,000 new officers, $9.7 billion for prisons, $6.1 billion for prevention programs, and took away higher education in correctional institutions. Gangs, drugs, and guns were key factors during this time—a time we call the "New Jack City" period in American criminal justice. The movie, *New Jack City*, depicted the crack epidemic in New York City and the effects of selling drugs and drug use in poor neighborhoods. The character Nino Brown, played by Wesley Snipes, was a kingpin drug lord. Freebased "crack" cocaine was cheaper to produce and more potent in comparison to powder cocaine. In the movie, this drug swept the neighborhoods, and eventually Nino and his brother and right-hand man Gee Money were able to take over an apartment complex with the amount of product they were "pushing." As with any other kingpin drug lord, the fast money and lavish lifestyle eventually caught up with Nino, and he was killed in the courtroom as he stood trial. The premise of the movie is to help viewers understand that Nino Browns exist everywhere, especially in the major cities and poverty-stricken neighborhoods. The movie also explains how it is imperative to enforce intervention and prevention methods to help combat illegal drugs or continue the epidemic.

The Community Policing Era: 1995 through 2015

The Get-Tough Era was ironically strengthened by federal legislation that established an office for community policing: The Omnibus Crime Bill of 1994 created the Community Oriented Policing Services (COPS) Office inside the United States Department of Justice. The community-oriented policing mission focused on building cohesiveness between police and members of communities. The primary elements of community policing are *community partnerships*, a collaborative partnership between law enforcement agencies and individuals and organizations; *organizational transformation*, organization management, structure, and information systems to support problem-solving; and *problem-solving*, a proactive and systematic approach to problems with effective responses.

The sunset of this phase injected race into the discussion with the arrest of Henry Gates, a senior Harvard professor arrested by Sergeant James Crowley of the Cambridge, Massachusetts, Police Department on July 16, 2009. Officer Crowley was dispatched to Gates's home as Gates, a slightly elderly man with a cane, was thought to be a burglar. An argument ensued, as Gates was incensed that he was suspected of burglary trying to enter his own house. Although some commended Crowley for responding to a 911 dispatch call, Gates viewed the event as racial profiling. For a few weeks, the United States was divided over who was right and who was wrong. The issue was determined to be a draw even after more dialogue over a beer at the White House with President Obama (Meares & Neyroud, 2015).

The 21st-Century Policing Era: 2015 to the Present

In recent years, city life has become chic and desirable, especially for youthful urban professionals. With many cities building up their central city areas with attractions such as sports arenas, shopping centers, parks, and entertainment venues, Zone 2 areas that were undesirable in the 1990s have become coveted addresses today, with many fearing gentrification as an undesired outcome. Gentrification is used by Whites (and in a limited way by non-Whites) to create urban ghettos in United States cities. The once socially disorganized areas dominated by poor Black and Brown people have been revitalized with new housing, restaurants, coffee shops, and retail markets and have become neighborhoods in which young, educated, middle-class Whites desire to live. In these areas there are still homes in need of repair, many abandoned, next to townhouse complexes and signs posted stating "we buy ugly houses," "cash for your house," "I buy houses in any condition," and so on. Property taxes then increase, and families sell their house for something like $100,000 only to find a year later that four town homes listed at $400,000 each are on the same plot of land.

Perhaps this change in urban areas adds to the need to change policing from an "us-versus-them" prospect to something beyond community policing. Identifying the "us" versus the "them" is not easy due to changes in geography. Race becomes the default separator as even middle-class Blacks and Hispanics living in these newly developed urban areas are seen as "them." Policing must treat all people equally. A term used to describe this new contemporary policing is "21st-century policing." While the term has been in use since the turn of the century, it took on new meaning and significance when President Obama commissioned the President's Task Force on 21st-Century Policing. The change is so significant that an entire chapter is dedicated to the subject (Chapter 4). It is important to realize that the world of policing and the interaction between citizens and police changed in a matter of a few short years. The United States emerged from a community policing model to a 21st-century policing outline that has as its foundation policing for all.

It is acknowledged that community policing was a step back toward the traditional policing model, but there are differences highlighted in the literature showing the transformation of community policing to 21st-century policing. Below, we define the differences in seven different aspects of policing: Relationship, Members of the Community, Diversity, Diversity in the Community, Technology, Police Operations, and Police Effectiveness.

TABLE 2.1 Comparing Community Policing to 21st-Century Policing

Aspect of Policing	Community Policing	21st Century Policing
Relationship	Establishing communication with neighborhoods supportive of the police.	Developing and maintaining two-way communication with all neighborhoods and people.
Members of the Community	Know the police are there. Community views the police as passive but responsive.	Move past passive interaction. Police department moves for more active involvement, especially from minority males under the age of 30.
Diversity	Acknowledge that diversity is a positive in policy.	Diversity is to be interwoven into the police department by actively inspiring all members of the police department to be represented through voice and leadership positions.
Diversity in the Community	Diversity is accomplished through the selection of highly vetted and trusted members of the community who gain access to the police. Their voice becomes the voice of diversity.	Focuses on the innate characteristic everyone has: implicit bias. From that start point, voice is desired and achieved through listening sessions and active interaction with many people in a group, not just one voice to represent the group.

Technology	Familiar with social media such as an active webpage and Facebook account. These social media tools are starting points moving social media toward being an integral part of police–citizen communication.	Social media is an active communication tool opening and facilitating communication for all groups but especially for those under 30 years of age. Police departments use the tool to peel back the veil of us-versus-them in policing, and sometimes showing the lighter side of police officers as people dancing, volunteering, and interacting with the public.
Police Operations	Top-down management with community policing as a unit, not as the ethos of the entire police department.	Procedural justice is the guiding ethos for the department with voice, transparency, impartiality, consistency, and fairness as guiding principles.
Police Effectiveness	Uniform Crime Reporting (specifically arrest) is the only way to measure police effectiveness.	Positive contact with the community allows for a measurement of effectiveness that goes beyond UCR data.

The first community policing models were implemented in the 1980s, championed by Lee Brown, and acknowledged with the creation of the Community Oriented Police Services (COPS) Office of the United States in 1994. Yet, after 30 years, there is still a high level of skepticism when one talks with line officers about community policing. Penn is reminded about a conversation he had with an officer with over 30 years of experience on the subject of policing. He stated, "You cannot treat all people the same; there are good and bad people. I must treat all people as if they are bad people first for my own personal safety." Many officers believe that community policing is "soft policing"—that is, not real policing—and when practiced too much, not at the right time, or at the wrong place, it could get one hurt or killed. Community policing is often viewed as "something nice to do for officers not cut-out for the street, the real police are on the street busting down doors and getting rid of the bad people on the street."

Perhaps police practices are most influenced by Presidential administrations. Richard Nixon pushed a "law and order" society; Ronald Reagan, a "just say no to drugs" media campaign; and George H.W. Bush and Bill Clinton, a war on drugs that saw the Federal Bureau of Prisons jump from 25,000 inmates in

1980 to 215,000 by 2012, of which 50% of the inmates were incarcerated for drug offenses, and of those drug offenses the majority were marijuana-related (Rosen & Brienen, 2015). The Clinton administration implemented the Community Oriented Police Services (COPS) Office in the Department of Justice. George W. Bush claimed to be fighting terrorism domestically and internationally. Barack Obama addressed the problems of police and citizen interaction with a Task Force that provided the context and support for movement beyond community policing into the second decade of the 21st century. Then the presidential election of November 2016 occurred.

To the surprise of pollsters and much of the American public, Donald Trump won the United States' presidency in November 2016. Hillary Clinton, the Democratic nominee, established clearly in her position statements that implicit bias, rollback sentencing, and community policing were priority issues (*The Washington Times*, 2016). This was not the belief of candidate Trump, who stated, "we need law and order, if we don't have it, we're not going to have a country" (Blake, 2016). Within his first week in office, Trump issued a ban on Muslims entering the United States, specifically from the following countries: Chad, Iran, Libya, Somalia, Syria, and Yemen. Trump's ruling was upheld by the Supreme Court, which he noted was a "great victory," granting him the authority to enforce the ban (Mallin, 2018).

Riding on an "America First" platform, Trump's position led to a decline in using the federal government's arm to provide mutual understanding and improvement for youth/citizen police relations. Introduced by the Obama administration, the COPS Office offered a less onerous alternative to consent decrees when asked to investigate local police conduct (Neuhauser, 2017). In September 2017, the COPS Office was redirected from reforming law enforcement agencies and improving police-community relations to what then-Attorney General Jeff Sessions stated was the COPS Office's original mission: providing technical training and assistance to combat violent crime at the request of local agencies (Neuhauser, 2017). The Department of Justice quickly moved from Obama's theme of building relationships while enforcing the law to a law-and-order doctrine, rolling back the strides toward improving citizen and police relations to return to an "us-versus-them" police/community relationship. Reflecting on what was learned from the 1968 Kerner Commission, the 9/11 Commission, and years of Community Policing through 21st-Century Policing, the lesson is that to be effective, policing to counter extreme groups, disenfranchised people, and those who may have anti-American values should be more rather than less inclusive.

The authors have attended dozens of "town hall" meetings, many in the United States, but some in other countries. In some communities, the police chief and others in command will sit in front as the audience throws out questions, examples, stories, and difficulties the police encounter. In an almost contest-like fashion, one person after another, in an attempt to shock the audience, will present a situation neither officer feels comfortable answering. Voices are raised, insults are hurled, and the result is more tension. This is because the narrator is usually a local pastor, defense attorney, or community activist, often on the side of the community rather than a neutral party facilitating solutions. The police leaders responding to the questions understand and publicly affirm the frustration felt by the community members. Sadly, at the end of such a meeting, the emphasis remains on the problems and stories about horrific encounters between police officers and youth—often with a sprinkling of stories from older citizens about something that happened 30 or 40 years ago—and little is solved. Perhaps the names of officers are known, and neighborhoods in need of services and care are identified. The solutions (if any) recommended may include additional training by officers to include: cultural sensitivity, attention to implicit bias, de-escalation, and knowing the community the officer polices. Yet, the general public spends little time getting to know the police officer and his or her culture.

Police Culture and Policing Methods

First, we must realize that police culture is made up of formal and informal norms established in the policing community. Membership is not guaranteed simply by joining the police department. Stages of acceptance exist, including recruiting, completing the training academy, rank, and experiences while in the academy; the feedback from field training officers during the first year on the job; and how well the officer handled stressful, dangerous, and difficult situations. In his 1998 *Criminology* article "Police Subculture Reconsidered," Steve Herbert (1998) discussed how there is a normative order for policing. It establishes rules and practices around six areas: law, bureaucratic control, adventure/machismo, safety, competence, and morality. As noted earlier, community policing is often viewed by police officers as "soft policing" or impractical for the harsh, dangerous, and traumatic events endured while doing "real" policing. This primarily male profession moves the police officer to be competitive, aggressive, sarcastic, crass, and tight-knit with their peers. Their view of the public can be characterized as cynical. They have seen the very worst of people, and this engenders social distance and negative feelings toward the general public, specifically minority group members, the poor, police management, new policing styles, and the criminal justice system (Cockcroft 2012). This tendency is often seen when training officers. In one training session, there was a welcome video by the chief of police informing the officers how the training they were about to receive would be important in making their job easier. Throughout the two-minute video, there were laughs at his gestures and his comments. In a room filled with 100 officers, comments came from the room including: "when was the last time he was on a scene?" "he does not know what we do," or "he does not have my back."

As we review history of policing in the United States, there have been various forms used in the literature to describe police methods. In June 2018, Penn was invited to attend the Center for Evidence-Based Crime Policy's symposium on evidence-based crime policy. The Center, led by Dr. Cynthia Lum, a former police officer who is now a highly respected police-practice researcher, provides an overview of definitions explaining police practice in the United States.

Hot Spots Policing

The term "hot spots" refers to socially disorganized areas in which higher levels of crime occurs. Perhaps it is within a certain 100 blocks of a street, near a club, or in a certain ward or district. The thought behind "hot spots" policing is to increase police patrols in those specific areas. This proactive policing increases patrols to deter and respond more effectively. Research indicates this type of policing produces short-term crime reduction going beyond simply displacing crime into surrounding areas. Studies show that crime in nearby areas reduces also.

Predictive Policing

In predictive policing, using computer algorithms, patterns of crime can be predicted to project exact locations where specific offenses are likely to occur next. Currently, there is insufficient rigorous research to support this method as a way to reduce crime.

Closed Circuit Television (CCTV)

Overall, closed-circuit television cameras provide a general deterrent because of the offenders' perceived risk of identification. Research shows that standing in as the watchful eye of a capable guardian, CCTV provides modest outcomes for reducing property offenses, but there are insufficient studies to conclude their impact on crime and disorder.

Problem-Oriented Policing

Problem-oriented policing seeks to identify and analyze the causes of crime. Once this is done, a response is provided using a wide range of methods and tactics. These methods range from Crime Prevention Through Environmental Design (CPTED) practices to improving citizens' recreational opportunities. Research shows short-term crime prevention gains with this method.

Third-Party Policing

Realizing that police cannot do it all by themselves, third-party policing seeks to persuade or coerce property owners, business owners, public housing agencies, and other organizations to take some responsibility for preventing or reducing crime. The research findings for this method show short-term reductions in crime and disorder.

Focused Deterrence

Police attempt to deter crime among repeat offenders by understanding underlying crime-producing dynamics and implementing a blended strategy that includes law enforcement, community groups, and social service agencies. Certainty, swiftness, and severity of punishment are essential for this method to be effective. Evaluations show consistent crime-control does reduce gang violence, street crime driven by drug markets, and repeat individual offending. This method shows short- and long-term areawide impacts in reducing crime.

Stop-Question-Frisk (SQF)

With the stop-question-frisk (SQF) method, police use their legal authority to engage in frequent stops of individuals. Officers question suspects about their activities, and often frisk and search the suspects. This is most likely to occur in places where severe and violent gun crimes occur. Issues of harassment and "netting dolphins with the tuna" are common complaints of this type of policing. Overall evidence of crime reduction of this method as a general, citywide crime control strategy is mixed.

Broken Windows Policing

Ensuring the small infractions do not become more serious in the future is the focus of the broken windows policing method. The belief is that if small infractions are addressed through police contact, the problems will not escalate to larger infractions in the future. Thus, police officers employ warnings, citations, and arrests as necessary to control actions and behavior. Using interventions that broadly apply aggressive tactics for increasing misdemeanor arrests to control disorder generates little or no impact on crime.

Neighborhood-Based Problem-Oriented Practices

Community-Oriented Policing

In community-oriented policing, citizens and police work together to identify and address public safety concerns. This method decentralizes decision-making to develop responses to concerns and works to solve them through community involvement; however, studies do not show a consistent benefit to this method.

Procedural Justice Policing

When the community legitimizes police officers' authority, they are more inclined to collaborate with the police and abide by the laws. Tyler (2001) states that people want to be treated fairly, with dignity, and desire all their rights as citizens to be recognized. Citizens want to feel that the police care about their concerns, their views are being heard, and cases are viewed and corrected in light of erroneous decisions. Brunson and Weitzer (2009) concluded that an arrest can take place, but the citizen arrested can feel the cops were "good cops" if the officers personally treated them with respect. Tyler (1990) tested the procedural justice model and concluded: "People who regard legal authorities as legitimate are found to comply with the law more frequently" (p. 64). The concept of procedural justice is paramount to reducing social distance between youth and police; it will be discussed in more detail in Chapter 4 as an important part of the President's Task Force on 21st-Century Policing.

Overall, when trying to reduce crime and reduce the social distance between community in general and youth specifically, effective strategies often fall under the general term of evidence-based policing. Lum and Koper (2017) articulate the many activities of evidence-based policing. They include rigorous evaluation; reflecting on research with management; training officers based on research findings; using crime analysis to guide the deployment of resources; generalizing from research knowledge and adjusting current practices; conducting rigorous surveys of community members to assess satisfaction with the police; using risk assessment instruments developed and validated by researchers to identify problematic situations; conducting surveys of officers to solicit their views on agency policies and strategies; using systematic social observations, ethnographies, or other systematic qualitative approaches to gain a detailed picture of police culture, practices, and behaviors; examining how technology is used in the organization to improve the acquisition and deployment process; and partnering with researchers and community members to carry out any of the above actions. In the 1960s, policing strategies emerged that moved policing organizations to develop and implement proactive techniques. In the short term, this strategy lowers crime, but with a concern about the cost to the community. Issues of legality, potential abuses of police authority, and equitable application of police services are in question.

Another policing option is the "no police" response. This philosophy was heard widely in response to the murder of George Floyd in May 2020 but was articulated to the lead author just a few months earlier through the heartfelt words of a young Black man after a Houston speaking engagement. There is a time when you are speaking to an audience—even on a difficult subject such as police and youth relations—in which you are in the groove of the talk: your points are dead-on; you are answering questions before doubters have an opportunity to ask them; you are listening and reading your audience so well that you have them moving with you, following your cues, and the presentation becomes a chorus of expression rather than a tug of war of ideas. While that was occurring at this Tuesday meeting, this young man, whom we will call Jack, jabbed every so often with remarks such as: "police do not make areas safer," "broken windows theory is not valid," and "having police officers in schools makes for more crime." He presented the no-police argument, that is, the belief that the entire system of policing is so corrupt and unjust to the African American and serves the interest of those in power that it is useless to those without power. This notion is certainly supported by Conflict Theory (Quinney, 1970) and the Colonial Model (Tatum, 1994).

Neil Websdale (2001) supports this position in his work titled *Policing the Poor: From Slave Plantation to Public Housing* by noting that the struggles related to poverty and public housing are so great in the Nashville projects he studied that community policing cannot overcome these devastating and deep-rooted forces. Similarly, "Jack" clearly believed it is not a criminal justice system led by police with a history of injustice that should respond to the deep-rooted problems of the African-American community.

> These are social problems, not criminal justice problems. Police were ill-equipped and wrongly placed as the response force to violence and crime in the Black community.
>
> *("Jack," a 20-something African-American male)*

In fact, Jack went on in a conversation after the meeting to explain that he believes the resources for policing should be placed in the Black community for prevention, intervention, and response programs and services. An older African-American woman participating in the discussion asked, "What are you going to do when 21-year-old Tyrone beats up his girlfriend or mother in the back room of the house?" Jack responded calmly, "You don't call the police, because they are going to kill Tyrone." He discussed how family, extended family, and close friends would have been there to prevent the problem in the first place, and if it did get to such a violent event, uncles, brothers, fathers, and "men" of the community would step in to control Tyrone. Jack described a shaming and self-control system at this time that, sadly, may be a vision of the Black community.

With these various forms of policing available, let us look at the difference between community policing and 21st-century policing. In general, 21st-century policing includes methods stemming from the President's Task Force on 21st-Century Policing. Community policing stops at police officers making their way to the community; it does not prepare the officer nor the public for confrontation by groups in the community through history. The concept of 21st-century policing looks at all members of the community as assets working together to find solutions to reduce crime and improve the community.

Summary

Issues of race and social class taint the history of policing in the United States. It is difficult to discuss reducing the social distance between youth and police without diving deeply into both elements. We find that policing in the United States has its origins in race, as slave patrols provide the first examples of organized policing. The social disorganization in the urban area created a patronage system that favored some groups over others. The benefits of the G.I. Bill provided relief for Whites to leave Zone 2 and "hot spots" of urban decay in order to create suburbs filled with the social buffers bonding youth to middle-class values and the reduction of crime. We find that the urban areas filled with Black youth saw increased social tension, fierce practices of the war on drugs, and riots that further distanced the urban youth from the urban police. Community policing emerged as a response, later to evolve into 21st-century policing, in which procedural justice motivates police departments to conduct operations in a manner to create legitimacy in the police to further compliance. The police culture is understood as a tight bond among officers in which they "have each others' backs." An officer wants to do the job and go home at night. The officer depends on fellow officers to ensure that that desire is realized. This produces and strengthens the us-versus-them mentality. We have also learned that some people have completely given up the notion that police can be fair and legitimate in the urban Black community, and thus they subscribe to the "no police" argument.

The 2012 case of Trayvon Martin, although not directly related to a police officer, truly sets the foundation of the modern-day police-youth conflict. While this chapter allowed us to focus on the police, the next chapter discusses youth, child development, and the juvenile justice system and its involvement in change throughout history. In relatively recent U.S. history, the youth has been known to be a "protected" class in need of rehabilitation. However, times have changed, and the pendulum in the juvenile justice system goes back and forth between retribution and rehabilitation. The next chapter dives into understanding youth culture. All adults were youth at one time, but they often quickly forget the creativity, invincibility, style, passion, and belief in oneself that is so prominent during the teens and early twenties.

Note

1   The original source gives the United Kingdom as the second of the two countries where drugs have been decriminalized, but it is actually Portugal.

3

YOUTH IS NEVER WASTED ON THE YOUNG

As a teenager, Penn would hear his mother often say "youth is wasted on the young" when he did something impulsive, dangerous, childish, or without rationally thinking through the consequences. This idiom, said to have originated from George Bernard Shaw, has been used to explain how, when one is young, one possesses the energy, the courage, and the qualities that could be used for something good, but some people "waste" their youth by making irrational and foolish decisions that they wish they could take back when they are older and wiser. In this chapter, let us take the time to understand the youth, those young men and women age 14 to 24, and answer the question: Is youth wasted on the young?

In Texas and other states, 14 is the age at which a youth can be tried as an adult; it also represents the first year in high school. The age of 24 is significant because adolescent psychologists define it as the age before true maturity when the brain fully forms at age 25. Some other age milestones include:

- 17: the legal age of maturity in Texas for the adult system;
- 18: the age to vote, smoke, or enter the military;
- 21: the age to drink legally.

So, now a new question is developing: What is an adult?

First, let us define an adult for the purposes of this book. When the question is asked in training or class, the answer usually encompasses someone able to take care of themselves, including being able to financially provide for themselves and their children. The next step in training is to look at the jobs available for a high school graduate, college graduate, and graduate school graduate. Finally, the students are asked to create a list of expenses needed to "take care

DOI: 10.4324/9780429424519-4

of themselves." They list food, shelter, clothing, car, car insurance, childcare, recreation, health insurance, travel, and so on. Then the cost is determined for each expense.

The differences between an all-inclusive $700-per-month apartment versus a luxurious high-rise apartment costing $2,000–$4,000 per month are discussed. The desires are almost always the same: nice place to live, expensive car, vacations, and name-brand clothing and shoes. Sometimes, members of the class or training session will add to the list items such as private school for kids, vacations in far-away destinations, two cars, investments, and good health insurance. The point is that often when one looks at the salaries available for high school and college graduates, the salary often does not meet the desired lifestyle. If being an adult means you can pay the cost for your lifestyle, what is the cost to be an adult? We find the answer in a "living wage."

"A living wage is the amount of money necessary for one to meet basic needs. These needs include food, housing, clothing, and other essentials with a small amount of money saved for unforeseen events (emergency savings)" (Grimshaw, 2004). In the United States, the basic but decent standard of living is calculated to be $3 to $7 above the federal minimum wage, which in early 2021 was $7.25. Thus, the living wage rate is calculated to be $15.84 per hour, or $633.60 per week, or $32,947.20 per year before taxes. In areas such as New York, San Francisco, or Los Angeles, the amount is higher, reaching $20.32 per hour, or $42,265.60 per year (Nadeau & Glasmeier, 2018).

With an understanding of minimum wage versus living wage, we can determine when a youth reaches maturity to be self-sustaining at 18 by looking at employment opportunities available for that 18-year-old. Below is a listing of the top ten jobs for people without a college degree (see Table 3.1).

TABLE 3.1 Ten Jobs for People Without a Four-Year College Degree, with Average Annual Salary, in 2018

Job	Salary
Administrative Assistant	$38,880
Appliance Repairer	$39,270
Carpenter	$46,590
Paralegal and Legal Assistant	$50,940
Computer Support Specialist	$53,470
Dental Hygienist	$74,820
Electrician	$55,190
Medical Records and Health Information Technician	$40,350
Respiratory Therapist	$60,280
Web Developer	$69,430

Source: 2018, U.S. Bureau of Labor Statistics. https://www.bls.gov/.

What is interesting to note about these high-paying jobs obtainable without a college degree is that although a bachelor's degree is not required, formal training is necessary. In other words, each of the positions requires a specific skill set in demand. As each of these positions are above the living wage annual salary of $32,000 to $42,000, they must be compared to more commonly held positions of people without college degrees. Here are a few examples of the median annual salaries for 2019 for various jobs (U.S. Bureau of Labor Statistics, n.d.):

- Food and Beverage Serving and Related Workers $23,000
- Retail Sales Workers $25,440
- Grounds Maintenance Workers $30,890.

Similarly, the average annual salary of an Uber driver in Texas was reported at $25,635, which does not take into account wear on car, gas expenses, how often people are in vehicle, and so on (Indeed.com, n.d.).

While writing this book, Penn purchased a new car. As part of the package, he received free Sirius service. Intrigued by the variety of music channels, he wandered up and down the dial but was surprised by the number of profanities heard in seconds on the rap and rock stations. He asked his younger co-author about the culture of "women getting paid" and "men getting played" that seemed to dominate in the lyrics. As she started to explain the artists and the music, he reflected on the 1990 work of Elijah Anderson's *Code of the Streets*. This powerful qualitative work of Blacks living in Philadelphia builds upon the work of *The Philadelphia Negro* to explain that there are two types of families in Zone 2 and in "hot spots" of the urban city: (1) what he called "decent" families, those who raise their children to follow the rules of society, and through hard work, social bonding occurs to overcome the negatives of a socially disadvantaged environment, as compared to (2) "street" families that succumb to the negatives of the environment, encouraging taking before being taken and holding that respect is the most important concept on the streets. People live and die for respect earned on the street (Anderson, 2019).

Davenport and Penn conducted a spur-of-the-moment research experiment while leaving a coffee shop. They went out to see what music channels were programmed in their cars. Penn's Sirius radio channel was programmed to 1970s Hits, Real Jazz, Pulse Alternative, CNN, MSNBC, and Fox News. On the other hand, Davenport's channels were programmed to Pandora, The Heat (R&B and Hip-Hop), and Heart and Soul. It is important to attempt to understand and appreciate the differences between different age groups, to look to reduce the social distance and understand the youth culture—because all adults experienced their own youth culture when they were teenagers and in their early twenties.

New to Penn and perhaps others over the age of 30 is the "influencer culture." The "influencer culture" consists of posting information on different platforms to reach a targeted audience. Social media influencers, such as the Kim Kardashians of the world, represent a third party who shapes perceptions and attitudes through different media such as tweets, blogs, and social media posts. Personal information is shared through these different social media channels and networks. The self-branding endorsed by social media involves individuals creating a distinctive public image for social and cultural capital. Self-branding is a focal point of social media that is popular and influential. There is a direct connection between brand, media, audience, and celebrity (Khamis, Ang, & Welling 2017). Celebrities with a vast following use social media to market or advertise to the targeted audience. When celebrities use their name for marketing a product or brand, they become synonymous with the item, and money is earned from endorsements.

Social media has created a world where regular individuals can create an alias and put up a façade of a perfect life. According to research conducted by Forbes, 78% of the U.S. population has a social media profile (Kerpen, 2016). Kim Kardashian West has 37.9 million followers and can make an estimated $300,000 to $500,000 for a sponsored Instagram post (Roberts, 2020). Many 18–24-year-olds are no longer interested in attending college; their dreams are now to become the next up-and-coming "social media influencer." However, the journey to becoming a social media influencer is not an easy one, and it does not happen overnight. It takes a lot of work and dedication learning what to post that will generate attention and appeal to followers. Reality check: Unless you are an athlete, famous actor, or an established social media influencer, people are not likely very interested in your life, what you wore to an event, or where you are going on your next vacation. Social media has allowed individuals to become "mini or micro-celebrities" by giving them the platform to amplify their popularity on social media by using different outlets such as blogs and YouTube channels. The influencers must continue to forge and sustain their relationship with their audience or "fan base" to keep their popularity high and remain relevant so their brand won't die or wither away. Success in this field is measured by the number of likes, follows, retweets, and shares generating more interaction.

Reality television is another platform that has allowed "regular" individuals to have the opportunity to gain fame. *The Real Housewives* and *Basketball Wives* are some examples of shows that allow women who have married into fame to use the television platform to showcase material wealth that has been acquired. These sorts of reality shows give some younger girls the impression that if you have the "Hollywood" or "Instagram model" look, it could attract a certain type of wealthy man that can provide a lifestyle of luxury. It's simple: Look good, work out, eat healthily, dress nicely, wear plenty of makeup, post pictures, and cross your fingers that your wealthy "knight in shining armor" will arrive.

Realistically, however, it is not that simple. The competition among people vying for that type of attention is extremely high; it is equivalent to being a famous athlete, singer, or actor. A more realistic plan would be going to college or trade school to get a certification or degree to give oneself a better chance of stability and a comfortable life. With education, one maintains control over one's own life. Putting trust in someone to provide a certain lifestyle is equivalent to giving someone permission to control your life. Nevertheless, the illusion promoted by social media and reality television has influenced much of the younger population to strive for the wrong things by placing too much emphasis on material wealth instead of education.

Becoming the next top athlete is another career that does not require higher education or a degree. To reach the status of an elite athlete, the individual must invest in rigorous training, eat properly, and maintain a physique that will allow them to compete with other athletes. Organized sports are heavily embedded in the United States school system, and many students prepare to make the transition from high school to collegiate sports. Many high school athletes neglect to put their focus on their studies and concentrate more on training to get the opportunity to make it to the "big league." Some of these students are told that having a degree is cool, but if they make it in their choice of sport, they could be set for life. Signing to a professional sports team will not only grant financial stability but will also allow those who have sacrificed to share in the stability and wealth. According to Spotrac.com, the average contract for an NFL draft in last year's top pick was worth $27.9 million, while the twelfth pick received $12.8 million (Spotrac.com, n.d.). Similar to the NFL draft, in the NBA draft, where players are ranked determines the pay scale when negotiating a contract. Deandre Ayton and the Phoenix Suns negotiated a contract for a rookie at $6,746,400 for his first year (Spotrac.com, n.d.). The media often glamorize avenues that afford instant gratification. Some younger people ask the question: "Why go to school, get into debt to get a degree that could potentially not be used, and work a job that I am unhappy with when I could make money being a social media influencer, reality star, or athlete?"

Societal values and morals have shifted attention to making fast, and sometimes dangerous, money rather than having something of substance such as a college degree or certificate from a trade school. Granted, school is not for everyone; however, finding something that you are passionate about can be its own reward. Today's youth culture is a clear example of how times have changed and how the value of school has shifted to accomplishing social status rather than obtaining a degree.

An average 18–24-year-old without a four-year degree will earn about $30,000, slightly less than the $32,947.20 living wage. Yet, there are positions where the living wage can be achieved. In comparison, the college graduate is expected to start at around $50,000. Yet often this college graduate has spent four years in school and is now four years and $120,000 behind his or her non-college graduate peers (Gleeson, 2018). Don't forget to add in the school loan debt accumulated, estimated to start around $27,610 for public university graduates (Association of Public & Land-Grant Universities, n.d.).

Another career to consider is the military. It is an option that many parents encourage because of the skill set and discipline that is developed through rigorous training. A private is a military soldier at the Department of Defense (DoD) paygrade E-1. At the time of going to press, the active-duty soldier receives a starting annual salary of $20,797. In addition, bonuses, allowance for housing and food, and special incentives for hostile fire and dangerous duties are included (goarmy.com, 2020).

In our culture today, a living wage to meet middle-class living standards may not be achieved until a youth has completed some form of training or has become college-educated. In either case, most people are not financially independent at age 18 to 24. According to this perspective, a person must be over the age of 25 to be defined as an adult. Interestingly, this age corresponds with the American Psychological Association's assertion that the brain fully forms by the time a person is 25 (Kersting, 2004). Thus, the years between being called an adult (18) and being age 25 can be filled with strain and tension. Robert K. Merton (1938), an American sociologist, developed strain theory to understand the strain that results from not having the means to attain or achieve goals. People are socialized to believe that achieving the American Dream can be easily done by working hard. These individuals would be considered "conformist"— the individuals who achieve their goals by sacrificing and working hard by legitimate means. However, not everyone is afforded the same opportunities that align them with the appropriate education or the necessary connections to place them in positions for specific jobs to make a living. These individuals would be what Merton considered "innovators." Innovators want to achieve the American Dream but do not have the means to do so, resulting in criminal activity. Seeking instant gratification can result in irrational decisions and risky behaviors. This concept is challenging to explain to adolescents because of the adolescent developmental process. According to research, adolescents lack the maturity to make rational decisions regarding self-regulation in emotional situations. Secondly, adolescents have a number of external forces that drive their decision-making, such as peer pressure. Lastly, adolescents lack the ability to use rational thinking for future orientation (Steinberg, 2007). Combining these factors can result in a high probability of lack of self-control that can lead to involvement in risky, deviant behaviors. Depending on the type of behavior or offense, this can result in the juvenile justice system enforcing punitive actions.

Since youth are impressionable at this stage, this is a time where parents or guardians have to be more hands-on by equipping their children with skills and tools to make rational decisions. A hot topic in the Black community is "The Talk," a tactic to help children, specifically Black males, know what to do when interacting with police. According to Cintron, Dawkins, Gibson, and Hill (2019), African-American communities have a deep mistrust of police. "The Talk" refers to the conversations parents have with their children about the "do's" and the "do nots" when interacting with police. During this time, parents equip their children with survival tools and strategies to help them navigate racial tension and bias experiences that may occur with the encounter. Barlow and Barlow (2018), in their timely work, *Policing in a Multicultural Society: An American Story,* discuss "The Talk" as "...a discussion about where to put hands, and eyes, how to manage tone, what not to wear, and generally how to make sure that African American children do not frighten armed police officers into shooting and perhaps killing them" (p. 137).

In the study of juvenile justice and juvenile delinquency, we see a shift in viewing teenagers and those younger as "little adults" toward an entire system created on the belief that those under a certain age, with some exceptions (waiver), are considered juveniles because they lack *mens rea* or lack of a guilty conscience.

Juvenile Justice

Youth are not responsible for their actions in the same way an adult is responsible for the same acts. The juvenile justice system in the United States has its origins in Europe but started to take shape in the United States with the opening of "houses of refuge" in large cities: New York in 1825, Boston in 1826, and Philadelphia in 1828. The houses of refuge were large homes for training that used various practices, such as indeterminate sentencing, skills training, and education, a hard-work ethic, religious training, discipline, and apprenticeships, to correct the wrongs of youth stemming from the ills of the city. Before these houses of refuge, there was no juvenile justice system. Youth were often housed with adults, there was overcrowding, and rehabilitation was often unsuccessful.

By the mid-1800s, the Industrial Revolution of the United States was moving Europeans and Americans from the South to the large metropolitan areas of the Northeast and Midwest, spurring tremendous growth (Deane & Deane, 1979). The American Industrial Revolution is marked by three major advancements: transportation, the control and use of electricity, and improved communication techniques such as the telegraph system developed by F.B. Morse in 1844. These developments moved people from an agrarian lifestyle to steady employment and income by living in the city, working in the factories, and producing manufactured goods (Hirschman & Mogford, 2009).

The unskilled male workers worked eight to ten hours a day for 10 cents per hour. Female unskilled workers earned about one-third to one-half of their male counterparts, and children worked the same six days a week for even less. Skilled workers would earn a little more (Economy Watch, n.d.). The factories were health hazards with little light, dark clouds of smoke put out by the machinery, and few if any safety precautions. Factory owners would push their workers to gain maximum production. Breaks existed only for lunch and dinner (Economy Watch, n.d.). When it was time to go home, life did not improve. Often workers needed to live very close to their factory because of the lack of transportation.

Accepting that those under the age of maturity are not responsible for their actions places strain on the youth population. These are the same youth who can physically do just about anything an adult can do: smoke, have sexual intercourse, drink alcohol, steal, drive, use illegal drugs, and perform numerous other activities.

Adolescent Development and Law Enforcement

In the United States, according to the United States Census, there were 64 million people under the age of 24 in 2015, with youth broadly defined as those between the ages of 10 and 24 (U.S. Census Bureau, 2015). In many states, the age of juvenile delinquency begins at 10. We use different terms to separate the juvenile justice system from the adult criminal justice system because of the legal principle of *parens patriae*, which means the state (government) is the ultimate parent. This principle was first legally tested in 1838 with the case of *Ex parte Crouse* in Pennsylvania. The Pennsylvania court concluded that *parens patriae* is a standard that allows the government to intervene in juveniles' lives without parental consent (Rendleman, 1971). It was later tested in 1905 with the case of *Commonwealth v. Fisher*. Again, the court concluded that the government, as "the ultimate parent," can intervene when trying to help a child (Rendleman, 1971).

The Juvenile Justice era (1899–1996) began with the work of the Progressives, who were called "Child Savers," in Cook County (Chicago, Illinois). This new system functioned as a true *parens patriae* model. The judges and other officials of the court were free to act in the child's best interest with or without parental involvement or due process protections of the law (Ratliff, 1999).

Anthony Platt, in his historical account of the formation of the United States juvenile justice system, *The Child Savers: The Invention of Delinquency* (1969), reminded us of the origins of a system planned to stop youth from being seen, treated, and punished as "little adults." This new system was created by the Child Savers to focus on rehabilitation and "fixing" a youth before he or she became an adult. Let us look at two points more closely with this definition: Child Savers and rehabilitation.

The Child Savers were described as Progressives, mainly women, living in urban areas who enjoyed middle-class to wealthy lifestyles. With the advancements in the home life of the mid-1800s and the ability to hire domestic workers, these women enjoyed free time to be ladies of society. Remnants of these women's social groups exist today in organizations such as The Professional Women's Club of Chicago. Platt (1969) explained that these society women would meet to discuss social problems of the day, and their solutions were then supported by fathers, husbands, and brothers of industry. As these society matrons made their way from their social club meetings, they observed youth whose parents may have been the domestics or workers toiling long hours at the industries owned and managed by their families. During the mid-1800s they may have observed a group of youth who, because of little to no adult supervision and no schooling, were loitering, stealing, harassing, and idling during the day. Perhaps some of the women observed them dancing or involved in promiscuous acts (Platt, 1969). The women took their concern to their social club meeting and discussed the need for a new system that would make these youth productive members of society. This system would modify the behavior of these youth and allow the government to be better parents to them than their working biological parents. Therefore, the system would call on the government to correct the wrongs by these new immigrants who committed deviant acts. Platt went on to describe the operation of the system through the actions of Judge Julian Mack, who believed that a judge was like a parent. Mack believed in rehabilitation, indeterminate sentencing, informal processing, and the use of probation in which members of the community would step in to be "better" parents than the biological ones so as to avoid future dealing with the justice system (Pisciotta, 1983).

The fate of youth who were not White was much less future-oriented. Fredrick H. Wines, a leader in the National Conference of Charities and Correction and the National Prison Association in the late 1800s and early 1900s, believed that crime and delinquency among Blacks was an "insoluble problem," and "because of their inherent biological, mental and moral primitiveness…neither punishment nor rehabilitation would work (Gabbidon & Greene, 2013, p. 289). Thus, Black children were treated differently and did not enjoy the juvenile justice system's rehabilitative principles. Black youth who did make it to houses of refuge, reformatories, or other facilities were often relegated to menial tasks of house labor for the facility's service, falling significantly short of the skills and apprenticeships often made available to White youth in these same facilities. Black youths were more likely sent to adult jails and prisons. There is little documentation about the treatment of Black youth in adult prisons, but we know the conditions in Southern state prisons. Here a system, begun in 1901, was described by Du Bois as the "convict lease system," in which penal institutions generated revenue for the state as well as those who ran the facility. Within this convict lease system, after the Civil War, inmates who were often Black, poor, and poorly educated would be leased out to private farmers. These farmers were in desperate need of laborers for long hours of work. Death rates were high, and sexual assaults and rapes were ignored (Gabbidon & Greene, 2013). Thus, Du Bois (1903), Gabbidon and Greene (2013), and Ward (2012) remind us that the story of Child Saving was not the case for all youth and perhaps provides an origin for issues such as the school-to-prison pipeline and disproportionate minority confinement.

The word "rehabilitation" is interesting because, by its very definition, the prefix "re-" means "to do again." Placed in front of the word habilitate, it would mean to reteach something that has been taught before. In aiming to rehabilitate these youth, the assumption was that they had the knowledge or skills at an earlier time. However, what if the reality is that the youth of the 1800s, whose parents were domestics and factory workers, never had middle-class standards to begin with (Cohen, 1955)? How could they be expected to meet a way of life that was unknown to them? This standard of values and norms was imposed on them through the work of the juvenile court judges in Judge Mack's time.

Platt challenged the reader to consider whether the Child Savers were more interested in creating a workforce for the business and industries of their fathers, husbands, and brothers. If the Child Savers believed there was a need to take these immigrants' raw talents and transform them into an American workforce filled with the middle-class values and an Anglo-Saxon work ethic, a juvenile justice system infused with these beliefs would do the trick. Perhaps "Child Slavers" is a more appropriate term than Child Savers (Platt, 1969).

By 1925 all states had a form of the Chicago model of Judge Mack-style juvenile justice, with little parental involvement and few of the due process rights we see today. However, with the case of *Kent v. United States* (1966), the days of that stye of juvenile justice were coming to an end. *Kent* was a landmark case in the juvenile justice system because it provided the fundamental basis for due process for juveniles and marked the end of the *parens patriae* approach. The "waiver of jurisdiction," critically important when determining the juveniles' statutory rights, was added. The waiver of jurisdiction (transfer of jurisdiction or certification) carries far-reaching consequences for the juvenile. For example, a juvenile can be released upon reaching the age of adulthood, tried as an adult in the adult criminal court, and subjected to incarceration. The *Kent* case was followed by *In Re Gault*, which was one of the most important juvenile justice cases ever to be decided by the Supreme Court because it focused on the rights of juveniles. The basis of the case provides for the fundamental approach that juvenile proceedings, even civil ones, require many due process protections that are afforded to adults (del Carmen, Parker, & Reddington, 1998).

Eventually, a slew of other cases would grant youth many of the same rights as adults, except the right to a jury trial, and would end the practice of the death penalty and life in prison. From its origin, the juvenile justice system was formed because, as a society, we believe youth do not have the ability to make sound decisions or possess *mens rea* (guilty state of mind). This is required for an act to be considered a crime. No *mens rea*, no crime. Of course, a youth may be waived to be tried as an adult, but the *Kent* case described above sets a standard for that action to take place. See Table 3.2.

The age of a youth also is a determinant of the function of the juvenile justice system. Although each state is different, a general understanding is that youth fall into two age groups: (1) under 10 and (2) 10 to 18. Using these two groups, let's examine a scenario in which a youth is in custody for another person's shooting death.

TABLE 3.2 Differences between Juvenile and
Adult Criminal Court

Juvenile Court Term	Adult Court Term
Taken into Custody	Arrested
Petition	Indictment
Hearing	Trial
Delinquent	Criminal
Adjudication	Conviction
Commitment	Sentence
Aftercare	Parole

Source: BrunoLaw,PLLC,2020,https://brunolaw.com/
resources/general-criminal-law/10-differences-
between-adult-and-juvenile-criminal-court.

Aged Under 10: Child in Need of Supervision

It may be hard to believe, but every so often, youth under the age of 10 commit a serious offense, such as murder. One case involved an eight-year-old boy (whose name was not released because of confidentiality and privacy rights due to his age) who was arrested and charged with shooting his father and his father's friend in 2008. The young boy confessed to killing the victims by shooting them with a .22-caliber rifle. He told the police he thought his dad was suffering and did not want him to suffer anymore. A motive was not found, but the police thought it was a premeditated murder. The child kept a journal of all the spankings he received over time. He was evaluated and found not competent to stand trial due to his age and not having the mental capacity to rationalize or understand the severity of the situation. He was sentenced to a residential facility; he will not be allowed to leave the facility and will receive intensive probation until age 18. He will also continue to receive psychological evaluations when he turns 12, 15, and 17.

Because *mens rea* requires a guilty state of mind and the juvenile justice system is based on the precept that youth do not have that, the youth therefore cannot be responsible for the act. Even with a body and a smoking gun in hand, the child would not be tried in adult court. However, some states will waive a juvenile under 10 to the adult system under certain conditions. A judicial waiver occurs when a juvenile court judge transfers a case from juvenile to adult court. In order for this process to occur, the offense is allegedly egregious enough for the case to be waived judicially, or else the individual has a long history of offenses. In 45 states, juvenile courts have jurisdiction over individuals to age 17, but the maximum age is 16 in five states (Texas, Michigan, Georgia, Wisconsin, and Missouri). All states now provide a judicial waiver and have set a variety of lower age limits based on the type of alleged offense committed, typically ranging from 12 to 14 (10 in Vermont and Kansas). However, roughly one-third of states have no minimum age requirement. Once a juvenile is transferred to the adult court, they fall under the principle "once an adult, always an adult." Going forward, if the juvenile commits any offense, they will be tried in an adult court, even if the offense is not serious.

In most cases in which a youth commits a shooting, the youth will be viewed as a "child in need of supervision." In other words, the child's home life is seen as contributing to the shooting of another person. This could be attributed to a gun not secured, thus allowing access to it by the youth, or perhaps a parent's negligence or actions, words, or deeds that contributed to the shooting act. In this case, removing the child from the home situation is often seen as the corrective action, and the parent is arrested and processed through the adult system for creating the factors that enabled a shooting death to occur.

Aged 10 to 18: Juvenile Justice System

Within this age group, *mens rea* may still be considered, but the focus is to correct the wrong and rehabilitate the offender before the youth becomes an adult. Thus, if adjudicated, the youth will be placed in a facility until the age of adulthood for that state. According to Anne Teigen (2020), in 45 states, "the maximum age of juvenile court jurisdiction is age 17." As stated earlier, the five states of Texas, Georgia, Michigan, Missouri, and Wisconsin have lowered the juvenile age to 16 (Teigen & McInnes, 2019). The youth could be waived to the adult system and face the maximum penalties, with the exception of life in prison and death as protected under the cases of *Roper v. Simmons* (2005), *Graham v. Florida* (2010), and *Miller v. Alabama* (2012).

Over the last 20 years, studies in the field of adolescent brain development (in training, Penn calls it "Teen Brain") have found the human brain is not fully developed until the mid- to late twenties. This includes the brain's functioning that controls impulses, calms emotions, provides an understanding of the consequences of behavior, and allows for rational decision-making. This directly relates to social control and the theory by Gottfredson and Hirschi (1990) purports that "people who lack self-control will tend to be impulsive, insensitive, physical (as opposed to mental), risk-taking, short-sighted, and nonverbal and they will tend therefore to engage in criminal and analogous acts" (Gottfredson & Hirschi, 1990, p. 90)

So how does a youth fail to gain self-control or lose it? Gottfredson and Hirschi (1990) present a multitude of factors, but the primary focus is that someone must monitor the child's behavior, recognize deviant behavior, and address it when it occurs to prevent the continuation of the behavior. Elements of Wilson's (1987) "lack of social buffers" and Anderson's (1994) Code of the Street, as discussed earlier, should resonate to support the theoretical foundation that positive social bonding acquired through family, especially parents, goes a long way to deter delinquent and criminal activity.

According to adolescent brain development studies, the area called the frontal lobe, and the cerebellum are still developing between the ages of 10 and 24 (Arain et al., 2013), directly affecting the output of logical reasoning. Because the frontal lobe is where the brain processes problem-solving, memory, impulsivity, and social behavior, it is the place that manages information processing. You demonstrate the maturity of your cerebellum and frontal lobe by reading this book, especially if it is assigned for a class or a training session. It is likely you would rather be doing something else, such as spending time with your family, enjoying a movie, attending a sporting event, or working out. But at this time and place, you are reading this book. What is motivating you to do that? What led you to read the previous pages and continue on to the conclusion of the book? You could humor us and say it is because the book is fascinating, and you are learning so much, but knowing most people have not reached the highest levels of Maslow's Hierarchy of Needs; you probably have a more primal motivation. Maslow's Hierarchy of Needs explains five levels of needs: physiological needs, safety, love/belonging, esteem, and self-actualization, and explains how people are motivated to achieve certain needs. According to Simons, Irwin, and Drinnien (1987), unless these needs are met, progression to the next level cannot be achieved.

The correlation between crime and age has been studied for a long time in criminology (Cornelius, Lynch, & Gore 2017). Quetelet (1833/1984) found that crime involvement tends to peak in adolescence and early adulthood and decline with age. Research and data from the National Crime Victimization Survey (NCVS) and self-report studies corroborate the effect of age on crime patterns. According to the National Crime Victimization Survey, the number of victims of violent crimes age 12 or older increased from 2.7 million in 2015 to 2.9 million in 2016, and 3.3 million in 2018 (Morgan & Oudekerk, 2019). Adolescents are likely to repeat the cycle of violence of victimizing others because of their own victimization (see Figure 3.1).

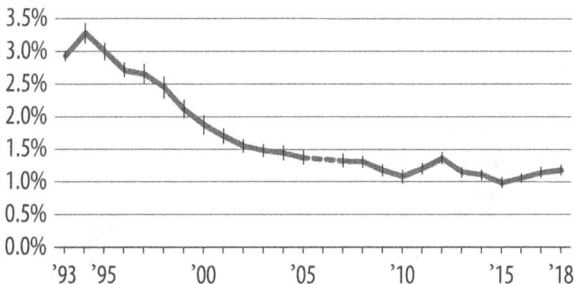

Note: See table 16 for definitions and appendix table 1 for estimates.
Source: Bureau of Justice Statistics, NCVS, 1993-2018.

FIGURE 3.1 Percentage of U.S. Residents Age 12 or Older Who Were Victims of Violent Crime, 1993–2018
Source: Morgan & Oudekerk, 2019.

Criminal involvement with the age group of 16–24 typically results from the strain and stress that results from the lack of access to opportunities. Merton (1938) explained this with his theory of goals and the means to achieve them. When strain, hardship, difficulty, or what Merton called "anomie" exists, there is a friction between the desire for the materialist goods of society and the means to achieve them. This anomic conduction creates the innovator who will use illegal means to achieve materialist goods. Youth are tied to the frustration of societal disparity that exists among different social groups. It was evident in Bernie Sanders' run for the Democratic Presidential nomination in early 2020. Although Sanders was 40–50 years senior to his base supporters averaging age 20–30, his message resonated with their feelings of strain and anomie. His message of radical change in American health care, social security, and education led youth to believe that they were being heard. "Younger people face the frightening realization that they may be the first generation to have a lower standard of living than their parents" (Kelly, 2020).

A concept called "Youth Bulge Theory" explains how a lack of employment opportunities creates a risk pool for violence. Population Action International (PAI) suggests a strong correlation between countries prone to civil conflicts and those with burgeoning youth populations over 20%.

> Youth Bulge contends that societies with rapidly growing young populations often end up with rampant unemployment and large pools of disaffected youths who are more susceptible to recruitment into rebel or terrorist groups. Countries with weak political institutions are most vulnerable to youth-bulge-related violence and social unrest.
>
> *(Beehrer, 2007)*

Penn witnessed Youth Bulge as a Fulbright scholar to Egypt in 2005, and during his half a dozen trips to Egypt with students before what was termed the "Arab Spring" in the early 2010s. One of Penn's tasks as a Fulbright scholar was to create mutual understanding and bridge the gap between the Western and Arab worlds after the terrorist attacks of September 11, 2001 (9/11). Riding in taxis in Tahir Square in Cairo, teaching college students at Cairo University, and traveling throughout Egypt allowed for great dialogue and conversation with a variety of people, including older men and women, middle-class professionals, and the very poor. Although Penn's command of Arabic was "shway shway" (a little bit/not that good), a constant rhythm of discontent was heard from individuals in their teens and early twenties. Youth remarked on how they finished school, went on to college, and could not find work that would supply enough income to start a family, buy a house, or live on their own. They felt they were being fooled by a system in which they followed the rules, but the payoff at the end was not worth the amount of time, dedication, and work they had put in to get to the goal. This sentiment came to a climax during the early 2010s as a series of anti-government protests, uprisings, and armed rebellions occurred in Tunisia, Libya, Yemen, Syria, Bahrain, and Egypt. The youth's frustration led to governments being overthrown, constitutional changes, and calls for democracy, economic freedom, and better employment (Dabashi, 2012). These events, collectively referred to as the "Arab Spring," when youth were involved in a series of anti-government protests, uprisings, and armed rebellions that spread across much of the Arab world in the early 2010s provided just one of many examples in history of the power of change that comes from youth.

The United States is not immune to such uprisings from its youth. Simply look at examples of civil rights, women's rights, labor rights, Black Lives Matter movements, as well as Native American, Black, and Latino protests—in all, the youth leaders are often experiencing Youth Bulge. Even the calls for justice in the wake of George Floyd's death have been led by youth. No social movement in the United States has existed without the youth's full participation. The average age of soldiers in World War I was 24, World War II was 26, and for Vietnam, the average age was 19 years old. Extend the definition of social change to the sciences, and you see this trend continues. The average age of the scientists involved in landing a man on the moon was slightly older at 28 (Hasler, 2009). Steven Jobs co-founded Apple at age 21. Bill Gates founded Microsoft at age 20. The frustrations, anger, and passion of youth must be heard and respected as those in their late teens and twenties historically have been the change agents of society.

Bump (2014) conducted research to identify six different generations and labeled their eras.

Coined by former news reporter Tom Brokaw in his book by the same name, the Greatest Generation includes those born 1924 and earlier.[1] These people fought and died in World War I and went through the Great Depression (Brokaw, 2000). The Silent Generation are those born between the years of 1925 and 1945. They are known as "silent" because they were more cautious than their parents (CNN, 2020). These individuals helped to shape pop culture, and the group includes many iconic filmmakers, television legends, and political satirists. Baby Boomers, an official title from the U.S. Census Bureau, includes those born between 1946 and 1964. During this period, there was a great number of births attributed to the soldiers, sailors, and other personnel coming home from World War II, beginning their lives, and starting families. Baby Boomers are currently 55–75 years old (and amount to approximately 76 million in the United States). George Masnick of the Harvard Joint Center for Housing Studies puts Generation X in the timeframe of those born from 1965 to 1984 (sometimes listed as 1965–1979). He also calls it the "baby bust," mocking "[p]undits on Madison Avenue and in the media" that call it Generation X (Masnick, 2012). Researchers Neil Howe and William Strauss (2000) use the term Millennials to describe those born 1982 through 2004 (sometimes listed as 1980–2000). They were nicknamed "the next great generation." Note that there are differences in opinion about the precise beginning and end points for these generations. According to the Pew Research Center, those who were born from 1997 to the present are considered Generation Z (also sometimes called Post-Millennials). This generation is the most racially and ethnically diverse generation (Dimock, 2019).

A recent study conducted by *Business Insider* determined that individuals in Generation Z started to build wealth earlier than Millennials because 9/11 divided the two generations on their values regarding money. Technology, mobile adaptations, a social justice orientation, and global interest are some of the results of the impact of 9/11 and how society shifted the path and trends of Millennials to Generation Z (Vogels, 2019). The aftermath of 9/11 created and shaped Generation Z's conservative views with regard to spending money and trying to avoid as much debt as possible. Millennials are in the process of "playing catch up" with their finances accrued from college tuition, while Generation Z is trying to stay ahead of the curve (Adamy & Overberg, 2019).

Understanding the power of youth is important, but we would be remiss if we did not touch upon race and youth. William Julius Wilson (1996) described anomie and how we can relate it to Youth Bulge in *When Work Disappears: The World of the New Urban Poor*. Chronic joblessness deprived those in the inner city of skills necessary to obtain and keep jobs. The disappearance of work has an adverse effect on the entire family and the neighborhoods where these individuals reside. Wilson explains how high joblessness is more devastating than high poverty levels because it creates social disorganization (Wilson, 1996). In contrast, children who are exposed to adults who are working consistently and have steady employment are more disciplined in comparison to children who do not grow up in a similar household. The sharp decline of jobs had more of an effect on Blacks than Whites because a substantial number of Blacks are unskilled compared to their White counterparts. Another factor to consider in large urban areas is that most working-age African Americans have criminal records that prevent them from having different job opportunities (Alexander, 2011).

Looking even more closely at urban areas and Black children, the Sentencing Project shows that the racial disparity in youth incarceration has increased since 2001. Juvenile incarceration fell by 54 percent from 2001 to 2015, with White youth declining faster than Black youth. In 2015 the Black youth population made up 16% of the incarcerated youth population, but of the 48,043 youth held in juvenile facilities (including residential treatment centers and detention centers) in the United States in 2015, 44% were African-American (The Sentencing Project, 2017). Black children are more susceptible to being arrested than White children, not because they commit more crime but because they are perceived as more dangerous (Equal Justice Initiative, 2017). The Uniform Crime Report (UCR) 2017 shows Whites (including Latinos) accounted for 61.6% of arrests of those under 18, while Blacks accounted for 34.9% of those arrested (U.S. Department of Justice, 2017).

In January 2017, the authors hosted a focus group with Black mothers in Houston, Texas, called "Mothers, Sons, and the Police." Twenty-one Black mothers and one White mother participated, ranging from their mid-thirties to 80 years old, with a median age of 65. One of the mothers expressed how she was going through a situation with her son being disrespectful at home and wanted some assistance; however, she was afraid to call the police for fear of them hurting or potentially killing him. This is one of the many stories told about the concerns they have with police. One of the Black mothers said, "the younger children in my household know that anytime they feel bold enough to be disrespectful, police will not get there fast enough before I knock them out." The mothers provided in-depth insight into the culture of the Black community and how hard it is raising a young Black male without the assistance of a Black father or male role model. Research explains the likelihood of incarceration for youth who reside in homes with absent fathers. Harper and McLanahan (2004) conducted a longitudinal study to examine the risk factors of adolescents with absent fathers. They determined that a sizable portion of the risk factors were added to by other factors such as poor education of the parent, poverty, and inequality. However, adolescents in households with the factor of an absent father still ranked the highest in incarceration risk (Harper & McLanahan, 2004).

In contrast, Suzuki (2002) revisited the "model minority" stereotype for Asian Americans. The article discussed earlier research that explained how Asian Americans as a single group compared to other groups (such as Blacks, Latinos, and even Whites) appeared to be doing well based on annual income while maintaining success by overcoming barriers imposed through racial discrimination (see Table 3.3).

Perhaps Asian success could be attributed to cultural factors such as being more educated and disciplined. This could also be why Asian-American youth are less likely to be involved in delinquent behavior. According to research, Asian-American youth are more likely to be victimized than other youth, with special emphasis on Asian-American immigrant girls enduring more school

TABLE 3.3 Median Household Income in the United States in 2019, by Race or Ethnic Group

Ethnic Group	Income
Asian	$98,174
Caucasian	$76,057
Hispanic	$56,113
Black	$45,438

Source: Duffin (2020a). https://www.statista.com/statistics/233324/median-household-income-in-the-united-states-by-race-or-ethnic-group/.

victimization (Koo, Peguero, & Shekarkhar, 2012). In addition, there was a rise in bias-related attacks against Asian and Asian Americans apparently related to President Trump referring to COVID-19 as the "Chinese virus" (O'Kane, 2020).

In comparison to other groups, some of the factors that would typically hinder individuals and cause strain seem to motivate Asian Americans in United States society. Throughout the literature on Asian success in the United States, the term "tiger mother" appears. Amy Chua (2011) defines a "tiger mother" as a Chinese mother who believes that:

1) Schoolwork always comes first;
2) An A-minus is a bad grade;
3) Your children must be two years ahead of their classmates in math;
4) You must never compliment your child in public;
5) If your child ever disagrees with a teacher or coach, you must always take the side of the teacher or coach;
6) The only activities your children should be permitted to do are those in which they can eventually win a medal; and
7) That medal must be gold.

These sentiments ally with the "decent family" as defined by Anderson (1994) showing strong social bonding and having social buffers (Wilson, 1987).

Summary

In this chapter, we wrestled with the definition of a youth and the issues related to psychological, cultural, economic, and social definitions of youths transitioning into adults. The debate is rich because the law may provide a chronological age in which one is an adult when we look closer in the justice system, but the definition is not clear. The power of youth is immense, as people in their teens and early twenties are filled with ambition, creativeness, feelings of invincibility, and courage that decreases as they become older. Perhaps those of us who have passed this young age admire or even resent those experiencing it because we reflect on ourselves as youth and have fond memories but also have some regrets. As both police and youth culture have been explored, the clash between the two is evident. The youth culture sees a world holding them back to be the norm, standard, vanilla, plain, and inside the lines. They desire to explore and expand. The youth culture sees a society made for those in charge but with little space for those trying to be in charge. They see the police as representative of the state. The police represent the ultimate authority figure of society. It is the police who enforce the laws created that place the youth culture's values in conflict with the established culture. What further develops the issue is who the police come in contact with as they do their job most often—youth. Consequently, belief and social distance prevail to create an "us" of youth versus a "them" of police in which daily contact is riddled with conflict-ridden interactions.

The first part of this book discusses the intersection of social distance, race, police, and youth culture. Through a social historical approach, the root of the social distance problem between youth and police is presented and displays policing as a foundation of traditional middle-class values as compared to youth culture questioning and challenging the old, and even displaying impulsivity compounded by issue of race and social class. Often academic texts bring the reader to the point of understanding the social phenomena and conclude with a few general suggestions for further research or conclusions. *Police and YOUth* moves beyond the traditional presentation of research to allow the reader to see the application, evaluation, and creation of new thinking on the subject. The second part of the text moves the reader to analyze implemented responses to the youth and police social distance question and concludes with a call for a new sub-discipline of criminology called Youth and Police Studies.

Note

1

Breakdown of Generations	
Greatest Generation	1924 and earlier
The Silent Generation	1925-1945
Baby Boomers	1946–1964
Generation X	1965-1980
Millennials	1981–1996 (sometimes listed as 1980–2000)
Generation Z	1997–present (sometimes called post-Millennials)

Note: There are differences in opinion about the precise beginning and end points of generations.

4

RESPONDING TO THE NEED

The President's Task Force on 21st Century Policing

The police and community events of 2012–2014 exposed rifts in the relation-ships between local police and the communities they protect and serve. All culminated on December 18, 2014, when President Barack Obama signed an Executive Order establishing the Task Force on 21st Century Policing.

In establishing the task force, the President spoke of the distrust that exists between too many police departments and too many communities—the sense that in a country where our basic principle is equality under the law, too many individuals, particularly young people of color, do not feel as if they are being treated fairly. When introducing the Task Force President Obama stated:

> [W]hen any part of the American family does not feel like it is being treated fairly, that's a problem for all of us. It's not just a problem for some. It's not just a problem for a particular community or a particular demographic. It means that we are not as strong as a country as we can be. And when applied to the criminal justice system, it means we're not as effective in fighting crime as we could be.
>
> *(Meares, 2016, p. 1)*

The task force provided a document designed to build trust between citizens and their peace officers so that all members of a community treat one another fairly and justly and are invested in maintaining public safety in an atmosphere of mutual respect. The Crime Bill of 1994 and the President's Commission on Crime in 1967 showed the importance of the formation of the task force as an important element in American policing. The 2015 President's Task Force on 21st Century Policing was partly in response to the uneasiness and social is-sues related to the Michael Brown incident in Ferguson, Missouri, discussed in

DOI: 10.4324/9780429424519-5

Chapter 1. The Task Force was co-chaired by Charles Ramsey, Commissioner, Philadelphia Police Department, and Laurie Robinson, Professor of Criminology, Law and Society at George Mason University. Each brought a unique perspective.

Penn once sat on a panel with Chief Ramsey at the American Society of Criminology in Philadelphia. He was reminiscent of a tough sailor—like an uncle who has aged a few years but still looks like he could scrap if necessary and beat you down if he had to. He brought a young conference delegate to tears in a discussion of crime and specifically the death penalty. The young woman said she was against the death penalty and believed it to be immoral. He quickly retorted: "Have you seen a dead body? Have you seen what these people do to other people?" In other words, he was making it clear that police officers have hellish images ingrained in their minds, unlike those college professors who have not lived through or seen the victim's side. With Ramsey's 30 years of policing experience, the exchange was a defining moment in the room.

Dr. Laurie Robinson, on the other hand, represents the refined academic co-chair. She is best known as the presidentially appointed Assistant Attorney General for the U.S. Department of Justice (DOJ) Office of Justice Programs, the research, statistics, and criminal justice assistance arm of the DOJ. The authors admire her not because of the title but for what she accomplished while in office. Robinson set up a Science Advisory Board, which launched an initiative to better integrate evidence into the Office of Justice Programs, CrimeSolutions.gov. The website serves as a "what works" clearinghouse for the criminal justice field and has become one of the best sources to search for programs that have been shown to work based on third-party empirical research. Programs strive to be rated "green" as successful. Other listings include "yellow," indicating some success, and "red," indicating no success. The days of simply throwing money at a problem and claiming success through anecdotal stories are gone. In addition, CrimeSolutions.gov directly attacks the statement often heard from patrol officers, community leaders, and even police chiefs: "If the program saves just one person, it is worth it." The information within the clearinghouse rebuts that thinking by comparing costs to benefits and outcomes. TAPS Academy is striving to be a green program in the near future.

2015 President's Task Force on 21st Century Policing included an additional nine members, including Dr. Cedric Alexander, Deputy Chief Operating Officer for Public Safety, DeKalb County, Georgia. Dr. Alexander came to the University of Houston as a keynote speaker for the University of Houston Law School. As one of the hosts, Penn took him to lunch and spent some time with him. Alexander was insightful about citizen and police interaction, basing his ideas on the belief that community resources exist, and if churches, parents, and others do their part, there will be less crime and friction between the police and community. He articulates his point of view in his book, *The New Guardians: Policing in America's Communities for the Twenty-first Century* (Alexander, 2016).

As a man who has dedicated his life to law enforcement, Alexander articulates that the police cannot guarantee the safety of communities. Instead, the police can and must work to build the community's capacity to reduce crime through fostering informal social control (p. 160). Values come from a community, and it is the police who should reinforce them both formally and informally. It is important to note that informal means occur through more casual interactions (p. 161). This provides significant support for the development of 21st-century policing as an informal means to a better policing end.

Other members of the task force included: Jose Lopez, Lead Organizer, Make the Road New York; Tracey Meares, Walton Hale Hamilton Professor of Law, Yale Law School; Brittany Packnett (now Cunningham), Executive Director, Teach for America; Susan Lee Rahr, Executive Director, Washington State Criminal Justice Training Commission; Constance Rice, Co-Director, Advancement Project; Sean Michael Smoot, Director and Chief Counsel, Police Benevolent and Protective Association of Illinois; Bryan Stevenson, Founder, and Executive Director, Equal Justice Initiative; and Robert Villaseñor, Chief of Police, Tucson Police Department. The backgrounds and expertise of the committee members formed a mosaic of diversity consisting of men, women, government, law, research, and the non-profit sector coming together to provide guidance to the President, law enforcement, and the United States during a time when issues of race and policing collided.

The task force recommendations were organized around six main topics areas or "pillars": (1) Building Trust and Legitimacy; (2) Policy and Oversight; (3) Technology and Social Media; (4) Community Policing and Crime Reduction; (5) Officer Training and Education, and (6) Officer Safety and Wellness. Two overarching recommendations emerged: the creation of a National Crime and Justice Task Force to examine all areas of criminal justice and the proposal of reforms and presidential support for programs that take a comprehensive and inclusive look at community-based initiatives addressing core issues such as poverty, education, and health and safety. The call is for a policing strategy that goes beyond community policing to bring procedural justice, recognition of biases, and fair and impartial policing to all citizens. Penn first presented these important concepts at a 2013 conference in a talk titled "Policing by TOTALS," which will be summarized and presented in Chapter 6. Policing by TOTALS places Transparency, Openness, Trust, Accessibility, Legitimacy, and Safety as guiding principles for policing in all neighborhoods and with all people.

Pillar One: Building Trust and Legitimacy

Research strongly indicates that most citizens believe that the police are fair; they trust them and defer to their authority. Furthermore, when trust and legitimacy are high, citizens will cooperate by reporting crimes and criminals, providing testimony, and otherwise holding offenders accountable (Davis, 2017; Tyler & Fagan, 2008). To gain legitimacy, law enforcement must be perceived as fair and as acting in procedurally just ways. Thus, policing agencies cannot be seen as an occupying force sent to control a group of people; instead, community policing concepts are applied, calling for law enforcement to be guardians rather than just warriors. Procedural justice emerges out of Pillar One by building voice, transparency, impartiality, consistency, and fairness into a policing process to develop public trust and legitimacy. Law enforcement proactively promotes public trust of all people by positively engaging communities with high crime rates, which are often the most investigated and have the highest rates of police presence. Policing becomes a two-prong warrior when necessary but actively moves to be a guardian.

Having traveled to some remote parts in Africa and the Middle East, Penn has seen the luxury enjoyed by American citizens: one simply dials three numbers (911) and in a matter of minutes, a stranger comes on the scene prepared to use deadly force to protect our lives. What a service! This is the warrior police officer often portrayed in recruiting posters and dramatized in television and movies. The protector or guardian image emerges in the practice of building relations to prevent and also mend warrior policing. Consider the United States foreign policy of war and nation-building as exhibited in Germany, Japan, Korea, Vietnam, Iraq, and Afghanistan over the last 80 years. After the warrior mentality weeds out the negative issues or threat, the guardian comes to seed in a plan to rebuild the country, in many cases making those countries strong, viable economic entities. In 1991 the U.S. Department of Justice's Weed and Seed program was developed to do the same: weed out violent crime, gang activity, and drug use and trafficking in target areas, and then seed the target area by restoring the neighborhood through social and economic revitalization. Weed and Seed integrated law enforcement, community policing, prevention, intervention, treatment, and neighborhood restoration efforts to achieve these goals. At its height, Weed and Seed programs were in more than 150 communities across the country. The last sites funded for Weed and Seed programming were in 2010 (The Weed and Seed Strategy, 2004).

Pillar One revitalizes Weed and Seed programming because it provides for unique crime prevention approaches. It is a strategy based on collaboration, coordination, community participation, and leveraging resources (The Weed and Seed Strategy, 2004). Trust, legitimacy, voice, transparency, impartiality, consistency, and fairness are words that move the foundations of community policing to 21st-century policing as all members of society, no matter race, gender, language, life experiences, and cultural backgrounds, are necessary as a part of building better police departments and community member partners.

Pillar Two: Policy and Oversight

A diverse group of people in the police workforce furthers dialogue between different groups and enables community members from disenfranchised populations to be heard so that policies will reflect the values of the communities being policed. Clear and comprehensive policies must be developed on use of force (use of de-escalation), mass demonstrations, consent before searches, gender identification, racial profiling, and performance measures such as the use of external and independent investigations. Policies should be made available to the public to ensure transparency. Just as with any policy, a review should occur periodically, and civilian oversight mechanisms should be put in place. The Community Oriented Policing Services (COPS) Office and the Office of Justice Programs (OJP) should provide technical assistance and funding to small agencies taking steps toward interagency collaboration, shared services, and regional training. Additionally, the reality of officers being relieved of duty from one agency and simply moving on to another is a problem. Thus, the International Association of Director of Law Enforcement Standards and Training (IADLEST) should be responsible for the National Decertification Index to serve as the keeper of national information on decertified officers with the goal of covering all agencies in the United States and its territories.

A reality of policing, just as with any field, is the credentialing of the employee. When a police officer is disciplined or removed from duty, it is a human resources issue. Thus, the officer deserving the protections of employment law and practices will have his or her dismissal kept as a confidential matter in most cases. A police department follows the same practice and usually does not disclose the specific details of the officer's discipline or dismissal. Here is where the recycling occurs. The officer leaves one police department to move to another part of the country and becomes an officer in a new department. Thus, an officer displaying traits contrary to 21st-century policing may move from department to department without stopping the officer's toxic behaviors.

Providing policy and oversight allows for training and administrative supervision for officers to guide their actions when interacting with the public. It is ironic that in many departments, the least experienced officers are often put into the most challenging situations. Policing, like many other forms of employment, depends on seniority. Thus, the most desired work times and days are coveted by the most senior officers. For police officers, Monday through Friday, day shift, 7 AM to 3 PM is "prime time." This shift allows an officer with a family to wake up with the family, work during times when a spouse is also at work and children are at school, and perhaps even pick up the kids from school, prepare dinner, and spend time with family before bed and doing it again the next day. Evening shifts, usually 3 PM to 10 PM or later, especially on Friday and Saturday evenings, are often avoided due to the influx of calls and criminal activity. Ironically, the officer with the least seniority often is placed, finally, either at the station or the city's geographical location that is most desired.

Nevertheless, Penn often hears from officers: "I am getting too old to chase down those criminals." Thus, the least experienced officers not only serve during the most active periods but also in the most crime-ridden areas. This reminds Penn of the response often heard when asking officers during a civilian interaction training course: How many years were you in the police department before you felt comfortable doing a routine traffic stop? First, he would usually be corrected by at least one officer in the audience in that there is no such thing as a routine traffic stop, but next, the consensus of the group was generally that it took three to seven years to feel comfortable doing a traffic stop. Police in training sessions also indicated that they did not handle all people the same when it came to civilian interaction. Height, weight, build, gender, and yes, even race, were mentioned as aspects that would cause them to move to a higher degree of aggressiveness. These answers made Penn realize that his 300-pound Black male frame was most in danger during the late evenings and nights when newer officers were on duty. Thus, policy and oversight are vital in order to allow 21st-century policing practices to become a motor memory practice in police operations.

Pillar Three: Technology and Social Media

The task force stated: "The use of technology can improve policing practices and build community trust and legitimacy" (President's Task Force on 21st Century Policing, 2015, p. 2). By fully using the advancements of technology and social media, law enforcement can move engagement and education of the community to a higher level in which dialogue can truly be a two-way communication in which expectations about policy, transparency, accountability, and privacy can be explored and discovered. With rapidly changing technology, assessment, evaluation, and adjustments must often occur. The Department of Justice, working with law enforcement, should establish national standards for the research and development of new technology including auditory, visual, and biometric data; less-than-lethal technology; and the development of segregated radio spectrums such as FirstNet, which was designed to operate, maintain, and improve the speed on a nationwide wireless broadband network dedicated to public safety. Technology should be developed with local needs assessed, including the need to communicate across agencies and jurisdictions while maintaining civil and human rights protections—all done with increasing community trust and access. Technology has affected policing because of the different strategies designed to assist with investigations and catching criminals. The impact of the development of social media has been two-fold. On the one hand, it has made it easy to catch "inept" criminals, that is, the ones who post their whereabouts while in the midst of committing an offense. On the other hand, it has made it very difficult to catch criminals involved with cybercrimes who commit identity fraud and theft, sexual solicitation of a minor, and so on (Pollock, 2017).

Pillar Four: Community Policing and Crime Reduction

This pillar emphasizes the importance of community policing as a tool to reduce crime. Community policing is often based on the belief that police should partner with community members to help prevent and reduce crime (Pollock, 2017). However, it can be referred to as "soft policing" as compared to the warrior policing style of breaking down doors and making arrests. This pillar argues, as we do in this book, that community policing is a crime prevention tool. When law enforcement works with community residents to identify problems and collaborate on implementing solutions, the results can enhance public safety. Community policing enables law enforcement to understand the complex causal factors of crime as emphasized in Chapter 2 when American policing history was discussed. As this pillar explains, 21st-century policing reflects the values of protection and promotes the dignity of all, especially the most vulnerable such as children and youth, who are most at risk of crime and violence.

> Law enforcement agencies should avoid using law enforcement tactics that unnecessarily stigmatize youth and marginalize their participation in schools (where law enforcement should have limited involvement in discipline) and communities.
>
> *(President's Task Force on 21st Century Policing, 2015, p. 3)*

It goes on to stress that police agencies should seek out and hear the voices of youth in the community by "facilitating youth participation" in research and problem solving as well as develop and fund leadership training and life skills through positive youth/police collaboration and interactions (President's Task Force on 21st Century Policing, 2015).

Chapter 6 directly relates the Task Force's recommendation about the proper use of police in schools to apply in Teen And Police Service (TAPS) Academy programming.

Pillar Five: Training and Education

The nation is becoming more pluralistic, and as the scope of law enforcement's responsibilities expands, the need for the most effective training becomes greater. Issues of international terrorism, evolving technologies, rising immigration, changing laws, new cultural mores, and growing mental health issues are just a few of the dilemmas modern policing faces today and in the future.

Law enforcement should engage community members, especially those with special expertise in the training process, and provide leadership training to officers throughout their careers. This training involves developing a national postgraduate institute of policing for the most senior executives. Within this learning environment, a standardized curriculum will be taught, preparing executives to lead agencies in the 21st Century.

One suggestion is that the Peace Officer and Standards Training (POST) boards make Crisis Intervention Training (CIT) mandatory, which is already the case for the more than 80,000 officers in the state of Texas. The description of the course states:

> With increasing frequency, law enforcement is being called upon to respond to individuals in serious mental health crises. It is necessary for law enforcement personnel to understand mental illness and the tactics and techniques that have been proven to work most effectively when responding to individuals in these situations. These tactics and techniques are different from those routinely taught to officers to manage conflict.

This 40-hour, five-day course was mandated for all Houston Police officers with the passage of the Sandra Bland Act (SB 1849) by the Texas Legislature in 2017. The Texas Commission on Law Enforcement (TCOLE) replaced the previous 16-hour course with the 40-hour TCOLE 1850 class. It is required training for all officers in the state of Texas licensed after April 1, 2018 (Houston Police Department, 2020). Pillar Five goes on to urge for more recruitment and in-service training in the areas of disease, addiction, implicit bias, cultural responsiveness, policing in a democratic society, procedural justice, and effective social interaction and tactical skills.

In Penn's experience, the most exciting training opportunities come when there is a mixture of civilians and officers in the same session. These training sessions often take twice as long, compared to officers-only or citizens-only training on the same subject. A special effort is made to break the ice and allow for free-flowing discussion. Some techniques must be employed to make the most of training police and educating civilian students. First, it works best when both an officer and a civilian are conducting the training. This technique allows audience members to identify with one or the other. It allows the trainers to make a case for both sides and ensure that all the pros and cons are heard. Second, the set-up of the room must avoid an aisle down the middle. An arrangement with an aisle creates an us-versus-them situation in which officers sit on one side and civilians on another. To further avoid a polarizing atmosphere, the leaders should assign breakout session groups in which officers and civilians are intermixed, so as to reduce the possibility that one group will be comprised of only police or only civilians. Third, it is best to avoid movie- or arena-style seating. Everyone should be level, ideally looking at each other with moveable tables and chairs arranged in a large square or rectangle. Finally, the presentation of information must be made without bias or accusations, and perhaps with an almost a Columbo-type fashion of stumbling and trying to understand thoughts, beliefs, practices, and issues of importance so that there is teaching from the audience, thus allowing the participants to dialogue, listen, and eventually educate each other on the subject. The Houston Police Department furthered the concept by creating a course titled "Building Trust from Trauma," a mandatory, eight-hour block of instruction for all 5,200 of its sworn officers. The course is co-taught with a sworn officer and community member. Penn is one of the community member instructors. Through applying procedural justice, the course defines trauma experienced by officers as well as by community members to support 21st-Century policing methods of building better relationships in the community to ease the devastating outcomes of trust-eroding events and practices in policing.

Pillar Six: Officer Wellness and Safety

Pillar Six makes clear that the wellness and safety of officers is critical for public safety. The call is for the U.S. Department of Justice to encourage and assist departments in the implementation of scientifically supported shift lengths; the collection of data on officer deaths, injuries, and near misses; and the tracking of preventive practices such as first aid training and wearing of tactical vests and seat belts. The safety of officers should be considered at every stage of the organization. The federal government should develop programs to provide financial support for law enforcement officers to continue to pursue educational opportunities. This is discussed further in Chapter 8 as a call for the establishment of Youth and Police Studies, thus supporting the close relationship between the college/university setting and policing. Finally, Congress should develop and enact peer review error management legislation.

The Officer Down Memorial Page (www.odmp.org/), which provides a memorial for officers killed in the line of duty, states that more than 24,000 officers have died while on duty since 1776. Causes of death and injury are vital to understanding the safety of the 800,000-plus law enforcement offices in the United States.

While teaching college and university courses, both authors have been shocked to hear the number of students expressing approval of the violent and brutal killings of officers and how they feel it makes for one less "crooked cop" they have to deal with. The most disturbing part of the conversation was how easy it was for them to say they knew people who would gladly kill a cop and sleep well at night. One of the students made the comment, "ain't nobody worrying about these stupid-a** pigs, that is what they get, we will do time if it cost one of them their life." This mindset that it is acceptable to kill an officer makes Pillar Six even more essential for officers to practice.

As we look at the Task Force Report for solutions, we reflect on an article a 20-year veteran officer gave us after several conversations on the topic of police shootings of unarmed Black males. The article, "Five Behavior Characteristics That Tend To Get Cops Killed" (Police Officers Association of Michigan, n.d.) resulted from a five-year study of officers murdered in the line of duty that led the Federal Bureau of Investigation research team to note that there are certain behavioral characteristics that tend to get cops killed. The article supports much of the Task Force Report by agreeing that while community-oriented policing is possible and even encouraged, there can never be a loss of police presence and, barring that, ensuring that the environment is known, controlled, and maintained for the safety of the public and the officers.

The five characteristics are:

1   **Overly Friendly**: Overly friendly behavior at an inappropriate time can backfire, researchers warn. That mindset can lull an officer into a sense of complacency, lead to the granting of dangerous favors or accommodations, and might be misinterpreted by an offender as a potential weakness or a sign of vulnerability.

2   **Service-Oriented**: Service to the community is part of policing, but on the street, your "customer" is not always right. To protect and serve the community, the researchers remind, "officers must realize that they need to protect themselves first" and not indulge a "misguided sense of service" that results in prioritizing prisoners' comfort over their own personal safety.

3   **Hesitant About Using Force**: The researchers found that officers killed in the line of duty tended to use less force than other officers felt they would use in similar circumstances. In addition, they engaged in use of force only as a "last resort." Their peers said they "would use force at an earlier point in similar circumstances." The Courts have confirmed that the use of force is justified in situations that officers perceive as threatening (e.g., *Graham v. Connor*, 1989).

4   **Given to Short-Cutting**: Officers killed in the line of duty often ignored or sidestepped rules, "especially in regard to arrests, confrontations with prisoners, traffic stops, and waiting for backup when backup is available." These officers were not viewed as slackers but more often hard workers seeking to be top performers. They were driven to make more arrests, receive more commendations, and be placed in desired assignments. Ironically, such rule-breakers are often rewarded after violating procedures designed to protect them and others.

5   **Trusting of "Perceptual Shorthand"**: Officers who ended up dead often relied heavily on their perceived ability to "read" people and situations. They depended on an abbreviated process by which they analyzed environments and subjects and chose their actions based on their quick perceptions. That is, they used their gut rather than what they learned in training. Their police presence was dropped when they saw signs of co-operation, heard promises not to cause trouble, enjoyed a prior history of non-violent contacts with a suspect, or sensed they had a rapport. A police presence that maintains a mind-set to stay open to subtle and not-so-subtle

shifts in every interaction was lost. The murdered officers made themselves vulnerable by failing "to recognize that their perception of an incident can vary greatly from the offender's perception of what is occurring" and what may occur before the contact is over.

It is important to understand that social distance needs to be removed in order for peaceful interaction between the two groups. Implicit bias is something that can create the social distance between police officers and a youth because it is instinctual. However, with the proper training and effective learning methods, it is something that can be addressed. According to research conducted by Hall, Hall, and Perry (2016), race has been a powerful factor surrounding the fatal encounters between police and Black civilians.

The President's Task Force for 21st-Century Policing was a significant accomplishment in helping the United States mend the rift between citizens and police. The tone of the task force was one of ensuring voice and procedural justice for all citizens.

On January 22, 2020, Attorney General Barr announced the establishment of the President's Commission on Law Enforcement and the Administration of Justice, established by President Donald Trump with the signing of Executive Order No. 13896 on October 28, 2019. The purpose was to create a Commission that would explore modern issues affecting law enforcement that have the most impact on U.S. police's ability to reduce crime. According to a government press release (U.S. Department of Justice, 2020):

> There is no more noble and important profession than law enforcement. A free and safe society requires a trusted and capable police force to safeguard our rights to life and liberty," said Attorney General William P. Barr. "But as criminal threats and social conditions have changed the responsibilities and roles of police officers, there is a need for a modern study of how law enforcement can best protect and serve American communities. This is why the President instructed me to establish this critical Commission, whose members truly reflect the best there is in law enforcement. Together, we will examine, discuss, and debate how justice is administered in the United States and uncover opportunities for progress, improvement, and innovation.
>
> *(U.S. Department of Justice, 2020)*

The Commission's focus was to research "important current issues facing law enforcement and the criminal justice system," and it recommended a variety of study subjects, such as, but not limited to:

- the challenges to law enforcement associated with mental illness, homelessness, substance abuse, and other social factors that influence crime and strain criminal justice resources;

- the recruitment, hiring, training, and retention of law enforcement officers, including in rural and tribal communities;
- refusals by State and local prosecutors to enforce laws or prosecute categories of crimes;
- the need to promote public confidence and respect for the law and law enforcement officers; and
- the effects of technological innovations on law enforcement and the criminal justice system, including the challenges and opportunities presented by such innovations.

(Executive Office of the President of the United States, 2020)

Commission members included Chair, Phil Keith, Director, Community Oriented Policing Services; Vice-Chair, Katharine Sullivan, Principal Deputy Assistant Attorney General, Office of Justice Programs; David Bowdich, Deputy Director, Federal Bureau of Investigation; James Clemmons, Sheriff, Richmond County, North Carolina; Chris Evans, Chief of Operations, Drug Enforcement Administration; Frederick Frazier, City Councilman at Large, McKinney, Texas, and Police Officer, Dallas Police Department; Robert Gualtieri, Sheriff, Pinellas County, Florida; Gina Hawkins, Chief of Police, Fayetteville, North Carolina; Regina Lombardo, Acting Director, Bureau of Alcohol, Tobacco, Firearms, and Explosives; Erica MacDonald, United States Attorney, District of Minnesota; Ashley Moody, Attorney General, State of Florida; Nancy Parr, Commonwealth's Attorney, Chesapeake, Virginia; Craig Price, Secretary of Public Safety, South Dakota; Gordon Ramsay, Chief of Police, Wichita, Kansas; David B. Rausch, Director, Tennessee Bureau of Investigation; John Samaniego, Sheriff, Shelby County, Alabama; James Smallwood, Sergeant, Metropolitan Nashville, Tennessee, Police Department; and Donald Washington, Director, United States Marshals Services (Executive Office of the President of the United States, 2020).

A gang specialist well-respected for his ability to work within gangs and throughout the community promoting crime prevention was asked to give testimony to the Commission. He contacted Penn to prepare for his five to ten minutes of discussion on the subject, conducted by phone due to COVID-19 safety concerns. The specialist's commander in anti-gang work was added to the call. The conversation was a three-part harmony of practice, policing, and theory as it moved through prevention, intervention, and subversion. Part of the discussion was the concept of police officers knocking down doors on one day but returning to that same family to provide understanding and restoration at another time. The deep roots of gang life have a strong tentacle hold on poor, African-American and Latino youth and their families. It may be difficult for those in the middle class to understand the pressing hold gang life has for survival in these communities. The creation of a Task Force and Commission moves the issue to a national discussion in which thought turns into recommendations, and recommendations can be turned into policy and practice.

Stark differences are apparent when comparing the 2015 Task Force to the Commission of 2020. The Task Force had 11 members compared to 18 members in the Commission. Of the 18 Commission members, six were members of the Executive Branch, serving at the will of the President. No members of the Task Force were a part of the Executive Branch. The Task Force had 90 days to complete their research, and the Commission had one year to report its findings. I asked my network of police chiefs about the Commission and one stated:

> At least President Trump established a Presidential Commission on Law Enforcement and the Administration of Justice. This Commission is definitely needed. President Obama refused to establish such a Commission, despite numerous requests and justifications. We'll have to see how this Commission functions, but it is a step in the right direction.
>
> *(Former Police Chief from a large urban city)*

Another chief stated: "It is a start, but the composition isn't the best. Better than nothing at this point. Time will tell." Finally, the authors talked with Cedric Alexander, a member of the 2015 Task Force, to learn his thoughts about the Commission. He pointed to his comments in *The Washington Post* on January 22 in an article titled: "Attorney General Launches Presidential Commission on Law Enforcement" (Jackman, 2020). In the article, Alexander said he hoped: "going forward that they would consider incorporating those from the civil rights and human rights community into their platform because they would be able to add valuable insight into their mission" (Jackman, 2020). Alexander went on to note that there were no big-city police chiefs on the commission. The largest city represented by a police chief on the panel was Wichita, Kansas, the 51st-largest city in the United States. In the same *Washington Post* article, Kristen Clarke, president of the Lawyers Committee for Civil Rights Under Law, said: "It's unclear whether this group has commissioners who bring to bear expertise on critical civil rights issues such as racial disparities when it comes to use of excessive or deadly force, stops and searches, and racial profiling."

Criminal justice issues rising to the point of a Presidential Commission is not new. In 2017, as part of larger criminal justice reform, the idea came up in the U.S. Senate. It was reintroduced in 2019 but had no success in moving forward. The 2020 Commission had a focus on promoting respect for law enforcement officers, but had no members from academia, non-profit entities, businesses, government service providers, or other individuals who are experts in community and criminal justice system interaction. Where some may believe the Obama Task Force was pro-citizen and others will believe the Trump Commission was pro-police, a balancing act in criminal justice will hopefully emerge in which issues from both sides will be heard and become policy for 21st-century policing.

The Commission's report was published in December of 2020. The voluminous 300-page document presents that the basic mission of police is to preserve the rule of law and that law enforcement cannot alone solve the problem of crime. The recommendation from the Commission was to enhance programs that address mental illness, homelessness, drug addiction, and youth from committing crimes "…so that communities can delimit and restore the mission of law enforcement to its core duty of preventing crime" (Executive Office of the President of the United States, 2020, p. xix).

The 2020 Commission pulls policing away from the collaborative working environment presented in the 2015 Task Force Report. It acknowledges social problems exist but states that the primary prevention of unwarranted force by law enforcement is for citizens to "Comply, then Complain" (p. xviii). It is ironic that "comply, then complain" was the prevailing conclusion by the 2020 Commission amid a time when the public witnessed George Floyd die on camera after he lay on a street for more than eight minutes with the knee of police officer Derek Chauvin on his neck.

Shortly after the murder of George Floyd, TAPS Academy and several other youth organizations in Houston were asked to gather the youth voice concerning what should be the next steps in police reform during the very turbulent time of May–July 2020. The think-tank group used selected recommendations from the President's Task Force on 21st-Century Policing (2015) to be the start point for gathering youth opinions. Here are the findings:

2015 Task Force Recommendation 1.3: Law enforcement agencies should establish a culture of transparency and accountability in order to build public trust and legitimacy.

Youth Voice:

Let us call our parents when we are stopped. Let us use our phones to video what is going on. Let us put our phone on the dashboard. We want to make sure our side of the story is told, and we will feel safer.

Recommendation Summary with Youth Voice:

Youth believe if police reform includes establishing a culture of transparency and accountability, youth should be allowed to call their parents and video their encounters with police.

2015 Task Force Recommendation 1.4: Law enforcement agencies should promote legitimacy internally within the organization by applying the principles of procedural justice.

Youth Voice:

Don't treat us like we are thugs. When we aren't doing something terrible, don't be so aggressive. Be fair and don't treat White people differently than Black or Brown people. My color is not a crime. We are all human, and we should all be treated the same. Give people of color a fair chance and the benefit of the doubt before making a judgment.

Recommendation Summary with Youth Voice:

Applying the principals of procedural fairness, youth recommend treating everyone fairly no matter what color. Youth do not believe they are treated fairly. Officers need to learn to de-escalate. Youth do not want to be treated like a mass murderer for a simple traffic stop. Police should receive training on how to treat everyone the same and should be able to discern the difference in approaching and interacting with an individual who is stopped or arrested for a felony offense or a traffic violation.

2015 Task Force Recommendation 1.8: Law enforcement agencies should strive to create a workforce that contains a broad range of diversity including race, gender, language, life experience, and cultural background to improve understanding and effectiveness in dealing with all communities.

Youth Voice:

I need police officers that look like me and understand where I come from. Don't use the N word when you talk to us. Police act scared of Black people. Police should be around more Black people so they will know I am not a threat. Police officers should have to spend hours in communities of color and learn how to interact with the people. Police should come around to spend time with the community, not just when there is trouble.

Recommendation Summary with Youth Voice:

Police should have cultural diversity training that includes time spent in minority neighborhoods. This would allow police to interact with other races and cultures to negate the "fear factor" that governs the officer's demeanor and unnecessary use of force. Police officers should be required to participate in community events.

2015 Task Force Recommendation 2.1: Law enforcement agencies should collaborate with community members to develop policies and strategies in communities and neighborhoods disproportionately affected by crime for deploying resources that aim to reduce crime by improving relationships, greater community engagement, and cooperation.

Youth Voice:

Have counselors in schools instead of police officers. We need people who can help us be leaders, not send us to jail. Help clean up our neighborhoods. Stop coming to our schools and scaring us when we haven't done anything wrong. "Us kids like people who will let us speak to someone instead of being scared that if we say something wrong, we go to jail."

Recommendation Summary with Youth Voice:

Youth would like to see a Community Oriented Policing Model wherein trained police focus on building police relationships with youth and the community. Through that relationship, police would teach them about equality and a positive path in life.

2015 Task Force Recommendation 2.2: Law enforcement agencies should have comprehensive policies on the use of force that include training, investigations, prosecutions, data collection, and information sharing. These policies must be clear, concise, and openly available for public inspection.

Youth Voice:

Give me time to respond before you try to hurt me. We are people, not animals. Get rid of the officers that always use force unnecessarily. The use of force scares people, and it makes them not want to talk to police.

Recommendation Summary with Youth Voice:

Youth believe firing should be an option to prevent officers from repeating discriminatory use of excessive force. They should be trained on use of force and de-escalation (comprehensive use of force training).

2015 Task Force Recommendation 2.9: Law enforcement agencies and municipalities should refrain from practices requiring officers to issue a predetermined number of tickets, citations, arrests, or summonses, or to initiate investigative contacts with citizens for reasons not directly related to improving public safety, such as generating revenue.

Youth Voice:

It seems like police are picking on my area. It looks like they are choosing random people to arrest. They seem to come in just looking for some little something to arrest someone for. They act like they want to get us in jail. The use of a quota of arrests is wrong. "From personal experience, many police are always in my neighborhood looking for people to put in jail for no reason. It is completely unfair to my community how the police choose to pick on us based on race and economic status."

Recommendation Summary with Youth Voice:

Youth see quotas as a deep-rooted issue sending the message that police are selectively riding in certain communities looking for youth and citizens to arrest just to meet quotas. Youth see this as a priority issue.

2015 Task Force Recommendation 2.13: Law enforcement agencies should adopt and enforce policies prohibiting profiling and discrimination based on race, ethnicity, national origin, religion, age, gender, gender identity/expression, sexual orientation, immigration status, disability, housing status, occupation, or language fluency.

Youth Voice:

Officers stop kids just because they are Black or Brown even though we haven't done anything wrong. Looking suspicious shouldn't be a reason to stop someone.

Recommendation Summary with Youth Voice:

Racial profiling is discriminatory and should be stopped, closing the loopholes for officers to use "he looked suspicious" to justify an arrest and/or stop youth.

2015 Task Force Recommendation 4.1: Law enforcement agencies should develop and adopt policies and strategies that reinforce the importance of community engagement in managing public safety.

Youth Voice:

Don't arrest us for little things. Give more warning tickets. Instead of driving without a license, tell us how to get a license. Send us somewhere for help, not to jail. We need a lot of help. Start talking to us and not just jumping to conclusions.

Recommendation Summary with Youth Voice:

Youth recommend that police should have certain policies (strategies) in place to prove that police are vested in the community. This would be demonstrated by police providing information to them on how to get jobs, get a license, and so on. Youth believe in Community Oriented Policing.

2015 Task Force Recommendation 4.4: Communities should support a culture and practice of policing that reflects the values of protection and promotion of the dignity of all, especially the most vulnerable.

Youth Voice:

Talk to me with respect. Don't treat me like I'm a criminal. Don't use the N word. Let me drive to somewhere safe in the light to talk if you want to question me. Police officers need to be more understanding. Don't assume we are doing something wrong because of our clothes or our skin color. Don't treat everyone like a criminal. Don't immediately label me. Treat people how you want to be treated.

Recommendation Summary with Youth Voice:

Police should be vested in the community and remember their job is to protect and serve and treat everyone with dignity and respect. They should use the Golden Rule.

2015 Task Force Recommendation 4.6: Communities should adopt policies and programs that address the needs of children and youth most at risk for crime or violence and reduce aggressive law enforcement tactics that stigmatize youth and marginalize their participation in schools and communities.

Youth Voice:

Help us in school to stay out of trouble and avoid getting suspended or sent to an alternative school. Help us not get arrested so we won't have to go to court or juvenile probation. We have problems we need help with at home, and that's why we get in trouble at school. No one asks us about what is going on at home. Teach us how to correct the mistake and not make it again. Police should have a task force of volunteers who can help kids with homework, sports, and medical and mental issues instead of pushing kids into detention centers or special schools.

Recommendation Summary with Youth Voice:

Unequivocally, youth ask for a Community Oriented Policing Model wherein police will talk to them and get to know them. It is clear from the comments that students have issues at home and need someone to talk to. They come to school to get away from what's happening at home, only to be sent to an alternative school, which is not the answer. Clearly expressed, they need police, mentors, and volunteers to talk to. It is a cry for help!

2015 Task Force Recommendation 4.7: Communities need to affirm and recognize the voices of youth in community decision-making, facilitate youth-led research and problem solving, and develop and fund youth leadership training and life skills through positive youth/police collaboration and interactions.

Youth Voice:

We shouldn't be scared of each other. They should just stop and talk to us for no reason. I saw on TV a police officer playing basketball with a group of kids. He was not afraid. He just wanted to get to know us. I would like to see us play a basketball game together. Get to know us and not just "roam around in a car." Police should get to know us. Talk to us to see how our day is going.

Recommendation Summary with Youth Voice:

Youth want programs that will produce positive interaction with police. This is the ultimate answer to much of our youth-police–related issues. The comments indicate that youth want a relationship with police based on mutual respect. Once a relationship of mutual respect and trust is developed, youth will become a valuable "partner" in policing the community.

Overall, when reviewing the recommendations from youth, common elements emerge. Youth want better communication with police, meaning that officers should show respect and not be fearful of Black or Brown youth. Better communication involves not using the "N" word, no racial profiling, and positive interaction with youth. It involves getting officers out of the schools for the purpose of arrests. It means that instead, they should be changing the dynamics of police and youth interaction to follow the pillars of the President's Task Force on 21st Century Policing.

(Youth Voice on Recommendations for Police Reform, 2020)

Summary

Chapter 4 presents the research that responds to the conflict between youth and police. As the death of George Floyd caused policymakers, youth, police departments, and the general public to search for answers to reform policing, we find that many have dusted off the President's Task Force on 21st Century Policing, a document written in 2015, as the guiding principles to reduce injustice and increase the fair and just treatment of all citizens. The document moves community policing to reach all people, including the most disenfranchised, allowing youth to see community-led policing as a strategy in a time when defunding or even eliminating police has made it to a national conversation. The remaining chapters of this text allow the reader to see these pillars in practice through the TAPS Academy's implementation to reduce the social distance between law enforcement and citizens and the enactment of the Community Safety Education Act of Texas.

5

TEEN AND POLICE SERVICE (TAPS) ACADEMY

The U.S. Department of Justice funded the Teen And Police Service (TAPS) Academy through a Community Oriented Police Service (COPS) grant in August 2011. Author Everette Penn still remembers when he received the email. He was teaching a summer Advanced Juvenile Delinquency course and while on a break, the Houston Police Department's email arrived saying that Penn's team had been awarded this challenge to start the Teen And Police Service Academy.

It was a challenge because the grant process is difficult, but what the future TAPS team set out to do was seen as impossible by many. "You mean you are going to put police officers and at-risk youth in the same room? Surely you are joking because someone is going to get stabbed, injured, or killed." To this day, after ten years, no such action has occurred. A process was established that made TAPS different and successful—a process of people understanding each other, gaining and using mutual respect, listening to each other, and providing opportunities for dialogue. This is not to say that TAPS is the time to start singing "Kum Ba Yah," hold hands, and give a group hug; rather TAPS Academy can be looked at as an advancement of police and community programming that builds upon the lessons learned from the past, from A to Z—Big Brothers Big Sisters, Citizens Police Academy, DARE, Explorers, GREAT, Officer Friendly, Neighborhood Watch, Police Athletic Leagues, Teen Courts, Youth Councils, and so many more. In fact, the principles of TAPS Academy's mutual respect and dialogue came to Penn as he served as a Fulbright Scholar to Egypt in 2005 in response to West and the Middle East tensions post September 11, 2001, terrorist attacks.

The terrorist attacks of September 11, 2001 (9/11) in Washington, DC, New York, and western Pennsylvania resonated with Penn because he was raised in Washington, DC, his family is originally from New York City, and he received

DOI: 10.4324/9780429424519-6

his doctoral degree from Indiana University of Pennsylvania, not far from Shanksville, Pennsylvania, where the last of the four planes was brought down by the passengers avoiding another target. The authors realize there are readers of this text who were not even born at the time of the 9/11 attacks, and may only know of the day on which nearly 3,000 people lost their lives through history courses, but for those who lived through it, it is an indelible memory. From that day, anti-Middle East, anti-Muslim, and anti-Arabic sentiments became prominent in the United States, and anti-American and anti-Western feelings have existed in the Arab world. As noted in Chapter 3, Penn was a Fulbright scholar teaching on the American criminal justice system at Cairo University in Egypt. Through his reading of literature on peace, conflict mediation, history, and even the Bible, as well as interacting, listening, and reflecting with dozens of those he would meet in his travels in the Middle East and Africa, the elements of reducing social distance, mutual understanding, active listening, and working toward peace and understanding became clear. He did not know his Middle Eastern travel in 2005 would lay the foundation for TAPS Academy six years later.

The Teen And Police Service (TAPS) Academy works like other youth and police programming to create a positive bond between youth and police. However, TAPS Academy does something unlike any of the other programs: it focuses on reducing the social distance between officers and highest-risk youth while building life and academic skills through its more than 20 modules. TAPS provides for the first time a curriculum aimed at building the relationship between youth and police and has been accredited to provide one high school credit in the state of Texas. TAPS Academy builds upon previous youth and police programs to take the very best out of each to specifically build a relationship with the most at-risk and disenfranchised youth—the youth who wants to kill police, the youth who believes there is no justice in the juvenile or criminal justice system, and the youth who has experienced vicariously or personally the very worst of the justice system and its agents. These are the desired TAPS Academy youth. No other youth program makes such a claim.

TAPS Academy participants showed significant improvement in social distance measures, with subgroups (such as Hispanic/Latino and male youths) reporting more favorable perceptions of police. However, the study was also limited by a lack of a comparison group, a short follow-up period, and a lack of behavior measures (Jones, Penn, & Davenport, 2015). It is important to note the "significant improvement" with hard-to-reach groups such as Hispanics and males, but the limitations of the research should also be noted. These limitations must be addressed if TAPS is to reach the prominence of previous programs, some of which met their demise or needed to re-tool because of the lack of strong research methods to test the model and practice. Let us look into five programs that preceded TAPS Academy to understand the TAPS methodology.

Drug Abuse Resistance Education (DARE)

The Drug Abuse Resistance Education program, better known as DARE, was developed in 1983 to bring police officers to the classroom for an hour a week for one semester. DARE was a drug prevention curriculum taught in schools across the 50 states, reaching more than 1.5 million students. DARE's curriculum seemed to be effective and impactful for all age groups, ranging from grades PreK-2, through elementary, middle, and high school. According to the U.S. Department of Justice, DARE was considered the bridge to build trust and positive police relations. According to DARE, the key to effective delivery is a "system" dedicated to training those who deliver the curriculum (DARE, n.d.). Schuck (2013) commends DARE's potential to improve youth's attitudes and perceptions of police by opening lines of communication, humanizing police, and enabling youth to see officers engaging with youth in a helpful manner rather than through law enforcement.

Positive evaluations for DARE are rare. Ennett, Tobler, Ringwald, and Flewelling (1994) found there was no statistically significant effect on student's perceptions of police. Crimesolutions.gov lists DARE as "not effective." Even with the evidence provided, it has little direct effect on the perceived outcomes by officers and youth. Still to this day the support of the DARE program is strong nationally and abroad. Today, it is not unusual to see a DARE bumper sticker or t-shirt about a program that has existed for almost 40 years. Thus, even with its overall negative effect, DARE provides the very foundation of bringing officers and youth together in a learning environment that TAPS emulate today.

Gang Resistance Education And Training (GREAT)

Gang Resistance Education And Training (GREAT) was founded in 1991 when Congress appropriated funds to the Bureau of Alcohol, Tobacco, Firearms, and Explosives (ATF) for a school-based gang prevention pilot program in Phoenix, Arizona. The program was designed to reduce gang activity by enabling law enforcement officers to teach life skills to middle-school students to help them resist the pressures to join gangs. In 1992 the first program was implemented. By 1994 GREAT had expanded to 900 officers representing 465 law enforcement agencies in 43 states. GREAT has three goals: (1) to teach youths to avoid gang life; (2) to prevent violence and criminal activity; and (3) to assist youth in developing a positive relationship with law enforcement (Esbensen et al., 2001).

During 1999–2000, GREAT underwent an extensive program and curriculum review (Esbensen et al., 2013). The outcome of changes moved the eight-lesson middle-school curriculum to 13 interactive facilitation-style lessons emphasizing active learning and increasing teacher involvement. According to Esbensen et al. (2013), practitioners and researchers who were well versed in gangs and school-based prevention were employed to assist with this revision. Along with the new curriculum, an elementary school curriculum for 4th and 5th graders and a new family training component were developed. In 2004 the GREAT program's administration and oversight were transferred to the Office of Justice Programs, Bureau of Justice Assistance (BJA). Four regions of administrative oversight were organized in 2009. The Phoenix Police Department and Portland Police Bureau leads the Southwest and West Regions. The La Crosse Police Department manages the Midwest Atlantic Region. The Metropolitan Nashville, Tennessee, Police Department manages the Southeast Region office. In 2011, the Office of Juvenile Justice and Delinquency Prevention (OJJDP) became an active partner of GREAT by providing funding and assisting in the national effort. In 2020, according to GREAT, since 1991 almost 13,000 law enforcement officers were certified as GREAT instructors, and more than 6 million students had graduated from the program (GREAT, n.d.). The revamping of the program in 1999–2000 allowed for an appreciation of the adolescent brain; the curriculum was revised to emphasize active learning, which counters being "easily distracted." GREAT provides TAPS Academy with a foundation of skill-building that can occur during youth and police interaction.

Police Athletic Leagues

The National Association of Police Athletic/Activities League, Inc. (National PAL) is self-touted as "the world's foremost leader in engaging kids, cops, and community." The Association states that it:

> exists to aid in preventing juvenile crime and violence by providing mentorship, civic/service, athletic, recreational, enrichment and educational opportunities and resources to PAL Membership Chapters. As a membership-based organization, National PAL seeks to provide its Chapters with resources and opportunities to aid them within their organizational growth and assist them in their pursuits of showcasing their unique programs and enhance the quality of individual youth engagement experiences.
>
> *(National Association of Police Athletic/Activities League, Inc., n.d.)*

National PAL has 300 chapters in the United States. The program brings youth aged five to 18 together through the guidance and influence of officers instilling positive values into youth. Leadership opportunities are provided for youth as their voice is heard with a goal of maturity, inclusiveness, and being a good citizen. Rabois and Haaga (2002) researched PALS and found that the program improved police attitudes toward youth but did not significantly change youth's attitude toward police.

Explorers

Explorers programming exists in two formats. The first is directly related to Boy Scouts of America. It is called Law Enforcement Exploring and provides a hands-on program for young men and women from sixth grade to the age of 20 interested in a career in law enforcement or a related field in the criminal justice system. In the program youth see the criminal justice system up-close through personal contact, training, practical experiences, competitions, and field trips. Personal growth occurs through character development, respect for the rule of law, physical fitness, good citizenship, and patriotism (Law Enforcement Exploring, n.d.).

The second form of exploring is Law Enforcement Career Exploring. An example is the Houston Explorers group operated by the Houston Police Department. It is open to young men and women aged 14 (and who have completed the 8th grade) to 20 interested in learning more about careers in law enforcement. By providing educational training programs for young adults' career orientation experiences, leadership opportunities, and community service activities, the program helps young adults choose a career path within law enforcement and to become responsible citizens of their communities and the nation. Activities include ride-alongs, pistol shooting, accident scene procedures, bomb threat response, equipment usage, college and career readiness preparation, team building, and community policing activities. (Houston Police Explorers, n.d.). Research on Explorers-type programming by Anderson, Sabatelli, and Trachtenberg (2007) studied competencies, positive adult-youth connections, and positive youth-community connections. Their findings were that there were no statistically significant differences between youth who participated and those who did not. Nevertheless, for TAPS Academy programming, the Explorers provides a foundation for working with older youth and the need to explore a wide range of topics to make up the TAPS Academy library of modules.

Citizens Police Academy

The concept of the Citizens Police Academy started in the United Kingdom in 1977. It began in the Devon and Cornwall Constabulary, England, as a police night school, allowing citizens to learn about police functions, police operations, and the police system's organization in England. Receiving an overwhelmingly positive response, it became a permanent part of the police department's public relations program. In 1985, the Orlando, Florida, Police

Department adopted the police night school concept for their agency and created the first Citizens Police Academy in the United States. Nationally the Citizen Police Academies are free of charge for 12–14 weeks for three hours in the evening. Weekly topics include History of the Police Agency, Roles of Criminal Justice Professionals, Patrol Procedures, Domestic Violence, Youth Services, Victim Services, Crime Scene Processing, Fingerprinting, Role of the Investigator, Use of Force, Shoot/Don't Shoot, Drug and Gang Investigations, Juvenile Investigations, Community Policing Strategies, and Police Defense Tactics, and then there is a graduation.

The concept has been modified across the United States to include ridealongs, jail tours, and other field trips. Responding to the need to be inclusive nationally, there are Spanish-speaking, Asian, senior citizen, and even teen police academies. Some Citizens Police Academies even develop alumni associations with a large pool of volunteers to assist police departments during disasters, large projects, and other times in which volunteers are needed. Overall, research indicates that graduates learn more about law enforcement and have more realistic evaluations of media accounts and are more willing to volunteer to help the police (Miller, Hess, & Orthmann, 2013). TAPS gains from studying Citizens Police Academies because it provides a cohort format in which learning occurs over a short period in a structured environment. By youth learning what the police do and how they do it (though never learning tactics), greater understanding and reduced social distance can occur.

The five community policing programs discussed above each provided building blocks for the development of TAPS Academy (see Table 5.1).

Add to the above the work of the Fulbright Association in which mutual respect, dialogue, and collective understanding work to reduce social distance (Penn, 2013), and you have the elements that make TAPS Academy a unique evolution of community policing for the 21st Century. Communities In Schools (CIS) cites "five basics" to keeping kids out of trouble—a one-on-one relationship with a caring adult, a safe place to learn and grow, a healthy start and a healthy future, a marketable skill to use upon graduation, and a chance to give back to peers and community (Communities In Schools, n.d.).

TAPS Academy programming fills the current gap as the next chapter of building youth and police relations as TAPS focuses on the most at-risk youth, including young African-American and Latino men in urban areas from poor backgrounds. When the Houston Police Department, the University of Houston–Clear Lake, and Texas Southern University combined their efforts to serve the youth in the most at-risk schools of the Houston Independent School District (HISD), TAPS brought together the practitioners with the academics. TAPS Academy moved beyond providing community policing to those citizens who respected police officers and went straight to those that describe

TABLE 5.1 Community Policing Programs Providing Elements for TAPS Academy Application

Name of Program	Element	TAPS Academy Application
DARE	Youth and police can have a positive interaction.	Youth and police desire positive interaction.
GREAT	Skill-building can take place while youth and police are interacting.	Recognition that the teen brain has its strengths and weaknesses. It is possible to gear programming to teens.
Police Athletic Leagues (PALS)	Active learning (through sports) allows for police to develop positive attitudes toward youth.	Can build positive attitudes from police toward youth, providing an environment of understanding.
Explorers	Interaction with police by teenagers and young adults.	Youth may desire to learn the jobs, tasks, skills, and a variety of subjects with police officers.
Citizens Police Academy	Weekly interaction with officers learning their jobs and tasks. Only available to adults and those passing a criminal background check.	Can teach teens in a weekly program about officers' jobs, skills and tasks. Can reduce the social distance and open the opportunity to the most at-risk and marginal populations.

police officers as "pigs," "OPs," "12," and so on. The TAPS program is not easy, and not all officers or youth make it through, mostly because the views held by each can be so entrenched. These negative perceptions can be seen clearly with the words and actions of the youth who physically try to run out of the classroom when four or five officers come in the room to begin the first day of TAPS. Sadly, that honesty is not received from the officers even after the training is provided.

There is a process to become a TAPS officer. First, current TAPS officers recommend potential TAPS officers to command staff. The command staff then checks each officer's personnel file to ensure there are no complaints against the officer that will indicate he or she will not treat youth, their parents, and community members with the utmost respect. If there is no negative finding, the officer undergoes a five-hour block of instruction. During this instruction period, usually taught by Penn and a senior TAPS Academy police officer, the following subjects are covered: history of TAPS Academy, implicit and explicit bias, working with at-risk youth, "teen brain," effective listening, teaching TAPS Academy, procedural justice, and role-playing. The program is based on the concept that the intrinsic values to support a TAPS program are found in the officer; the training simply guides and brings out the best in each TAPS officer. Not every officer is a TAPS officer because it is difficult for some to take off the police protective layer that leads to the swagger and presence of a traditional officer who perceives youth as "lesser than" or as potential offenders. Bias creates a wall, limiting the ability to create mutual respect and understanding.

Finding, training, and watching a new TAPS officer flourish is a masterful experience. What adds to it is knowing that the officer is on patrol, in the anti-gang unit, or in command, sharing the values of TAPS Academy with other officers while at the same time conducting their police duties safely and with justice for all. Officers were asked: Can officers mentor youth and do their job on the street? In other words, does being a mentor to at-risk youth make the officer too soft or unable to do the law enforcement aspect of policing? More than 95% said they can be both mentor and street officer. In fact, many noted that being a mentor to at-risk youth enhanced their ability to do their job as a patrol officer because they better understood the needs of the youth and community (Lumpkin & Penn, 2013).

There is a sadness upon seeing an officer mentor serving as a TAPS officer for 11 weeks or an entire semester or year's work but not want to return for the next TAPS class. For some, it may be because of a promotion, shift change, or simply finding it "too difficult." Being a TAPS Academy officer is hard. In some cases, entire departments stop the program because not enough officers make themselves available. Author Davenport, who volunteered with TAPS for several years in the mid-2010s, shares an experience demonstrating the difficulty of the program:

> After graduating with my master's in Criminology, I began volunteering with the program to acquire experience to work in the field. It was something different, especially working with at-risk youth and police officers, which can be challenging to work with, especially at the same time. I quickly learned about the police culture that I was constantly reminded of by the officers in the program, which frustrated me because being a part of that culture was the last thing I wanted. I enjoyed my time while working with TAPS; however, many things would disturb me. For example, some officers only volunteered because of the compensation they received. I often thought to myself, if funding were eliminated from participating in the program, how many officers would participate. Another incident that was disturbing was while working at one of the schools; we were doing our regular routine, stating the "TAPS creed," and introducing the topic of discussion for the day. On this particular day, one of the students had his head down, and because he was not participating in

the TAPS creed, one of the officers decided to throw a quarter at him to get his attention to sit up and participate. The infuriating part about this matter is that other officers witnessed this as well, and nothing was done. I was told early on: the program is about the officers, and that was restated to me several times. However, as many times as that was reiterated, I felt that I was the buffer between the youth and the police. I could see both perspectives while remaining neutral. There was nothing I could do to vindicate this young man, and I began to see why they viewed officers the way they did, and this situation surely did not help to change that. The young man was angry and told the officers, "just because you wear a gun, and a badge doesn't mean you can throw things at people. If I did that, it would be considered assault. If you must know, my head was down because I suffer from migraines." At that moment, I sympathized with the young man because he was right; if the roles were reversed, that officer would have charged him with assault from throwing an object at him. Honestly, I do not think the officer did it intentionally. I think it was a spur-of-the-moment decision that was made, like we all make, and it was something not well thought out.

This was the moment when I realized not all officers were a good fit for the program. It also helped me realize both perspectives of youth and police officers and why respect was such an important component when bringing the two groups together. The officer was reprimanded and removed from the location following the incident. During my experience working with the program, there were some outstanding officers; however, I have seen a few that should have never been allowed to work with the program and even questioned if they should carry a gun and badge. There are other experiences I can share, good and bad, I experienced while volunteering with TAPS; however, the experience allowed me to see the ins and outs of working with officers and at-risk youth. It also allowed for me to see first-hand what needs to be done to continue to help bridge the gap between youth and police.

We hope by explaining the fundamentals of TAPS Academy in this chapter, police department leaders, policymakers, teachers, school districts, and the general public can move past those first uncomfortable feelings to spend time with these youth who are not understood. Remember the President's Task Force on 21st Century Policing clearly states: "Communities should adopt policies and program that address the needs of children and youth most at risk for crime or violence and reduce aggressive law enforcement tactics that stigmatize youth and marginalize their participation in schools and communities" (President's Task Force on 21st Century Policing, 2015, p. 47). It goes on to say: "Communities need to affirm and recognize the voices of youth in community decision making, facilitate youth-led research and problem-solving, and develop and fund youth leadership training and life skills through positive youth/police collaboration and interactions" (p. 49). Finally, the report states: "Communities and law enforcement agencies should restore and build trust between youth and police by creating programs and projects for positive, consistent, and persistent interaction between youth and police." Listed as the final Action Item: "Communities should develop community-and school-based evidence-based programs that mitigate punitive and authoritarian solutions to teen problems" (p. 50). TAPS Academy does all of the above, and was created four years before the final Task Force report.

The Origin of TAPS Academy

In 2011 Assistant Chief Brian Lumpkin was a 28-year police veteran leading 1,000 police officers as the commander of East Patrol in Houston, Texas. Penn was an Associate Professor of Criminology and the Division Chair for Social and Cultural Sciences at the University of Houston–Clear Lake. As the Chair, Penn led the hiring of adjunct professors. He believed that the Criminology programs, both graduate and undergraduate, should produce students who could demonstrate their criminology acumen against the top schools of Maryland, Rutgers, Albany, and Cincinnati, but at the same time, he was quite realistic about a fact that took him 10 years to develop. The uppermost goal for most of the students in the program was to be employed in the criminal justice field. While they wanted to learn the subject matter, just as important was the fact that they desired employment to raise their standard of living, and they believed the criminal justice field would provide them that opportunity. However, as Division Chair, Penn was in a position to do something about it. So, he stacked his adjuncts with professional, real-world credentials. Holding a master's degree became the baseline; what he was looking for were professionals in criminal justice who would take his students higher by giving them the insight along with the credentials to get hired. Thus, a list of the adjuncts read like a "who's who" of Houston criminal justice. Police chiefs, district attorneys, juvenile justice facility administrators, public defender lawyers, and investigators were teaching the courses. Penn even offered a position to then-retired Mayor Lee Brown, who politely refused his offer, probably because the pay was insulting. One of the professionals serving as an adjunct was Assistant Chief Brian Lumpkin, who was teaching the Police and Society course. This coming together of practice and academics led to Lumpkin's call in February 2011 asking if Penn would like to work with him and the Houston Police Department on a Request for Proposals from the Community Oriented Policing Services (COPS) Office.

Penn said yes, partly because of his personal ethos that the university should be interwoven with the community. A divide between "town and gown" serves no purpose; instead, concepts such as internships, co-ops, and service learning should be required practices for the university to serve the community better while at the same time providing opportunities for the students. After the call, Lumpkin, Penn, and a team of officers and staff worked for weeks researching, discussing, and debating citizen and police relations. During that time, nationally, the story of Rodney King was a reference of the strife, but it was two Houston, Texas, cases that provided the impetus to create TAPS in Houston: the Joe Campos case of 1977 and the Chad Holley case of 2009.

On May 5, 1977, Joe Campos Torres, a 23-year-old Mexican-American, Vietnam veteran, recently released from serving in the United States Army, was fighting in a Houston bar called The Hole. Police were called to the scene, and Torres was beaten by six Houston police officers and charged with disorderly conduct. The officers took Torres to jail for booking, but the authorities at the jail refused to take him because he needed medical attention. The officers were instructed to take Torres to Ben Taub Hospital. They did not; instead, they took him to a remote part of the Buffalo Bayou and pushed him into the water. Two days later, on Mother's Day, Torres's body surfaced. His cause of death was drowning.

The two arresting officers, Terry Denson and Steven Orlando, were fired and convicted of non-negligent homicide. Convicted by an all-White jury, they received a year's probation and a $1 fine. The three other officers were fired and had no formal criminal charges filed. One rookie officer on the scene cooperated with authorities and served as a key witness. A juror in the conviction of Denson and Orlando, Deborah Penny, stated: "they were not reckless, all we could prove is that they were negligent in not making sure Torres was on the other side [of the Bayou]" (KHOU-TV CBS, 1978). Ann Westmoreland, another juror, stated as she left the courthouse: "We gave it our best effort." When asked by the reporter if she had any regrets, she stated, "No!" (KHOU-TV CBS, 1978). In response to public demand, federal charges of civil rights violations were brought against Denson and Orlando in 1978. They served nine months in prison (Watson, 2005).

Chad Holley was a sophomore at Elsik High School at the time of his arrest in 2010. He was accused of burglary and was beaten and kicked by Houston Police Department officers when apprehended. What is interesting about the Holley case is that a surveillance camera caught the event. Neither Holley nor any of the 12 officers involved reported the beating. In the video (LaPuertorra69, 2011) it is clear that Holley is in a surrender position with his hands on top of his head, yet the officers continue to beat and kick him. All 12 officers involved were fired by then-Chief Charles McClelland, who said the Holley beating gave the department a black eye and lent ammunition to anyone looking to criticize the department (Rogers, 2013). Four officers were charged. Phil Bryan and Raad Hassan pleaded "no contest" and received two years on probation. Bryan received a $500 fine and Hassan, a $750 fine. Drew Ryser was convicted of a misdemeanor oppression charge. He received two years on probation and a $1,000 fine. Finally, Andrew Blomberg was found not guilty (Rogers, 2013). After the investigation, a total of 12 officers were disciplined as a result of the case. Seven were fired, two got their jobs back, while four officers and one sergeant remained fired. Four officers were indicted for official oppression. Two took plea deals and were sentenced to two years deferred adjudication. One was convicted by a jury and sentenced to two years of probation, and one was acquitted by a jury.

In 2011 when the TAPS Academy proposal was written, both cases haunted the history of police misconduct at the hands of Houston police officers. The Holley case was especially important because it involved a youth. Holley was 15 years old and African-American. Knowing the history of the divide between African-American young men and the police, the proposal focused on the words, feelings, thoughts, and aftermath of the Holley beating to form TAPS Academy.

It was determined that TAPS Academy should have a citizen's police academy type of format with a developed curriculum. It would be compressed like a police academy to keep logistical issues to a minimum. Through an 11-week academy, law enforcement officers and the most at-risk youth in the community would participate in a curriculum designed around modules to teach the most pressing subjects of strife between the two groups. The literature was researched to define what it means to be "at-risk," and it was decided that the Texas Education Agency (TEA) provided the best example, with their 13 characteristics for a child to be considered at-risk of dropping out of school. Since the literature articulates that dropping out of school leads to a litany of risky behavior including delinquency and crime (Cox et al., 2017; Sweeten, Bushway, & Paternoster, 2009; Lawrence, 2006), TAPS Academy used these characteristics to define the youth for which the program would be most focused on in reducing the social distance with police.

Defining At-Risk Youth

A student at risk of dropping out of school is aged under 21 and meets one or more of the following criteria:

1) is eligible for free or reduced-cost school lunch (this was added by TAPS Academy because the original first criteria for at-risk involved primary grade students);
2) is in grades 7, 8, 9, 10, 11, or 12 and did not maintain an average equivalent to 70 on a scale of 100 in two or more subjects in the foundation curriculum (language arts, math, science, and social studies) during a semester in the preceding or current school year or is not maintaining such an average in two or more subjects in the foundation curriculum in the current semester;

3) was not advanced from one grade level to the next for one or more school years;

4) did not perform satisfactorily on an assessment instrument administered to the student under Texas Education Code (TEC) Subchapter B, Chapter 39, and who has not in the previous or current school year subsequently performed on that instrument or another appropriate instrument at a level equal to at least 110 percent of the level of satisfactory performance on that instrument;

5) is pregnant or a parent;

6) has been placed in an alternative education program in accordance with TEC §37.006 during the preceding or current school year;

7) has been expelled in accordance with TEC §37.007 during the preceding or current school year;

8) is currently on parole, probation, deferred prosecution, or another conditional release;

9) was previously reported through the Public Education Information Management System (PEIMS) to have dropped out of school;

10) is of limited English proficiency, as defined by TEC §29.052;

11) is in the custody or care of the Department of Protective and Regulatory Services or has, during the current school year, been referred to the department by a school official, officer of the juvenile court, or law enforcement official;

12) is homeless, as defined by No Child Left Behind (NCLB) Act, Title X, Part C, Section 725(2), the term "homeless children and youths," and its subsequent amendments; or

13) resided in the preceding school year or resides in the current school year in a residential placement facility in the district, including a detention facility, substance abuse treatment facility, emergency shelter, psychiatric hospital, halfway house, or foster group home.

(Texas Education Agency, n.d.)

TAPS Academy offered its first Academy at Beechnut Academy (the alternative middle and high school for the Houston Independent School District) in February 2012, almost three years before the President's 21st Century Task Force described in Chapter 4 advocated for this type of programming for youth and police.

In the *Journal of Juvenile Justice* article titled "Social Distance Between Minority Youth and the Police: An Exploratory Analysis of the TAPS Academy" (Jones, Penn, & Davenport, 2015), the foundation that supported TAPS goals and structure is presented. As the basis for TAPS Academy, the theoretical foundation for better relations between the most at-risk youth and law enforcement was based on work by Travis Hirschi (1969), who discussed social control/social bond theory and hypothesized that the development of social bonds (through mechanisms such as mentoring) can be used to decrease social distance. Social distance was conceptualized using Emory Bogardus's research from the 1920s (Bogardus, 1925), which indicates that as contact and familiarity increase, social distance decreases. Thus, as people spend more time around those of or from a different race, ethnicity, age, geographic location, or sexual orientation, the stereotypes and damaging preconceived notions held about them decrease or are eliminated. Thus, when social distance is reduced, the person's characteristics, rather than the image of the group, become most dominant. People learn to appreciate the similarities rather than the differences.

Research clearly indicates that minority teens demonstrate the least trust for law enforcement (Cobbina, 2019; Davis, 2017; Jones, Penn, & Davenport, 2015; Unnever & Gabbidon, 2011). These distrustful feelings develop out of negative (involuntary and voluntary) contacts with law enforcement. Additionally, when these contacts occur, they are shared with family and friends, often to lighten the burden because regular channels of regress are thought to be blocked or inaccessible. The shared experiences create a domino effect of anguish and anger toward the police, often existing in and expanding out to the entire group. Thus, others within the group who may not have had any contact with the police, assume vicarious experiences that become their own, thus creating minority group hostility and distrust for the police (Brunson, 2007).

The social bond explains why individuals conform to moral and socially acceptable behavior rather than deviate. Hirschi (1969) contends that conformity results from integration into prosocial groups and a personal internalization of social norms and values. In other words, bonds form between individuals and their societies that prevent them from engaging in deviant activities. These bonds include attachment, commitment, involvement, and belief. Attachment involves positive connections between individuals and significant others (family, friends, mentors) and purports that deviant behavior would damage these relationships. Commitment involves engaging in conventional activities and establishing positive goals that will constrain deviant behavior. Involvement includes the time and energy invested in conventional activities, which then limits opportunities for engaging in deviant behavior. Finally, belief involves the personal internalization of social norms and values. Social control/social bond theory suggests that the stronger an individual's social bonds, the lower the likelihood of deviant behavior. The weaker an individual's social bonds, the greater the likelihood of deviant behavior. Research has provided support for social control theory by finding a negative relationship between social bonds and delinquency (Li, 2004; Longshore, Chang, & Messina, 2005). TAPS Academy provides a mentoring mechanism for reducing social distance through social bonds development between at-risk youth and law enforcement. Although several studies have explored the effectiveness of mentoring programs with at-risk youth (DuBois & Karcher, 2013; Longshore, Chang, & Messina 2005; Li, 2004; Keating et al., 2002), few studies, notwithstanding one completed by

TAPS ACADEMY:
A Community-Led Policing Program

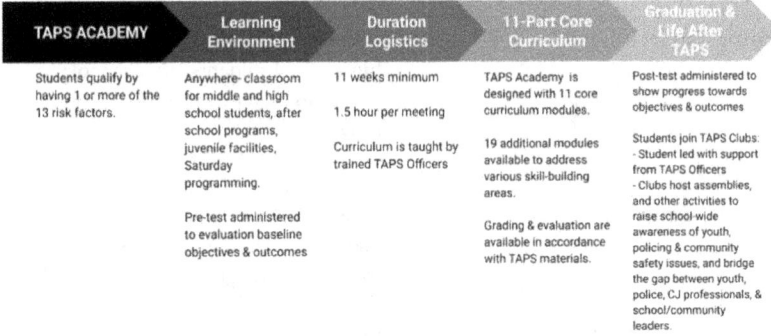

TAPS ACADEMY	Learning Environment	Duration Logistics	11-Part Core Curriculum	Graduation & Life After TAPS
Students qualify by having 1 or more of the 13 risk factors.	Anywhere- classroom for middle and high school students, after school programs, juvenile facilities, Saturday programming.	11 weeks minimum 1.5 hour per meeting Curriculum is taught by trained TAPS Officers	TAPS Academy is designed with 11 core curriculum modules. 19 additional modules available to address various skill-building areas.	Post-test administered to show progress towards objectives & outcomes Students join TAPS Clubs: - Student led with support from TAPS Officers - Clubs host assemblies, and other activities to raise school-wide awareness of youth,
	Pre-test administered to evaluation baseline objectives & outcomes		Grading & evaluation are available in accordance with TAPS materials.	policing & community safety issues, and bridge the gap between youth, police, CJ professionals, & school/community leaders.

FIGURE 5.1 TAPS Academy Community-Led Policing Program Model

Lumpkin and Penn (2013), have explored the benefits of mentoring the most at-risk youth using police as mentors in order to improve negative perceptions of the police among minority youth and create increase social bonding to pro-social society.

Through positive contact between at-risk youth and law enforcement concepts of procedural justice, legitimacy, providing youth with voice, fair and impartial policing all become elements to reduce social distance. When these concepts become a reality for youth and law enforcement, social bonding occurs, thus creating increased public safety and pro-social behavior. See Figure 5.1 and Table 5.2.

TAPS Academy began as a twice-a-week, two-hours-a-week, 15-week program on Tuesdays and Thursdays at Beechnut Academy, the alternative school for youth who were removed from their home middle and high schools. Youth would be removed for various offenses including truancy, incorrigibility, fighting, and drugs. Their time at Beechnut Academy, which was a large converted Walmart, could be as short as a month and as long as an entire school year. Beechnut Academy was a place where fighting, cursing, and yelling were common occurrences. The staff, mostly African-American teachers in their late thirties and forties, knew their student population and often displayed a mixture of care with in-your-face confrontation. The program's time was right after lunch, and the time was used discussing the curriculum of pressing issues between youth and police on subjects such as police interaction, date violence, bullying, anger management, avoidance of gang life, drug usage, police interaction, human trafficking, conflict management, future goals, and many other topics.

TABLE 5.2 TAPS Academy– A Community-Led Policing Program

Student Selection	*Students qualify by having one or more of the 13 risk factors as prescribed by Texas Education Agency.*
Learning Environment	Classroom setting for middle and high school students, after school programs, juvenile facilities, Saturday programming. Pre-test administered to evaluation baseline objectives & outcomes
Semester Logistics	11 weeks minimum 1.5 hour per meeting/class session Curriculum is taught by trained TAPS Officers
11-Part Core Curriculum	TAPS Academy is designed with 11 core curriculum modules. 19 additional modules available to address various skill-building areas. Grading and evaluation are available in accordance with TAPS materials.
Graduation and Life After TAPS	Post-test administered to show progress toward objectives and outcomes Students join TAPS Clubs: • *Student led with support from TAPS Officers* • *Clubs host assemblies, and other activities to raise school-wide awareness of youth, policing and community safety issues, and bridge the gap between youth, police, CJ professionals, and school/community leaders*

TAPS Academy Day

Through these interactive sessions, students gained valuable skills in managing life situations while both the youth and law enforcement officers built positive relationships. The program starts with the TAPS Creed, which was created by students in the very first TAPS Class. The creed embodies the idea of change in a positive direction as youth move from at-risk to at-promise:

> We are going where we have never gone.
> To do what we have never done.
> To have what we have never had.
> And to no longer be an at-risk kid,
> But an at-promise teen.

The term "at-promise teen" was borrowed from a book edited by Swadener and Lubeck called *Children and Families "At Promise": Deconstructing the Discourse of Risk* (1995). Penn first read the book when he was invited to the summer session of the Poverty Research Center at the University of Michigan in 2005. The text was applied to TAPS in order to channel youth, parents, teachers, and community to evolve from lacking cultural and moral resources and refocus to the ideas of "at promise," in which negative stereotypes, definitions, and images are reduced or removed in order to mobilize their current and newly found cultural, community, family, and personnel resources and capital to achieve new goals, and a level of excellence.

Correct knowledge is a powerful tool for youth. Through TAPS Academy, youth discovered the ability to make positive decisions in their daily lives. Interaction with highly trained mentor officers and community leaders moves the youth from street answers to correct answers about the variety of subjects that unwrap themselves in a TAPS session. Take, for example, a TAPS Academy graduate we will call "Chance," a heavyset, African-American young man whose physical size could be intimidating to others. Penn related to him because he, too, was always the bigger guy in a group. From TAPS, Chance learned that his size put fear in people, even police officers. He learned the reality that if he is coming at an officer, the officer may respond more quickly with deadly force. He stated: "TAPS program changed my life. I really hated cops before, but now I know what they do, and why they chose to do that job. I look at the police a lot differently now."

TAPS provides an opportunity for the veil of policing to be lifted. For example, in an open session some teens asked: "Why do you cops always have your hands on your gun when you come to the car?" This is a question the officers get quite often. Some go the route of safety by stating: "I do not know what is in your car, and I have to be ready." Another was honest and put a little humor into the dialogue by saying: "This gun belt is heavy and I am just trying to keep my pants up." The response got a laugh and successfully broke the ice to discuss a subject of contention: the traffic stop and how TAPS teens believe they are the target of racial and social discrimination. It took the officers off their perch of looking down upon the teens to be within the mix as many of the officers relate how they came from poverty backgrounds, and they themselves are Black or Latino, and how they themselves are concerned about their safety when they are out of uniform and stopped by the police.

TAPS Academy also enables youth and law enforcement to build their communities through a meaningful service-learning project, using a methodology by Penn (2003) of EAR, which stands for Education in the classroom, Action in the community, and Reflection about the experience. TAPS Academy is transformative. For many of the teens, community service is seen as something court-ordered. Thus, their perception of volunteering is skewed to the belief that you are either required to do it or are foolish for doing anything for which you will not "get paid." Service-learning projects were purposely created to be removed as far as possible from court-ordered community service. There was no trash pick-up or construction work; instead, there are projects to build the community and allow the community to see the youth as constructive members of society.

Take, for example, Gardens of Greatness, in which the EAR methodology invited an agricultural specialist to come to the class to discuss the concept of food deserts, getting the youth to think where the "good" food stores are located. They were asked to think: Does your local food store have a florist, seafood department, and lots of fresh fruits and vegetables? Does it have a meat counter? Often they would say: "No, those are the stores in the 'White neighborhoods.'" They discussed the foods more prominent at their local food store. They describe the corner store with three or four rows of canned goods, potato chips, pickles, and bread. In the back, there is a refrigerator case with withering lettuce, some tomatoes, and potatoes. There may also be a lady in the back to cook up an order of fried fish and French fries. You point to the item you want and tell the lady your order. You pay her and she gives you a little piece a paper with a number on it. You wait to the side for 10 to 15 minutes, never making eye contact with others, also waiting for their food. She yells out a number. It's not yours, but you see the guy approach the steel cage. She opens the Styrofoam container to show the contents are what was ordered—burger with fries. The guy demands more ketchup and another hot pepper. Finally, your number is called, and you inspect your food and find it acceptable, but then you needed something cold to drink, so you order your fruit punch soda. You pay and go. Over and over the youth tell how this is their dinner or how the people who own the store "treat them mean." The goal is to understand a world that to most of us is in the past or simply an experienced accident because we are traveling or need of gas or gum.

The first week of March is the week to plant in southeast Texas. The Action of the EAR was planting the seeds and physically accomplishing the labor to create raised gardens and mix soil with manure to create the rich ingredients to make for good crops. Those running the program learned to inform the youth well in advance of the Action day that they were going to get dirty, wanting to avoid the drama of youth getting their Jordans dirty.

The Action of planting took the youth to new areas and experiences. While one participant, Sharonda, was planting potatoes, she stated: "I do not eat anything that comes from the dirt." An officer working alongside her during the service-learning project asked her: "Do you like McDonald's French fries?" She said: "yes." It was then explained to her that fries are made of potatoes, and potatoes grow in the dirt. Through TAPS Academy, Sharonda learned a valuable lesson of where the food she enjoys comes from before she buys it. Reflection came when ordering pizza for the youth as the program came to an end in late May, serving them a salad made from the tomatoes and cucumbers they grew or watermelon that came from their own gardening.

For interactive and innovative programming service-learning, TAPS Academy won a Jefferson Award for its creative, urban gardening project to combat food store deserts. The service-learning project annually culminated in a Gardens for Greatness community festival, which brought together TAPS graduates, law enforcement, and community for a day of food, fun, and celebration.

The first TAPS Academy was exhausting for the officers and staff. Doing the program twice a week for two hours per week meant a total of four hours of interaction for officers who were doing their other duties. One of the TAPS officers was involved in a widely broadcast officer-involved shooting the Wednesday before the Thursday afternoon TAPS class. He came to TAPS with scars on his face and arm. That day the discussion ventured off topic (which is a part of the TAPS methodology) so he could express his thoughts about being in a shootout—the danger and the fear. Of course, he did not talk specifically about the case, but it did allow the youth to know the human element of a shooting and that officers have families and are human beings with emotions.

The learning in TAPS is not one way. The program is about mutual understanding and respect. Take, for example, Kisha (a pseudonym). Kisha was a beautiful, 15-year-old African-American girl whose parents were involved in drugs and crime. They both were in correctional institutions. Kisha lived with her grandmother. Kisha's grandmother placed a padlock on the refrigerator door with a cup attached. She informed her granddaughter in order to get food out of the refrigerator she must place some money in the cup. A 15-year-old girl was living in a situation that forced her to pay for food to eat in her home. Kisha thought about the men and boys who admired her looks and began equating her looks with a means to raise money for food and other things in life. She was at Beechnut Academy for prostitution. TAPS teaches the officers, teachers, and staff that their lives are different from the youth we serve, and although the law has a responsibility to respond, the available choices are different. Penn flinches when he hears someone say: "TAPS is for the kids who made bad choices." Is there really a choice when the right turn is blocked or not conceivable? It is a question they should have asked Kisha.

TAPS officers were asked in a survey whether they felt connected or disconnected to the TAPS teens (pre and post TAPS Academy). Some 84% of the officers felt very connected to the teens at the beginning of the program. That rose to 87% post-TAPS. Great recruiting, command oversight, good training, and a dedicated officer core can be credited for such numbers. What was interesting about this was at the other extreme. The number rose from 7.7% pre-TAPS to 12.5% post-TAPS in reference to feeling "very disconnected" to the youth. When asked about this after one of the early TAPS Academies an officer said it best: "The more we spent time with the teens the more we learned how disconnected we were to them and their lives."

Reaching understanding through listening, communication, and learning allows both the officer and the youth to grow. Shortly after starting TAPS Academy at Beechnut Academy, they were asked to bring the program to

Youth Village, the Harris County Juvenile County Probation facility. This facility, located south of Houston in the Clear Lake area near NASA, housed 90 teenaged boys whose offense or home life found them unfit to remain in the home. The Academy would meet on Thursday afternoons. The officers would have to undergo the same criminal background checks as civilians and would have to leave their weapons securely locked. There are two issues officers do not like. The first is to have an outside agency conduct a background check on them, thus exposing where they live and other personal information. The second is an giving up his or her weapon while in uniform. Added to that was going into a secure facility with youth who absolutely despise and hate the very existence of police officers. Yet, for years we had a team of officers that willingly took on the change to the point that TAPS was in all three Harris County Juvenile facilities providing programming.

The Teen And Police Service Academy curriculum, which has been approved by the Houston Independent School District and the Texas Education Agency, awards one high school credit to students upon completion. The course is listed as TEEN POL (N1130025) under the Innovative Courses for the Texas Education Agency (Texas Education Agency, n.d.). Any student in the state of Texas may take the course. The course is offered just like any academic offering. There must be a teacher of record certified as a high school social studies teacher. Depending on the school's academic schedule, it may be offered two to four times a week through a collaborative effort of a team consisting of a teacher of record, TAPS educational specialists, TAPS program manager, community partners, and, of course, TAPS officers. The course is offered to students displaying one or more of the risk-factors described above. Usually, the principal, wrap-around specialist, or counselor selects students to be in the course. Course size is usually 15–30 students. See more on TEEN POL in Appendix 1.

Having the certification of the Texas Education Agency to award one academic credit did not come easily. There is a long process that involves the submission of outlines, lesson objectives, planned outcomes, and other learning criteria. With the idea of gaining certification and the success of offering it at Beechnut Academy, other Houston Independent School District schools desired TAPS Academy but could not fit the program (for non-credit) into the busy schedules of students. In those early years, once the program was expanded past Beechnut Academy in 2013, TAPS Academy occurred during whatever available time the school would provide: lunch time, study periods, gym classes, homeroom, after school, and even in-school suspension. These times were often unreliable, unscheduled, filled with distractions, and unproductive. A positive solution was sought for these problems. The result came after talking with Shannon Weigel, who worked for Beechnut Academy as their registrar. She suggested applying for an innovative course listing. Through her guidance, research, and assistance, TAPS Academy submitted its course credentials and was certified as an innovative course in Texas. This is an important factor in youth and police education because TAPS represents the first time a course to build youth and police relations has been certified by a state to provide one high school credit to students upon completion. TAPS Academy owes much to the work of Ms. Weigel.

Emotions run high the first day the TAPS officers meet with youth inside the juvenile facility, or even in high schools or middle school. Penn remembers a first day at one of the juvenile facilities. The officers were in the room first, waiting for the youth to file in with their hands interwoven behind their backs. The first came in, and soon the rest of 20 approached. TAPS officers had become used to the jokes, the negative words about officers, and the youth's belief that it was a set-up that they were going to be taken away for crimes committed. However, this first day's interaction was different. There were two young African-American males who placed their hands at the door and would not allow themselves or others to physically move them into the room. They called out: "Hell no, I am not going in there" and other expressive words indicating their opinion about police officers. One of the young men held on to the door as his bottom made the way to the floor as he protested being in the same room as police officers. Probation officers at the facility took the young men away. They re-joined in week two. It was later learned that they were from New Orleans and came to Houston after Hurricane Katrina. What they had seen police officers do in New Orleans created a fear, dislike, and lack of trust of all police. Progress was made with these young men, but it echoes the sentiment made clear in the training of TAPS officers: with the availability of social media, the questionable act of an officer in Milwaukee can directly affect the contact a Houston officer has on his evening shift. In other words, the vicarious interaction of police and youth creates the belief that all police officers will treat them unfairly and without justice. This belief, which comes from images of unarmed Black and Brown young men being shot, creates a mind-frame that a young man of color may have a better chance of fairness and escaping the criminal justice system by running away when confronted by police. As one TAPS student said in 2015, "You got to understand something. Police don't care about us. We are Black men. I can outrun them, and I will!"

Through 30 modules and the honest conversation that takes place during the breakout sessions, the youth are implored to understand the multiplying negative effects of running. Their response is look at Trayvon Martin, Michael Brown, or a number of other cases. At the conclusion of TAPS, there is usually a "like" for the officers who were with them for the duration of TAPS and even a statically significant rise in like, trust, and connectedness with police in general, but there is still an underlying belief there is unfairness, targeting, and illegal profiling that makes them victims of police oppression. An 11-week or semester-long, 18-week program consisting of 20–60 hours of contact (depending on the TAPS format offered) has a long way to overcome years of personal, vicarious, and family experiences and beliefs about the negative feelings related to police.

In 2016, TAPS Academy responded to this issue by starting the TAPS Center. A place was needed to focus in on the problem of social distance between youth and police by carrying the mission into four distinct areas: teaching at the college, university, high school, and middle school areas; training of law enforcement, civilians, youth, parents, and adults; programming that connects research to practice; and, finally, research to build the field of Youth and Police Studies with theory and use of sound methodology to support the science of youth and police coming together to make for better understanding and society. The primary TAPS Center activities are found below.

Chenelle Jones serves as the Lead Evaluator for TAPS Academy. Below she presents the largest sample of TAPS evaluation data. In order to assess the effectiveness of the TAPS Academy, youth engaged in the program were administered a 13-item social distance survey during week one (pre-test) and week 11 (post-test). In the survey, participants were asked to indicate the extent to which they agree with several statements on a four-point Likert scale ranging from 1 (strongly disagree) to 4 (strongly agree). The survey includes statements like "I respect the police" and "I feel connected to the police." Data was analyzed using an independent samples t-test in SPSS. Effect size was measured using Cohen's D, which assesses the standardized difference between two means. Results from the study have consistently found that youth who participate in the TAPS Academy have significantly more favorable opinions about the police at the conclusion of the program. In other words, the TAPS Academy successfully reduces social distance between youth and the police. The data presented below includes a sample of 500 youth from TAPS Academy locations in Texas, Ohio, and Alabama from 2014 through 2019 (see Table 5.3).

With the exception of the item "I feel nervous around the police," the TAPS Academy successfully reduced social distance on the other 12 items by 16–34%. One potential explanation for the lack of change on the "nervous" outcome is that many youths were not nervous when they initially encountered officers at the start of the program, and their subsequent interactions with the officers over the 11-week period helped youth become more comfortable and even less nervous around officers. These findings are consistent with other studies (Jones, Penn, & Davenport, 2015) that suggest the TAPS Academy successfully reduces social distance between police and youth.

Although the outcomes continue to be promising, there is a need to conduct a randomized control trial to examine the impact of social distance on both a control and experimental group and compare the outcomes. TAPS is seeking funding to accomplish such a high degree of research, and also has a goal to conduct future research to examine the impact of the TAPS Academy on delinquency. Findings could help inform diversion programming and other initiatives to improve police/youth relations, and youth behavior. According to Jones, with these recommendations in mind, the TAPS Academy aligns with

TABLE 5.3 TAPS Academy Outcomes 2014–2019

	Test Pretest=1 Post-test=2	Mean	Std. Deviation	t-value	Cohen's d
I respect the police	1	2.2600	1.00631	-4.198★★	.81
	2	2.9800	.74203		
I feel close to police officers	1	1.6400	.77618	-5.200★★	.92
	2	2.3800	.83029		
Police officers will treat me fairly when I get into trouble	1	1.7000	.78895	-5.267★★	1.0
	2	2.5200	.70682		
Police officers will help me when I am in trouble	1	2.0000	.90351	-3.746★★	.75
	2	2.6400	.77618		
Police officers will listen to me when I get into trouble	1	1.8200	.87342	-3.500★★	.71
	2	2.4200	.81039		
I care what police officers think of me	1	1.4000	.67006	-5.002★★	.84
	2	2.1400	1.04998		
I want to get along well with police officers	1	2.1000	.93131	-3.525★★	.72
	2	2.7200	.78350		
I don't want to disappoint police officers by getting into trouble	1	2.1600	.95533	-1.804[+]	.39
	2	2.5200	.86284		
I feel connected to the police in my community	1	1.5800	.78480	-3.293★★	.65
	2	2.0800	.75160		
I believe the police respect me	1	1.6600	.74533	-5.824★★	1.1
	2	2.5600	.76024		
I believe the police do their job of fighting crime well	1	2.0200	.89191	-3.625★★	.80
	2	2.6800	.74066		
The police treat all people fairly	1	1.6000	.78246	-5.112★★	1.0
	2	2.4000	.75593		

★p ≤ .05 (two-tailed); ★★p ≤ .01 (two-tailed);[+]p ≤ .10 (two-tailed).

the pillars of 21st Century Policing practices. As the TAPS Academy continues to grow, additional research will continue to inform best practices for reducing social distance between youth and the police.

The TAPS Center program works to break the current cycle of negative interaction with law enforcement that has become all too familiar for many youth. It creates an environment where law enforcement and youth learn from each other, build relationships, and discuss better ways to manage adverse situations. The TAPS Center forges a path for these traditionally opposing groups to build a solid foundation of trust and mutual respect.

The benefits of reducing social distance between youth and law enforcement are many, but one of the most significant is that better community policing can occur, especially regarding young Black and Latino males. TAPS Academy moves community policing one step further by taking its tenets—organizational transformation, problem-solving, and partnerships—to the most removed group of citizens, enabling them to be full participants in their own community through positive interaction with their local law enforcement officers. By reducing social distance, these youths develop respect for authority and pro-social behavior, all leading to reduced crime. At the same time police officers learn youth culture and activities in order to separate truly criminal or delinquent activities from cultural norms and labeled activity.

The original TAPS Academy grant called for, and surpassed, the following ten deliverables:

1. Produce a body of literature about the need, perceptions and feelings of youth, specifically minority youth related to law enforcement, crime, and crime prevention.
2. Create a national curriculum that teaches at-risk youth all the topics under Children and Youth.
3. Create a website for training and implementation of TAPS Academies internationally.
4. Develop a website for current and alumni students to stay connected with TAPS Academy.
5. Develop a Facebook site for current and alumni members to stay connected.
6. Develop a tested TAPS Academy curriculum through five classes (250 youth) in two large metropolitan areas (Houston, Texas, and Washington, DC).
7. Provide over 500 community service hours implementing crime prevention programs in the communities that need it the most.
8. Create an environment for law enforcement to better understand the at-risk population and see them as assets to their community.
9. Create youth graduates who understand the roles and tasks of law enforcement.
10. Prepare youth members of the community to build, develop, and grow their community by erasing prejudicial thoughts previously held about law enforcement personnel.

Findings

Goal 1. Produce a body of literature about the need, perceptions and feelings of youth, specifically minority youth related to law enforcement, crime, and crime prevention. TAPS Academy has created a body of literature in both practical and scholarly areas, which can be found through TAPS TALK (www.tapsacademy.org/tapstalk). These TAPS Talk citations have created short, easy-to-read findings related to youth, police, TAPS programming, social distance, implicit bias, research findings, and a variety of other closely related topics. Additionally, TAPS Academy has appeared in several media outlets including the *Houston Chronicle, Chicago Times, El Paso Times,* NPR, and several local television broadcasts in the greater Houston market (see http://www.tapsacademy.org/About_Us/TAPS_News). TAPS Academy has over 20 media citations. For scholarly work, TAPS Academy has one article in print in the *Journal of Juvenile Justice,* 2015, titled "Social Distance Between Minority Youth and the Police: An Exploratory Analysis of the TAPS Academy." The literature continues to grow as TAPS appears in textbooks, articles, and other outlets.

Goal 2. Create a national curriculum that teaches at-risk youth all the topics under Children and Youth. The TAPS Academy Curriculum is available at http://www.tapsacademy.org/Programs/TAPS_Modules_login. Information about the curriculum and a short description about each of the 11 weeks is found at http://www.tapsacademy.org/Programs/Curriculum. This curriculum meets the rigor of the Houston Independent School District as well as the Texas Education Agency, thus allowing all students who complete the course and all academic requirements to receive one academic credit toward graduation. A story about this accomplishment, "Teen and Police Service Academy Program Earns Texas High School Accreditation," appeared in *Police Magazine* (2014).

Goal 3. Create a website for training and implementation of TAPS Academies internationally. The TAPS Academy website—www.tapsacademy.org—was created and is maintained and operated by Vistra Communications of Tampa, Florida. On this site, users can find a wealth of information about the program as well as the various locations where the program is offered.

Goal 4. Develop a website for current and alumni students to stay connected with TAPS Academy. The TAPS Academy website maintains a page for alumni and former officers to stay connected: http://www.tapsacademy.org/About_Us/Alumni. Additionally, TAPS clubs have been created to further the involvement of alumni after the 11-week TAPS Academy experience. TAPS Clubs are to be set up in schools, churches, and other community organizations to provide opportunities for TAPS alumni to stay connected while they serve their community. More information about TAPS Clubs can be found at: http://www.tapsacademy.org/Programs/TAPS_Clubs. This has been one of the most difficult goals to overcome. Youth are highly mobile and active. Keeping them engaged past graduation is a task that deserves further study.

Goal 5. Develop a Facebook site for current and alumni members to stay connected. TAPS Academy's Facebook page was developed in 2012 and has over 2,500 followers. It is the primary way to quickly inform the TAPS Academy community about activities, important events, and salutes. TAPS Academy Facebook can be found at https://www.facebook.com/TAPSAcademy.

Goal 6. Develop a tested TAPS Academy curriculum through five classes (250 youth) in two large metropolitan areas (Houston, Texas, and Washington, DC). TAPS Academy has developed a tested curriculum that has surpassed the objectives listed in this goal. The grant was originally designed to serve 250 students in academies located in Houston and Washington, DC. Houston developed and flourished. Although attempts were made, developing TAPS in Washington, DC, was unsuccessful. However, TAPS Academy was developed in El Paso, Texas, and Columbus, Ohio, early in its development, thus allowing it to surpass the number of 250 in its first four years.

Goal 7. Provide over 500 community service hours implementing crime prevention programs in the communities that need it the most. Each class has completed a service-learning project which has included gardening, creating TAPS Academy T-shirts, creating bookmarks for elementary school–aged children, and designing art projects for injured veterans. Over 550 students from various academies in the first four years completed one and a half hours of service-learning, totaling 825 hours of service-learning as the youth worked side-by-side with their TAPS officer mentors.

Goal 8. Create an environment for law enforcement to better understand the at-risk population and see them as assets to their community. Throughout the TAPS Academy curriculum, interaction between officer and youth is paramount. The primary source of this interaction is the breakout session that occurs after the lesson of the day. Here youth and officers discuss the subject matter in detail. Research findings regarding connectedness are indicated in Table 5.4:

TABLE 5.4 Self-Reports of Connectedness Before and After TAPS Academy

	Pre-TAPS Academy	*Post-TAPS Academy*
Very Connected or Somewhat Connected	84.7%	87%
Somewhat Disconnected or Very Disconnected	15.5%	12.5%

Goal 9. Create youth graduates who understand the roles and tasks of law enforcement. Through the 11-week TAPS Academy, students learn about the tasks officers perform for the public safety. In the first module, officers introduce themselves and explain what they do. One of the areas in which the highest amount of change occurs with TAPS Academy pre- to post-test is respect. When asked, the students make statements such as: "Now that I know what they do, I can respect them"; "They (police officers) have a hard job"; "Now that I know them better, I just might want to be one (police officer)." Testimony is found throughout TAPS Academy Facebook postings during graduations and on TAPS Talk.

Goal 10. Prepare youth members of the community to build, develop, and grow their community by erasing prejudicial thoughts previously held about law enforcement personnel. Although TAPS Academy needs to do more research focusing on police officers, findings indicate the officers acknowledge being a TAPS officer is difficult and that some academies are more difficult than others. In Houston, which has the largest concentration of TAPS officers, a core group of eight have completed more than five academies. This compares with several officers who have chosen not to continue. When asked why officers do not continue, the answers include: "Busy work schedule"; "Newly promoted"; "Youth do not listen"; and "We cannot help them." See Table 5.5 for a timeline of TAPS Academy/TAPS Center milestones.

Beyond the Deliverables of the Grant

Having the TAPS Academy grant affiliated with the University of Houston–Clear Lake has provided great dividends for programming. The university provided a constant stream of talented and eager students interested in the subject matter. They often provided direct and indirect support for TAPS Academy. Over 30 University of Houston–Clear Lake students in the fields of Criminology, Public Service Leadership, Psychology, and Behavior Sciences interacted in TAPS Academy programming through service-learning, internship, or volunteering. The interest in the subject matter stimulated the creation of a minor in Youth and Police Studies which began in the Department of Social and Cultural Sciences in Fall 2015.

The original grant called for two, two-hour sessions for 15 weeks. However, after the first TAPS Academy, this was found to be draining on the officers as well as interfering into the student's academic time. The curriculum was redesigned to be a single 90-minute to two-hour session for 11 weeks.

TAPS Clubs developed as a means to keep the contact going after TAPS Academy and as a way to initiate contact between youth who were not in a TAPS Academy environment. TAPS Clubs are student-led, high school organizations teaching the important social issues in a service-learning format

TABLE 5.5 Timeline of TAPS Academy/TAPS Center

2011	• Grant received by COPS Office for Houston Police Department.
2012	• First TAPS Academy Class meets in Houston, Texas.
	• Webpage and Facebook page created.
	• TAPS Festival and Conference held in Houston, Texas.
	• TAPS Academy wins Jefferson Award for Community Service.
2013	• Houston Independent School District grants permission to award one high school credit for students completing TAPS Academy.
	• TAPS Summit held in Houston, Texas.
	• TAPS Academy implemented in Miami, Florida.
	• TAPS Clubs created in Houston, Texas.
2014	• TAPS Academy implemented in Columbus, Ohio, and Ponce, Puerto Rico.
	• TAPS Academy implemented in Galveston, Texas; El Paso, Texas; and Tampa, Florida.
	• TAPS Camp implemented in Houston, Texas.
	• TAPS Academy implemented in the nation of St. Kitts/Nevis.
2015	• TAPS Academy implemented in La Marque, Texas, and Chicago, Illinois.
	• TAPS Academy implemented in New York City.
	• University of Houston–Clear Lake offers a Minor in Youth and Policing.
	• TAPS Academy receives Internal Revenue Service 501c (3) status.
	• Original COPS Office grant ends with over 30 academies, 14 different locations, and 606 Academy students taught.
2016	• TAPS Academy implemented in nation of St. Maarten.
	• TAPS Academy implemented in Richmond, Virginia.
	• TAPS Academy gains approval from the Texas Education Agency to offer the academic TEEN POL course, thus granting one high school credit to students upon completion.
	• TAPS Center created in Houston, Texas.
2017	• TAPS Academy implemented in Tuscaloosa, Alabama.
	• TAPS Academy implemented in the nation of Barbados.
	• Community Summer Camps offered in Houston, Texas.
2018	• TAPS Academy implemented in Norristown, Pennsylvania.
	• TAPS Academy leads the teaching of the Community Safety Education Act of Texas.
2019	• TAPS begins teaching the TEEN POL course to eighth graders for high school credit.
	• TAPS Academy implemented in Kansas City, Missouri.
2020	• TAPS Academy implemented in Mocksville, North Carolina.
	• TAPS Academy implemented in Marion, Ohio.
	• The TAPS YouTube channel begins in response to COVID-19.
2021	• TAPS Academy implemented in Las Vegas, Nevada.
	• TAPS Academy implemented in the United States Virgin Islands.

as youth and law enforcement work together to build their community. More information about TAPS Clubs can be found on the TAPS website at http://www.tapsacademy.org/Programs/TAPS_Clubs.

Additionally, the original TAPS Academy grant has spawned the growth of four other TAPS programs.

TAPS Summits provide a day of engagement for high school and college students, parents, and community members to connect with law enforcement in a conference and breakout session format. Several summits have been held in the Houston area in partnership with the Houston Police Department, Houston Independent School District Police, and Prairie View A&M University. A story in the *Houston Chronicle* in 2015 reported that the program aims to reduce "social distance" between police and youth (Wermund, 2015).

TAPS Conferences provide a condensed TAPS Academy curriculum, usually in four-hour formats. Conferences have been held in the Houston area with several law enforcement agencies. Additionally, the conference at the University of Houston–Clear Lake in 2015 was supported by the Houston-area United Way and brought together over 250 youth. Information about TAPS Conferences can be found at: http://www.prweb.com/releases/TAPSAcademy/2015Conference/prweb12627168.htm.

TAPS Festivals provide a fun, carnival-type environment for community and law enforcement to come together. The festivals in the Houston area have highlighted the Gardens for Greatness program of TAPS Academy at Beechnut Academy. Information about TAPS Festivals can be found at: http://tapsacademy.org/join-us-for-the-taps-gardens-for-greatness-festival-this-Saturday.

TAPS Camps are intensive TAPS Academy sessions, usually five to eight weeks during the summer. TAPS Camps are infused with leadership and team-building activities, skill building, and community enrichment. El Paso, Texas, has conducted several TAPS Camps including an academic component in which students complete courses for their high school graduation. In Houston, TAPS Academy has established a relationship with the Harris County Juvenile Probation to provide TAPS Camps for all three facilities. In the summer of 2016, TAPS Camps provided five weeks of programming for 300 adjudicated youth. More information can be found at http://www.tapsacademy.org/TAPS_Talk/now-hiring-for-the-taps-summer-camp.

TAPS numbers as of June 2021:
- Over 3,200 youth have graduated from the TAPS Academy/ TEEN POL
- Over 1,000 youth have participated in summits or conferences
- Over 1,000 youth have participated in camps
- Over 500 youth have participated in TAPS Clubs
- Over 350 have completed TAPS training
- 20 cities have implemented TAPS programming

One of the greatest challenges is sustaining a program, especially a successful one, as administrators change and funding issues emerge. Chief Brian Lumpkin, the co-founder of TAPS Academy, served as an Assistant Chief of the Houston Police Department and the commander of East Patrol, which had about 1,000 officers under his command. In his more than 30 years of policing, he experienced the various eras discussed earlier in the book. He told Penn about the way policing administration works with limited budgets. The chief would call his assistant chiefs in for a strategic planning meeting. The room would be filled with ten or so officers, each with over 20 years of experience. The chief would have three flip charts, labeled "Things We Must Do," "Things We Should Do," and "Things That Are Nice to Do." The officers would fill out the charts accordingly. Of course, under "Must Do" were 911 calls; under "Should Do" were investigations, but consistently under "Nice To Do" were the youth programs of DARE, GREAT, Explorers, and other programs such as storefront police stations, Crime Prevention Through Environmental Design (CPTED), and other community policing crime prevention activities. If these programs were done at all, they were often relegated to a public affairs unit and not seen as a "Must Do" of the department. As a result, activities that would help to reshape policing, and enable community policing and 21st-century practices to become a guiding philosophy rather than a police program, do not become permanent activities and are often cut when budgets get tight or philosophies change. Some say this is the case because policing is about being a paramilitary force, but is it possible to be both warrior and protector, moving between two worlds to serve the public? Penn wrote an article for the Department of Justice along with another Assistant Chief (ret.) Vicki King, titled "Moving Police Officers from Enforcers to Protectors." The article presents the position of the warrior officer and the protector officer and how they can both coexist in to-day's law enforcement personnel (Penn & King, 2016).

Some police officers will argue that they are only warriors by training, with practices such as stop-and-frisk, zero tolerance, and saturation patrols. Additionally, they claim these practices have reduced crime. They cite the "Broken Windows" theory of James Q. Wilson and George Kelling, which linked the prevalence of petty crimes and disorderly conduct with high-crime areas known to police as "hot spots" (Wilson & Kelling, 1982). The reality is that when police cast a wide net in these hot spots, they catch (as was mentioned earlier in the book) "the dolphins with the tuna." Average citizens are questioned along with career criminals. Indiscriminate suppression of criminal activity and alienation of local residents who were caught up in these crackdowns begin to undermine police authority, credibility, and respect. An us-versus-them mentality and practice is the result. People who could escape from these hot-spot areas fled to new neighborhoods, taking with them a wariness of the police. Those leaving for greener pastures would be replaced by a new generation, plagued by crime and distrustful of the police. William Julius Wilson calls these citizens "The Truly Disadvantaged" (Wilson, 2012). In these areas, nothing changes, except the faces. The good people of the community try to mind their own business, staying away from criminals and police alike. Criminal activity flourishes, unrestrained by social convention or police activity. In the absence of citizen input, the police find no reason to abandon their tried-and-true methods of stop-and-frisk, zero tolerance, and saturation patrol. So, the cycle continues.

To turn the tide, the police must concentrate on those within the community who pose the greatest threat to public safety, such as violent offenders, domestic batterers, burglars, gangs, and others involved in criminal enterprises. Nuisance offenses should not be ignored, but a protective approach can yield greater benefits than the traditional enforcement model. For example, a warrior police officer seeing a group of teens hanging out in public before the nighttime curfew will circle back after midnight for some easy citations. A protector will engage the teens before they are in violation, seeking a dialogue before warning the teens of the looming curfew. Officers can gain important information from both contacts, but the protective approach is less adversarial and more likely to yield a positive outcome.

Police must understand that the Ferguson incident was not born of one flashpoint but of thousands of negative police encounters that chipped away at legitimacy, trust, respect, and fairness. The U.S. Department of Justice report on civil rights violations by the Ferguson Police Department showed that "Patrol assignments and schedules are geared toward aggressive enforcement of Ferguson's municipal code, with insufficient thought given to whether enforcement strategies promote public safety or unnecessarily undermine community trust and cooperation" (Justice.gov, 2015). Even if these actions were lawful, the effect was awful.

As protectors, officers tackle crime and disorder issues to enhance the quality of life for all residents. No longer confined to select officers assigned to specialized community outreach programs, the protective model requires street officers and investigators to be engaged with school officials, business owners, religious leaders, and civic associations. Officers must become part of the neighborhood fabric, protecting their constituents from criminals and those who seek to harm others for their own gain. This paradigm shift moves policing away from a prosecution-centric purpose to a collaborative community protection model. The difference is clear. Protectors are proactive. Enforcers are reactive. Protectors build relationships by acting in the best interest of all stakeholders. Enforcers use authority to gain compliance. Protectors do their best. Enforcers do their job. Protectors keep us safe. Enforcers keep us in line.

Shedding a warrior identity and focus will help police evolve new strategies and tactics designed to protect rather than simply enforce. Programs such as

TAPS Academy increase officer safety and police legitimacy because the pillars of procedural justice (voice, transparency, fairness, and impartiality) are at the core and practiced for all citizens.

Summary

Upon completion of reading this chapter we hope you see the evolution of TAPS Academy as the best elements of DARE, GREAT, PALS, Explorers, and Citizens Police Academies, and even serving as a prequel to the President's Task Force on 21st Century Policing. The Teen and Police Center founded in 2016 extends the work of TAPS Academy programming and training to move into research and teaching—all for the purpose of reducing the social distance between youth (especially those most at-risk) and the police. It is not an easy task. Research shows that the TAPS Academy program yields statically significant increases in "like," "respect," and "trust" to improve understanding between police and youth. TAPS creates the opportunity for mutual understanding and dialogue to take place where naturally these interactions do not occur. TAPS moves the conversation of police reform and community-led policing past us-versus-them to a collaborative working together in which youth have a voice and use that voice to make for better policing in their schools and community.

6

POLICING BY TOTALS

In the summer of 2013, Penn was invited to give a speech at the national conference of the National Organization of Black Law Enforcement Executives (NOBLE) in Pittsburgh, Pennsylvania. Although Penn has given speeches to the International Association of Police Chiefs, American Society of Criminology, and Academy of Criminal Justice Sciences, there was a special feeling about giving a talk about what was learned from one full year of TAPS Academy programming to a room of African-American police executives, especially in light of his reading of the works of Dr. Lee P. Brown, known by many as the "father of community policing," a trailblazer for NOBLE whose works provide theoretical support to reduce the social distance between youth, communities, and police.

NOBLE is the leading police leadership organization for Black officers, with over 3,000 members. It meets annually and conducts training sessions and forums to understand Black and urban crime. Its origins in 1976 arose from a meeting of 60 top-ranking Black law enforcement executives in Washington, DC, as a symposium co-sponsored by the Police Foundation and the Law Enforcement Assistance Administration (LEAA). The Joint Center for Political Studies (JCPS) coordinated the meeting to discuss crime in urban areas. The Black executives realized they could have more of an impact on the criminal justice system as a unified voice. They departed from the symposium with an agenda to create the National Organization of Black Law Enforcement Executives, electing Hubert Williams, then-Director of the Newark, New Jersey Police Department, and the first Black police chief of a major city, to be the temporary chairman of NOBLE. During that meeting, the initial purpose and the objectives of the organization were developed and a working committee to devise the organizational structure was formed (National Organization of Black Law Enforcement Executives, n.d.).

DOI: 10.4324/9780429424519-7

Brown comments that in the 1980s NOBLE changed its membership requirements, thus allowing any officer at supervisory level to join the organization. Its professional orientation is much like Police Executive Research Forum (PERF) and the International Association Chiefs of Police (IACP), but NOBLE is different because it has a specific focus on issues of racism, career development, and equal justice. In its mission statement, NOBLE claims it was instituted to "ensure equity in the administration of justice in the provision of public service to all communities of law enforcement by being committed to justice for all" (Brown, 2012, p. 58). Thus, Penn was highly honored to address such a highly esteemed group of men and women on the front line of building positive relationships between youth and police. Remember the Trayvon Martin death had occurred just one year earlier, on February 26, 2012. Although the Martin case was not an event between a law enforcement officer and a youth, the outcome helped to create the Black Lives Matter movement and stands as a bookmark commencing a chapter of tense race relations between police and Black and Brown youth. Below is the foundation of Policing by TOTALS, which refers to Trust, Openness, Transparency, Accessibility, Legitimacy, and Safety. This chapter will expand upon the idea, as some seven years have passed since it was first written.

Equality in society depends on government agents being legitimate while providing opportunities and protections for all citizens. Citizens' perceptions demonstrate their understanding of whether their interactions and contacts with government agents in the mainstream arena reflect a fair and just process. Arguably there is no system today under more scrutiny concerning questions of equality than American policing and its interaction with African-American and Latino youth. As director and a co-founder of TAPS Academy, Penn presented a perspective from both youth and law enforcement.

As noted in the previous chapter, TAPS Academy provides an 11-week curriculum to the most at-risk youth in juvenile facilities, alternative schools, and low-performing high schools in which police officers and teens learn together about subjects affecting them most, including youth and police interaction, conflict resolution, drugs, teamwork, bullying, truancy, dating, and other topics, including a service-learning project. Pre- and post-program evaluations show 30–50% positive changes for youth as compared to control groups in areas of trust, connectedness, like, and respect. In addition, post-program evaluation shows that police officers increase their understanding of youth, which enables them to more effectively handle interactions with youth in the community (Lumpkin & Penn, 2013).

A host of literature confirms that minority youth, especially African-American youth, has the lowest amount of trust, like, connectedness, and legitimacy for police (Jones, Penn, & Davenport, 2015). Overall, 59% of White Americans have confidence in the police, as compared to only 37% of Black Americans (*The Economist*, 2014c). This poisonous relationship erodes public trust and weakens the social contract that holds a society together. Citizens must believe they have equality with law enforcement in order for the groups to bond and the citizens to become law-abiding. They must believe that "playing by the rules" pays off justly and fairly and is rewarded (Hirschi, 1969)]; the fact that many do not raises questions about perceptions of authority and the law in general (Laub, 2014). Penn conducted research in area high schools in the fall of 2011 before starting TAPS programming in 2012. He found in some minority communities in the United States that police are seen as "an occupying force fighting a war against us just because we live in a poor neighborhood," according to one African-American male teenager. This legal cynicism (Sampson & Bartusch, 1998) has been found to correlate with the disadvantaged as well as with high rates of violence (Kirk & Papachristos, 2011).

Violence, crime, and victimization rates make for constant contact among minority youth and the police. With this reality of race and place, the African-American young man quoted above has a one in three chance of going to prison in his lifetime (*The Economist*, 2014a). This ongoing, daily struggle between members of minority communities and law enforcement has the characteristics of war, as death occurs on both sides. Stories such as those of Michael Brown and Eric Garner have triggered public protest, but other deaths should also be noted. For example, John Crawford was in an Ohio Walmart toy aisle holding an air rifle he planned to buy. As he talked on the phone and looked at other items, he passed several children and their parents. Video footage shows there was no concern from the parents or children. When police responded to a 911 caller stating "a Black man with a gun was threatening people," they shot the 22-year-old Crawford dead. In addition, the mother of some of the children died of a heart attack in the aftermath. The grand jury declined to indict the officers who shot Crawford (*The Economist*, 2014a).

The statistics are grim for both African Americans and the police: roughly 29% of Americans shot by police were African-American. African Americans make up about 13% of the U.S. population and 42% of those who kill the police ("cop killers") when the race of the offender is known. In 2014 alone, more than 46 police officers were shot dead (*The Economist*, 2014b). Recall that in retaliation for the killing of Mr. Garner, Ismaaiyl Brinsley wrote on his Instagram account: "I'm putting wings on pigs today. They take 1 of ours, let's take 2 of theirs" (Long & Peltz, 2014). Brinsley would later assassinate New York City officers Rafael Ramos and Wenjian Liu before taking his own life. Hatred for the police is so embedded in the minds of many minority youth that self-protection is seen as the logical response. With the pre-TAPS research Penn found that one Black teenage girl stated: "I have more faith in my papa's gun than the police. They ain't no good."

Social distance, procedural justice, social-historical analysis, the work of Brown (2012), and criminology theory were synthesized to present Policing by TOTALS in 2013. It was well received by the NOBLE audience and later reprinted in an 2016 article by the COPS Office (Penn, 2016). It consists of the following:

Trust: Starting from the premise that bias (explicit and implicit) exists, the question becomes what is being done agency-wide to build relationships and understanding between the most disenfranchised communities and the police? Citizens must believe in the legitimacy of the agency and the local law enforcement officer.

Openness: Is the agency seeking and pursuing opportunities to listen and learn from the most disenfranchised? Theories such as Developmental Theory, Minority Threat Theory, and Social Distance Theory provide an understanding for fears, misunderstandings, and biases. All citizens have value, and venues must exist to enable dialogue and discovery.

Transparency: What are the procedures for all citizens to engage in due process? All people should have voice, and access to information is important to facilitate interaction. Access to information and interaction among groups promotes accountability. The use of body cameras, outside investigations, and reports will assist in creating opportunities for citizens to know the functions and operations of their law enforcement agencies.

Accessibility: Community policing in its simplest format brings policing to the citizen. Yet there must be an understanding at the citizen level and throughout the agency command of what community policing means in practice. What is being done to bring policing to the most disenfranchised and those with the greatest social distance from the police? Additionally, are those communities being oriented to understand, implement, and respond to community policing?

Legitimacy: Citizens comply when they feel local policing is legitimate. Procedural justice practices of voice, respect, neutrality, understanding, and helpfulness advance individual police actions into citizens' perceptions of fairness by law enforcement, moving citizen and police relations beyond "us versus them" practices.

Safety: Crime is at its lowest levels for over 30 years, yet the positive perceptions of law enforcement have not risen and have even dropped in minority communities. Because the perception of safety is one's individual reality, the question is what is being done to make people feel safer beyond Uniform Crime Reports (UCR)? Are there ways to reward officers beyond the number of arrests? Finally, men and women in over 12,500 law enforcement agencies in the United States provide society's line of authority; going past that line would be chaos and an end to society as we know it. Those officers must have the training and authority to best perform their duties honorably and safely every day.

Policing by TOTALS provides a starting point to bridge the gap that currently exists between minority youth, their communities, and law enforcement.

COPS Office-funded programs, such as the Teen And Police Service (TAPS) Academy, Fair and Impartial Policing, and Coffee with a Cop, are tools to bring community policing to the most disenfranchised citizens (Penn, 2016).

Police departments following Policing by TOTALS entail the work of an entire police department, not just a public affairs division or special officers completing the job of "being nice to the citizens." As Penn noticed as he traveled around the United States and abroad to meet and train thousands of hardworking officers, the job of building community relations is often seen as "less than" policing. Minority and female officers in the ranks may have a lead on relating and interacting with young Black and Brown men.

It is a plus that so many Black, Brown, and female officers focus on elements of 21st Century Policing and Policing by TOTALS. Their affinity for these elements grows even stronger when they themselves receive unfair treatment when not in uniform or learning about how their children or other family members were treated by police officers. Some officers, especially Black officers, have privately shared with the lead author horrific stories of harassment, foul language, and rough handling taking place until they identify themselves as a police officer. One Black male police sergeant shared:

> I was sitting in the stands watching a high school football game while dressed in civilian clothing. All of a sudden, several police officers approached me and demanded I leave the stands. I asked, why? They continued to shout at me to get up and leave as they had their hands on their guns. They grabbed my arms to lift me out of my seat. I kept asking why? I decided it was in my best interest to comply. So I left my seat as the incident attracted the attention of those friends, parents, and spectators around me. The officers took me to a secluded area under the stands and told me to remove my gun. I then identified myself as a police officer. It appears someone saw my weapon and called the police to say "there is a Black man in the stands with a gun." I would not like to imagine the outcome of this incident if I did not keep my cool. Would they have treated me this way if I were a White officer?

Those officers pushing beyond community policing to go further to evolve into 21st Century Policing and Policing by TOTALS report feeling like outsiders running against a current of us-versus-them and traditional warrior policing. One female officer stated:

> They know I don't play. You see I was the officer that took time to explain things and correct officers on the scene. I understood. You see I have two Black men as sons, and I know these cops can be dirty.

What police officers must remember is what makes for police legitimacy: providing citizens with voice, transparency, impartiality, fairness, and consistency ultimately creates good police officers and public safety. When the public has stronger feelings of legitimacy there is a higher level of following police directions and obeying the rules of society. Tracy Meares, a member of the President's Task Force on 21st Century Policing, writing with Tom Tyler in Angela Davis's edited work titled *Policing the Black Man: Arrest, Prosecution, and Imprisonment* (2017), discusses how the body of evidence called the social psychology of procedural justice has been widely replicated. They discuss how the public wants to be listened to, they want explanations for police actions, and they need to have information that will allow them to make an assessment about whether they feel that the law is applied consistently and appropriately across people and situations.

> If people believe that the police are fair, they will trust them and defer to their authority. They will also cooperate by reporting crimes and criminals, providing testimony, and otherwise helping to hold offenders accountable.
>
> *(Davis, 2017, p. 164)*

Thus, improving legitimacy and following policing by TOTALS decreases crime and increases police safety. One way to ensure legitimacy in youth is to remember what we studied earlier about the adolescent brain development and recognize that these characteristics of youth thinking must be considered:

1. Trouble considering consequences
2. Confused or disorganized thinking
3. Thinking blocked by emotions
4. Impulsive decision-making
5. Short-sightedness
6. Feeling invulnerable
7. Seeking short-term rewards and not considering long-term consequences
8. Prioritizing thoughts differently
9. Misinterpreting social clues
10. Emotionally driven decisions
11. Different body clock (more alert in late afternoon/evening)
12. Easily distracted
13. Lack of long-term planning
14. Less oriented toward the future

(International Association of Chiefs of Police, n.d.)

Now this does not mean youth receive a pass or get-out-of-jail-free card because they are experiencing "teen brain"; rather, it calls for an understanding of this population not as outsiders but as members of the community who with proper mentorship, mutual respect, and positive interactions can be productive members of society.

School shootings by youth presents an excellent case study to understand the application of teen brain and policing by TOTALS. These tragic realities that we have seen across the United States demonstrate the need to have rational adults available for youth who may believe violence is the "teen brain" response. Houston alone had experienced a 27% increase in homicides in 2018 (Ucr.fbi.gov, 2019). In 2019, according to the Uniform Crime Reports, there were a total of 7,495 people including adults, juveniles, and individuals whose age was unknown. A school shooting at Santa Fe High School in the greater Houston area as well as others have created an environment in which youth, parents, teachers, and other citizens need answers in order to feel more secure and safe on their school campuses.

In response, the Texas legislature put out a request for proposals (RFP) for $100 million in funding for schools, governments, and non-profits to purchase cameras, locks, guns, and other items to protect students, faculty, and school facilities. The RFP clearly stated that no part of the monies could be used for training or programs. A few months later, the COPS Office issued an RFP of $50 million dollars in funding, and its wording did allow for police training:

> School Violence Prevention Program (SVPP) will provide up to 75% funding for the following school safety measures in and around K-12 (primary and secondary) schools and school grounds:
>
> - Coordination with law enforcement
> - Training for local law enforcement officers to prevent student violence against others and self
> - Metal detectors, locks, lighting, and other deterrent measures
> - Technology for expedited notification of local law enforcement during an emergency
> - Any other measure that the COPS Office determines may provide a significant improvement in security.
>
> (*Cops.usdoj.gov, 2020*)

With an increase in population imminent and challenges in resources for local police departments, there need to be solutions that promote the training of police officers, prevention, diversion, and treatment of youth in order to reduce elements that lead to crime, specifically crimes of bullying, violence, and mass violence on school campuses. Hardware alone will not do the job. There need to be "peopleware": qualified, trained, and experience officers prepared to use their people skills first through communication, mentorship, skill-building, and positive interaction.

In May of 2018, CNN reported that there had been 23 school shootings in the United States so far that year (Ahmed & Walker, 2018), thus, averaging one each week. For the greater Houston area, the tragedy of the Santa Fe High School shooting, in which 10 people were killed, resonates. Sadly, that was not the only school shooting in the greater Houston area in 2018. Evidence-based programming must be implemented in order to prevent such tragic events.

PBS reported 10 ways for schools, communities, and parents to prevent school shootings in a 2018 report. The top three are the fundamental blocks of TAPS Academy programming in middle and high schools.

1) *Teach social and emotional skills.* TAPS Academy teaches police officers about youth and youth about police officers. Through a curriculum that encourages dialogue, mutual understanding, and learning, both groups learn social and emotional skills to cope with issues faced by students and police officers.

2) *Hire more counselors and school resource officers.* TAPS Academy brings additional officers to a school campus. Beside the presence of more police officers (their cars and equipment on campus), TAPS provides officers with training on how to be the most effective when interacting with students. TAPS officers receive eight hours of training in teen brain, implicit and explicit bias, procedural justice, teaching and training teenage youth, classroom management, and community resources. TAPS Academy believes more police officers on campus will deter school violence, but that is only half the solution. It is imperative that police officers on campuses are highly trained to create positive interactions with youth in order to prevent violent acts.

3) *Use technology to identify troubled youth.* TAPS Academy officers are a presence on campus one to four times a week. Officers provide youth with contact information in order to discuss problems, concerns, and issues on campus or in their lives. TAPS Academy has an active social media presence to inform and educate youth, parents, officers, teachers, and the public. In one case, TAPS Academy prevented a horrific event when after a bullying module a student told her mentor officer she was carrying a butcher's knife in her book bag because people in school were bothering her. The TAPS officer took the knife, assisted with counseling between the students, and prevented what could have been the tragic loss of life for one or more students.

(PBS, 2018)

Summary

Policing by TOTALS, in which each police department earnestly works to build Trust, Openness, Transparency, Accessibility, Legitimacy, and Safety in their daily operations, relies on the performance of every officer, not just a team or division. Policing by TOTALS was presented in 2013 but finds support in the President's Task Force on 21st Century Policing. In this chapter, Policing by TOTALS was applied to one of the challenges faced by police in school safety. This moves to a new level of importance as calls for defunding and even the elimination of police are a part of the national conversation. Policing by TOTALS answers the call for more community-led policing so officers can have a place in the school for safety as well as mentoring and building positive relationships. By allowing more characteristics of 21st Century policing to take place (voice, procedural justice, transparency, legitimacy, and safety), the traditional, warrior police officer sheds us-versus-them practices to become the protector that communities demand in their law enforcement.

7
THE COMMUNITY SAFETY EDUCATION ACT OF TEXAS

On a warm July evening in 2018, TAPS Academy received the William H. Hastie Award from the National Association of Blacks in Criminal Justice. Judge Hastie was the first African-American federal judge with his appointment to the Virgin Islands in 1939. A graduate of Harvard Law School, Hastie would become the Dean of Howard University's law school, the first African-American federal appellate judge in 1950, and was considered for the US Supreme Court in 1962. TAPS received the award because their work was viewed as "effecting changes in policy in the area of criminal justice at a national level." Upon reflecting about that award, the authors decided to include this chapter about the Community Safety Education Act of Texas because this Act has the "bones" of being a true national policy as states, districts, and localities wrestle with implementing solutions to improving youth, citizens, and police relations. Texas offers a policy for the rest of the United States. This chapter explains how.

In June 2016, TAPS Academy staff met with State Senator John Whitmire's staff to introduce the TAPS Academy philosophy, training, and programming. They discussed the events of the previous four years and the social distance that existed between minority youth and police that manifested in horrific acts of violence between citizens and police. It became clear that policy at the state level could be a solution to the problem. State Senator Whitmire was the Dean of Senate, serving since 1983; nothing criminal justice-wise in the state occurred without his review and blessing. Several weeks later, the senator introduced legislation calling for instruction to improve citizen and law enforcement relations by requiring ninth graders in the state of Texas to receive instruction (Ward, 2016).

As Chair of the Senate Committee on Criminal Justice, Whitmire called for a hearing in the Fall of 2016. Penn testified and explained to the committee

DOI: 10.4324/9780429424519-8

the importance of both sides (law enforcement and youth) receiving education, training, and programming to improve the relationship; his recurring theme was: "By learning from each other, youth and police can reduce their social distance." From the lessons learned through directing TAPS Academy, Penn believed it was imperative to have instruction in which police, youth, and citizens were equal. Yes, all officers are required to learn what to do during a traffic stop, but a refresher/retraining was needed state-wide. For youth and citizens, there was also a need to be instructed on what should occur during a traffic stop. Think about it; who taught you what to do during a traffic stop? Penn recalled his own experience learning how to drive in Washington, DC, in the mid-1980s. His mother enrolled him in the Easy-Method Driving School. There was an overview of the traffic stop, but a major difference from his instruction as compared to the current practice in Texas was that he was taught to assemble license and registration in those few moments after the car comes to a complete stop and before the officer comes to the driver's side of the car. Drivers were taught to have these items ready to give to the officer once he or she arrived at the car. In Texas today, however, such a practice could be detrimental to your health. In Texas you are not to move while the officer has your car stopped or while he or she approaches the car. You are to follow the officer's instructions and keep your hands at the 10-o'clock and 2-o'clock positions on the steering wheel.

Testimony in front of a Texas Legislative Committee is formal, much like a courtroom. The committee members sit in a half-circle behind a raised platform. The witness sits at a table with a microphone, and there is stadium seating for the audience behind the person giving testimony. When giving testimony, Penn spoke for the full allotted time about the work of TAPS and the need for both sides to be educated. It was evident that his testimony sparked the interest of the community members as he blended research with practice, and included heartfelt stories of building relationships between youth and police while making a point that Texas can lead the way with a course for both officers and youth. After he spoke, several staffers came to Penn before he could take his seat and asked for his card so that they could learn more about TAPS Academy and the philosophy of bringing youth together with law enforcement. The side conversations were so loud as he spoke while others testified that Senator Whitmire had to remind them that the committee was still in session and that they needed to take the conversations outside the room.

Among the entourage of distinguished police chiefs, pastors, and community leaders was the president of the National Association for the Advancement of Colored People (NAACP). Since he flew to Austin from Houston for the meeting, Penn offered him a ride back to Houston as he wanted to spend more time with him to gauge his feelings about the proposed legislation and the need for both officers and citizens to receive the same training. As a very stately and wise man who teaches at Thurgood Marshall Law School and has even served as the dean of the law school, his comments were calculated and measured. One statement was that Black people are always the ones receiving the education and supposedly the ones who needed to change. It was very important to make sure the officers received the education and training that they needed. A traffic stop has two parties: officers and citizens. The citizens cannot be in the wrong all the time.

The following months were filled with emails, telephone calls, and office visits in which Penn communicated with legislative officials throughout the state informing committee members, government officials, and the general public about TAPS Academy programming in relation to the proposed legislation. He spoke boldly and proudly about the TAPS Academy, noting that it was the only national program approved by the Texas Education Agency to grant academic credit to high school students and pointing out the evidence-based research demonstrating the program's success for youth and law enforcement involved.

Eventually Senator Royce West from the 23rd District took the lead of Senate Bill 30. West wanted to make learning what to do during a traffic stop mandatory for those receiving original or corrective driver's education. His leadership, along with other legislators including Representatives Garnet Coleman, John Wu, and others, created the Community Safety Education Act (CSEA), which passed the 85th Texas Legislature and was signed into law by Governor Greg Abbott on June 9, 2017. The passing of CSEA was a triumph with one limitation: it was an unfunded mandate. Penn quickly learned just how many people the law would touch:

- approximately 2 million high school students in Texas;
- approximately 80,000 peace officers; and
- approximately 1 million Texans receiving driver's education or taking a driver's safety course.

Senate Bill 30, The Community Safety Education Act, follows the philosophy of TAPS Academy, in which both citizens and law enforcement work together to improve relations and reduce their social distance because they become better informed and learn from each other. Not only was Penn gratified that the law passed the Texas legislature, he was honored when in August 2017 he was appointed a member of the state-wide implementation committee. Over the next few years, TAPS Academy staff worked with several Texas agencies to implement the law so that citizens and law enforcement could improve relations in Texas. A very important aspect of the Community Safety Education Act is that it acknowledged that all three populations—officers, youth, and adult citizens—needed a course on what to do during a traffic stop in order to alleviate confusion.

If Texas can do it, so can other states. Texas has the second largest land mass as well as second largest population in the country. Its vastness creates a diversity in both land mass and people. Texans are often identified as coming from one of its six regions:

1) City Dweller—from Houston, Dallas, San Antonio, or one of the other major cities;
2) From the Valley—from Brownsville/South Texas;
3) Hill County—from central Texas, non-city;
4) West Texas—from that vast amount of land west of San Antonio, which has more cattle than people;
5) East Texas—from the area northeast of Houston heading toward Arkansas and Louisiana; and finally
6) The Panhandle—from Amarillo and the area northwest near Oklahoma.

These six different regions create diversity in thought, beliefs, practices, and ideologies. As a member of the state-wide committee to implement the Community Safety Education Act, Penn would attend meetings in which urban-versus-rural, farmland-versus-city, and small town-versus-large city speed limits of 70 miles per hour, compared to 35 miles an hour or less, would make for heated debate. There was no consensus throughout the state on how a traffic stop should be conducted. Thus, conversations and decisions had to center around common ground as members defended the part of Texas with which they are most familiar. A committee of 12 worked for ten months with the charge of implementing the legislation so that each of the three groups taking driving instruction (law enforcement, high school students, and citizens) received the same course materials. The meetings were filled with police officers from around the state, Texas Commission on Law Enforcement (TCOLE) leadership, Texas regulatory personnel, and Texas Education Agency officials. At the first meeting, Penn clearly remembers being the only civilian as well as the only African American in the room. He thought to himself: How did this happen? He felt he alone was carrying the torch of the true spirit of the Act: for citizens and officers to improve their relationship by making a curriculum that teaches understanding the issues and points of view and concerns on both sides during the potentially confrontational traffic stop. As Penn listened to the concerns held by the different police officers in the room, it became clear to him their feeling was: "just do as you are told during a traffic stop, and everything will work out fine." Yet, the faces of the TAPS youth continued to remind him that this was to be a two-way street of education and the citizen should not be considered the enemy. Both officer and citizen needed to be educated. Penn fell back on the works of Dr. Martin Luther King, who stressed the need to find the good in all. He thought about ways he used his time as a Fulbright scholar to find points of mutual respect and dialogue. He began to speak at the meetings as the voice of the citizen—the Black and Brown citizen, the youth citizen, and all others looking for voice and Policing by TOTALS.

Over the course of six meetings, participants listened to each other—disagreeing on some points but finding common ground to create a curriculum. It was decided to create a short film demonstrating a traffic stop. Penn was tasked to develop a segment of the training film that provided the citizens' voice through a series of questions asked by citizens and answered by police officers. Working along with the Houston Police Department's Public Affairs video production unit, a group went to Discovery Green, a park in downtown Houston, and talked with citizens. People were asked if they wanted to ask a question for the video; some did, and some did not. What was most valuable was the incredible dialogue between the officers and the people that occurred that day.

One Black man in the park, setting up a display with a team of other workers, conversed with the officers for several minutes before feeling at ease enough to be on camera. His questions were about procedure, the feeling of being uncomfortable around officers, ways to reduce the stress, and learning why officer procedures are as they are. The dialogue was so valuable that telephone numbers were exchanged, and both the officer and citizen believed they learned from each other. The citizen commented, "This was good because I now understand what the police are trying to do." He agreed to be on the video when he saw the good of the project.

They also did a question-and-answer (Q&A) session at the then-named Robert E. Lee High School, a Houston Independent School District high school, where Penn had been asked to serve on the Shared Decision-Making Committee. At the first meeting, Penn introduced himself and stated: "We need to do something about the name." Within a year, the name was changed, and Penn happily attended the inauguration in May 2018 for the new Wisdom High School, named after a prolific Houston Independent School District educator.

Wisdom High School is probably the most diverse high school in Houston. Sitting just west of The Galleria, an upscale mall, the school boasts students who speak over 40 different languages, but the school is a far cry from the opulence of the mall. At Wisdom there is poverty, gang life, conflict, immigration issues, poor performance, and other elements of social disorganization. A TAPS Academy has been in the school for years. In the first year, one young TAPS student was lost through gang violence just after he graduated. Special girls-only TAPS Academies are often held at Wisdom. Usually, they include a select group of girls ranging from victims of violence to those who are actively involved in delinquency. TAPS is about understanding each other and reducing the social distance.

The school administration had gathered about 30 students (some of them TAPS graduates) for the Q&A session. Officer Treva Mott of the Houston

Police Department, known as the Big Sister of TAPS Academy for her work in 2011 to the present with the Academy, was there. She is the longest-serving TAPS officer. Mott answered the students' questions that were mostly focused on driving and the "what ifs," including questions about immigration. Some of the students were nervous in front of the camera, but just as we learned with the adults in Discovery Green, the students wanted opportunities to talk to officers to receive correct information and move beyond the us–versus–them attitude to see officers as real people doing a dangerous public service.

The training film came together with students from Austin Community College as the actors for the two scenarios. The Q&A section was inserted in the middle, and an introduction by State Senator Royce West was placed at the beginning. The 16-minute video is called "Flashing Lights: Creating Safe Interactions between Citizens and Law Enforcement" and is available at: https://www.texasgateway.org/resource/flashing-lights-senate-bill-30. Officer Jason Knox is one of the officers answering a question in the film. Sadly, in May 2020, while on patrol, Officer Knox's helicopter crashed. He ended his watch on May 2, 2020. Tragically Knox appears to have lost his life to a 19-year-old, drunk, undocumented immigrant from Honduras who fired his weapon in the direction of a police helicopter (*The Houston Chronicle*, 2020).

The curriculum was created based on the SB 30 Statutory Guidelines and Recommendations (2017), which originated from Texas State Senator Royce West's office. Although it was written for law enforcement and citizens of Texas its usefulness is for all drivers. It states:

> The Role of Law Enforcement and Duties and Responsibilities of Police Officers.
>
> - Officers should treat motorists with dignity and respect.
> - Drivers should be advised that officers are not required by state law to provide their names or badge numbers to a driver but may do so if required by agency policy.
> - It is recommended that an officer explain to a driver that when a citation is issued, it is with the implied agreement that the driver will appear in court or make the arrangements necessary to satisfy the court appearance. Or, the officer should instruct drivers to read the information provided on the citation regarding the driver's obligation to appear in court.
> - When seeking to perform a consensual search, officers should elicit clear consent for the search, including when practicable, a signed statement or video recorded affirmative consent to the motorist.
> - While it is not required by law, it is recommended that an officer inform a driver or passenger of when they are no longer being detained.
>
> Proper Behavior for Civilians and Officers During Interactions.

- While being stopped by an officer, a driver should be instructed to slow down immediately and pull over to the right side of the road as soon as possible.
- When being stopped by an officer, it is recommended for a driver to park the vehicle on the right shoulder or to the right of the road as far as safely possible. If safe parking is unavailable at roadside, a driver should move slowly to a side street or parking lot away from high-volume traffic.
- When being stopped by an officer, when visibility is limited, it is recommended for a driver to activate vehicle hazard lights and/or interior dome lights.
- Drivers should be advised that an officer may approach their vehicle from the passenger side for reasons of safety.
- When their vehicle is stopped, a driver should place the vehicle in park and engage the emergency brake. It is recommended for drivers, except for certain circumstances, to turn their engines off.
- If a driver is uncertain that the vehicle performing the traffic stop is a police car, the driver should be instructed to drive slowly and carefully, below the speed limit, to a well-lighted and populated location. A driver may contact 911 and remain on the line until the officer's identity is verified. However, drivers should be advised that it is a violation of state law and the driver can be arrested for not stopping when the vehicle performing the stop is a marked law enforcement or emergency response vehicle.
- During a vehicle stop, drivers should be instructed to keep their hands visible or on the steering wheel, and passengers should keep their hands in plain sight. State law requires the driver to lower their window.
- During traffic stops, all drivers should be instructed not to reach or search for their license(s) or insurance documents before or while the officer approaches the vehicle. Before attempting to access license or insurance documents, a driver should be instructed to notify the officer of the location of those items.
- Drivers should be instructed to follow the officer's instructions and should be informed that certain movements as the officer is approaching, or has arrived at their vehicle, such as reaching and searching for required documents, could be interpreted as a threat to the officer's safety or indicate possible criminal activity.
- During a traffic stop, a driver and passengers should be instructed to remain inside the vehicle unless instructed to exit by the officer. If instructed to exit the vehicle, drivers should check traffic and do so safely.
- Drivers should be instructed to not attempt to leave a traffic stop until it has been indicated by the officer that the stop is complete. At that

time, a driver should give the appropriate signal and re-enter traffic safely.

- All drivers should receive instruction on how to safely interact with law enforcement if there is a firearm inside the passenger compartment of their vehicle. All drivers should be advised that they should store their required documents in a different location from that of the firearm.

A Person's Rights Concerning Interactions with Police Officers.

- Law enforcement and drivers should be instructed to respond with courtesy during traffic stops and other officer/citizen interactions.
- Drivers and passengers should be instructed that although it is lawful for them to remain silent during a traffic stop, they are required by law to truthfully identify themselves when asked to do so by an officer. A driver of passengers can be arrested for giving false identifying information to an officer.
- Drivers should be instructed that if they are placed under arrest, it is an offense to refuse to identify themselves, to not provide their address, or to refuse to give their date of birth to an officer.
- A driver should be instructed that although they have the right to remain silent, it may be beneficial to verbally provide identifying and address information to an officer if they cannot present their license.
- A person who a passenger in a vehicle should receive instruction advising them that they can be asked questions by an officer while they are being detained. However, a passenger can ask an officer if they are being detained or if they are free to leave and have a right to leave if they are not being detained.
- A driver should receive instruction advising them of their right to refuse to have their vehicle searched if asked by an officer. However, a driver must also be instructed that if an officer has reason to believe that the vehicle contains evidence of a crime, the vehicle can be searched without the driver's consent.
- A driver should receive instruction that if an officer suspects that a weapon is on their person, the officer may conduct a pat-down search of their clothing. A driver may not physically resist the search but has the right to notify the officer that they do not consent to any further search. Instructions should include that consent to a search may later be used in court.
- Drivers and passengers should also be advised that an officer may conduct a non-consensual search based on an officer's observation that the subject detained has responded in a way to make the officer believed that the subject has engaged in a criminal act or is about to engage in a criminal act.

- Drivers, passengers, and other citizens should receive instruction on how to respond if they believe that an officer has acted inappropriately during a traffic stop or other officer/citizen encounters. These instructions should inform a driver, passenger, or citizen on the appropriate governmental body for a complaint to be filed, whether the law enforcement agency is a municipal police department or a Sheriff's Department or if the complaint involves the Texas Department of Public Safety.

To summarize what should be done during a traffic stop there are three basic rules

1. Do what the officer asks you to do. Understand it is a very tense moment for you and the officer. Thus, safety for you and the officer are the greatest concerns.
2. Understand you have rights to refuse and not to self-incriminate, but such refusal can and will be used against you if the case goes further.
3. Officers are not required to provide names or badge numbers, so do not make a big deal out of that if they refuse. Instead, look to see if the camera is on and look for the badge number, agency, and name of officer. Note the number of the police car as well as your location, time of day, and whether other cars stopped or passed by whose drivers may have seen the event. These details will be useful if you believe you were treated inappropriately during the interaction with the officer. Report all of this information to the department's internal affairs department, the NAACP office, Crime Stoppers, or the FBI as necessary.

One final note. Be very careful with cell phones recording the interaction. While it is permitted to record the interaction as long as it does not interfere with the work of the officer, a cell phone could be mistaken as a weapon by another officer. It could put your life in danger if another officer believes the officer conducting the stop is in danger. You may record the event or call a family member to hear the interaction, but it is important not to point the phone/camera in a way that it could be perceived as a weapon, especially if lighting is poor.

By September 2018 the curriculum was approved, the film had been edited, and everything was ready. The law stated that all Texas Commission of Law Enforcement-certified officers in the state of Texas were required to complete the course by January 1, 2020. The course became mandatory for all high school seniors starting with the class of 2021. TAPS Academy received a grant from the Governor's Criminal Justice Division to train 7,000 citizens in the state. From October 2018 through September 2019, they trained over 12,000 people, including all of the 5,200 Houston Police Department officers.

The Texas Legislature meets every other year. Each session leads to changes to procedures and laws related to police. TAPS was placed in the mandatory course rotation. Every Wednesday there was a four-hour block of instruction to train 150 officers in a large, auditorium-style room. Training 150 officers with a variety of rank, backgrounds, experiences, and job duties can be challenging, but TAPS created a methodology that worked well for officers as well as citizens.

TAPS Academy assembled a symposium consisting of former chiefs, training officers, traffic officers, public affairs officers, and patrol officers. When shown the curriculum they were asked: What is the best way to teach this course to officers and citizens? The feedback was tremendous. Hearing the issues officers have to overcome with traffic stops was insightful in giving the training a balanced approach. The following elements were agreed on:

- The course would be taught with a knowledgeable civilian and officer, thus ensuring that all points of view are expressed and covered in the class. Each would make sure the tough questions were asked and answered.
- It would incorporate a video showing a traffic stop as a starter for the course to allow both citizen and officer to see how improvements could be made.
- It would incorporate a video of a particular officer who had given over 25,000 tickets and never received a complaint, in order to show his demeanor and presentation. In the video of this officer, who has been featured on national news, citizens remark about how they were never so happy to receive a ticket in their life. When the officer was asked what he does differently from other officers, he discussed how he treated people equally and fairly. The video clip shows him talking to people in a respectful but firm manner. It provides a lesson for officers and citizens alike.
- The course also included some information on procedural justice and the President's Task Force on 21st Century Policing.

These four elements complimented the four parts required to be in the course:

1) Explain the Community Safety Education Act.
2) Explain the seven steps of a traffic stop.
3) Explain procedures, actions, and laws as they occur during a traffic stop.
4) Provide information on how to file a compliment or complaint after a traffic stop.

Officer Mott and Penn usually taught the course. In the first hour, Penn introduced the course, with information about the Community Safety Education Act, the basics of the police stop, and traffic officer videos as well as procedural justice and 21st Century Policing. After a short break, Officer Mott taught the seven steps of a traffic stop, as well as procedures and laws applicable during a traffic stop, especially those pertaining to the search of a vehicle. The Commander of the Internal Affairs Unit taught the "Citizens' Complaint and Compliment" part of the course. This aspect of the course articulated the need for citizens to file complaints and compliments, and explained the process and what occurs internally once complaints are filed through the Internal Affairs Office all the way through to the Chief of Police. They ended the course with the Community Safety Education Act film and review. Officers were required to take a test. In all of the training, no officer failed the test.

Some people reading this may believe the officers did not take the course seriously. Penn has two assurances that they did. First, this was a mandatory course in which rosters, a test, and signatures were required. If an officer does not follow the instructions of a mandatory course, he or she is reprimanded because being on the course and passing the test states there was understanding and retainment of the information. Thus, if any citizen believes an officer is not conducting a traffic stop correctly, a complaint to the Internal Affairs Unit (IAU) should be filed. The officer is required to follow protocol presented in class. If not, he or she is in violation and will be reprimanded. Second, the evaluation scores were, in the words of one senior instructor, "some of the highest we have seen for a mandatory course." See Appendix 2 for the scores from Houston Police Officers as well as from high school and college students. Overall, course instructors were rated highly, especially by officers. Higher scores were maintained in the content area with a 4.68 out of 5 from the officers and a 4.54 from the youth. Narrative comments provide some nuance and insight. It was felt the course needed to be taught by a knowledgeable civilian and a police officer. As indicated by the comments, officers can be very hard on each other. There were compliments for the civilian instructor, but often the officers believed the police officer instructing was too far removed from life on the street. Officers often define themselves by "years on the street" and the area of the city in which they work. Tougher areas receive more respect. More time on the street leads to more respect; special assignments such as SWAT or gang enforcement amount to more respect; and so on. Conversely, public affairs, juvenile units, supply, and administration are rated lower among officers in this informal ranking. Penn has even been told that those duties are "not real policing." Refer back to the discussion about police culture in Chapter 2 to understand this as an ongoing issue in police evolution.

Further comments mentioned role-playing. In training, two traffic stop scenes would be conducted, and officers would be called on to play the role of citizens. The officers would play the stereotyped role of drivers in an extremely exaggerated manner. *Boyz in the Hood* had nothing on these police actors. Penn found it interesting to see them mimic street behavior and mannerisms, loud talk, smoking of illegal substances, curse-filled language, girlfriend and boyfriend fights, and issues over money, cheating, and children. Evaluations indicated that some officers thought it was too light-hearted and should be made more realistic to be taken more seriously. Interestingly, the youth enjoyed the role-playing and thrived on acting as officers. They played the role of stereotypical officers in the "hood." They were rough, they used bad language, and they were quick to get the drivers out of the vehicle and pull their weapons out. Both examples showed what each culture thought about the other.

The officers made it clear that there were technical issues. The equipment at the Houston Police Academy is in dire need of replacement. There were often Internet freezes, audio stops, and the inability of some videos to play without stopping. These technical issues take much away from a class. The youth did comment that they thought some of the videos were not relevant or were outdated. This was part of the challenge of using the same course for both officers and youth.

The course has been presented to over 15,000 Texans, including high school students, government employees, law enforcement personnel, juveniles and adults on probation, social and civic club members, citizen groups, and those in each TAPS Academy/TEEN POL course. The information, exchange of ideas, and rich information about how to better the relationship between citizens is the stuff of a future book.

Summary

The Community Safety Education Act of Texas was a 2017 policy response by the Texas Legislature after many horrific events in the years between 2012 and 2017. The bill, unlike so many other responses, required both officers and civilians to receive education to correct and improve the interaction between citizens and police. The intent of the legislation was to ensure that both officers and citizens have the same information, are following the same directions, and know the responsibilities of the other during a traffic stop. The course must be taken by all 80,000 officers in the state, all high school seniors starting with class of 2021, and those preparing for a driver's test or receiving corrective driving education. The philosophies of Policing by TOTALS and TAPS Academy lay a foundation that positive results can come when civilians and police officers are provided an opportunity to actively listen to each other through dialogue and training. Penn taught all of the Houston Police Department 2018–2019 and several other departments in the state of Texas as well as dozens of youth, justice, government, social, and civic organizations—over 15,000 people. Yet, he is reminded constantly by citizens that "that is not the way they do it in my neighborhood," and hears consistently from officers that "your attitude determines what I as a police officer will do to you during a traffic stop." This is concerning because issues of social distance, stereotyping, and bias may determine an attitude or behavior of a driver to be out of the norm, which will elevate the traffic stop into a violent situation. The Community Safety Education Act is a movement in the right direction, but policy often dies when in practice. Enforcement, evaluation, and retraining are remedies to ensure that policy is implemented into practice.

8

FUTURE

Building the Field of Study for Youth and Policing Studies

Police and youth stand at a pivotal moment. As noted earlier in the book, Cedric Alexander, a member of the President's Task Force for 21st Century Policing, discussed the need for a proactive approach in his book *The New Guardians*. He provided examples supporting that safety on the road requires preventive maintenance of brakes, steering, lights, and tires. The proactive approach to a leaky roof is to perform repairs at the first sign of a leak, and the proactive approach to good health is to exercise, make healthy food choices, and visit a doctor regularly. He states:

> In "co-producing public safety" the most proactive approach is to create policies and programs that address the needs of children and youth most at risk for crime and violence and reduce aggressive law enforcement tactics that stigmatize youth and marginalize their participation in schools and community. Much of who we are as adults is formed, maybe even determined, through our childhood and youth.
>
> *(Alexander, 2016)*

Today juvenile justice is a subdiscipline, but its very definition focuses on the *system* responding to juvenile delinquency. There is even a College of Juvenile Justice and Psychology at Prairie View A&M University just outside Houston, Texas, where Penn served as one of the founding faculty and where Davenport will earn her Ph.D. The program offers undergraduate, masters, and doctoral degrees at the College of Juvenile Justice and Psychology and the Texas Juvenile Crime Prevention Center. The College and Center offer a diverse curriculum training empiricists, educators, and practitioners in juvenile justice and psychology. A primary aim is to assist with the understanding of human behavior

DOI: 10.4324/9780429424519-9

and the reduction of juvenile crime in the State of Texas (Prairie View A&M University, n.d.).

The study of Juvenile Justice looks to understand youth behavior to reduce juvenile crime, but another field that provides a background is Youth Studies. As defined by the Children and Youth Studies course at Brooklyn College, a goal of Youth Studies is to be aware of the distinct place in society for children and youth, as a culturally specific cohort, both historically and in the present. One of the goals is to understand the complexity and diversity of social conditions experienced by children and youth across the globe. Finally, it looks to link theory to practice by engaging students in multidisciplinary opportunities for research, advocacy, and professional development in traditional, non-traditional, and emerging areas of children and youth studies (Brooklyn College, n.d.). As the founding institution of Children and Youth Studies, Brooklyn College provides a listing of programs in the field on their website http://www.brooklyn.cuny.edu/web/academics/centers/children/resources/colleges.php).

Overall, when surveying Youth Studies programs, the mission and goals focus on an interdisciplinary academic field devoted to the study of children and youth up to the age of 24, as this relates to the age at which the brain is fully formed. Through a study of their development, history, culture, psychology, and politics, relationships and roles emerge defining where youth fit in society. Scholars for the field come from education, literature, history, political science, religion, and sociology.

As discussed earlier, Juvenile Justice provides an understanding of why delinquency and criminal behavior occurs as well as the system developed to respond to and prevent such acts in the future. Usually Juvenile Justice is found as a course inside of Criminology or Criminal Justice programs, both popular majors on campuses. Criminology studies the theoretical foundation explaining why crime occurs and secondarily the criminal justice system that responds or tries to prevent the criminal act from occurring. On the other hand, Criminal Justice focuses more on the system. This discipline, which came to prominence after 1967, when there was an influx of Law Enforcement Assistance Administration (LEAA) funds earmarked for implementing criminal justice programming, focuses on the management of the system, including police, courts, and corrections. Nationally there are a few programs that specifically focus on Police Studies. One such program is at Eastern Kentucky University (EKU). They state that their course of study is designed to provide students a balanced blending of academic and professional preparation in the areas of criminal investigation, ethics, operations, administration, terrorism, predatory crime, computer technology, human relations, criminal law, criminal evidence, and criminal procedure (Eastern Kentucky University, n.d.).

As we view the strengths of these three areas of study—Youth Studies, Juvenile Justice, and Criminology/Criminal Justice (focusing on Police

Studies)—there is no synergy between the study and practice of youth work and the study and practice of policing, in combination to improve interaction, mutual respect, dialogue, training, and understanding. Strategies for Youth, a national organization dedicated to improving police/youth interactions, reports the shortfall that existed in 2013 in the training and the preparation of police officers:

- 40 states' juvenile justice curricula focus primarily on the juvenile code and legal issues and provides no communication or psychological skills for officers working with children and youth.
- It appears that only two states' written curricula included training on youth development issues, such as communication techniques with juveniles, understanding the problems adolescents face, and recognizing the sources and triggers of their behavior.
- The majority of academies do not teach recruits how to recognize and respond to youth with mental health, trauma-related and special education-related disorders.
- Only eight states address the federally mandated obligation to reduce disproportionate minority contact.
- In spite of the number of young officers assigned to schools right out of the academy, only one state (Tennessee) provided specific training for officers deployed to schools.

(Strategies for Youth, 2013)

There is no indication there has been a major change in the amount of training occurring in police academies since 2013. There are organizations such as the National Association of School Resource Officers (NASRO), which states that since its founding in 1991 school-based policing is the fastest-growing area of law enforcement. With 3,000 members, NASRO provides training and conference opportunities for law enforcement officers assigned to school communities. A review of the NASRO website and promotional material indicates that the organization follows more of the warrior police practices, but it does provide training to prepare the officer for a school environment. Courses include: Basic and Advanced School Resource Officer, Adolescent Mental Health Training, School Crime Prevention Through Environmental Design, and School Safety Officer (SRO). It describes its basic SRO course: "The course provides tools for officers to build positive relationships with both students and staff. The course is also beneficial for educational professionals dedicated to providing a safe learning environment and provides a more in-depth understanding of the role and functions of an SRO" (National Association of School Resource Officers, n.d.).

All this is to say the pieces are out there but not in one centralized location. Chapter 9 provides a list of resources to understand many organizations involved in Youth and Policing. The list is in no way exhaustive, but it does provide a layout of the vast number of partners in this subdiscipline.

A Youth and Police Studies field will allow for juvenile justice workers, court personnel, after-school program workers, child care workers, teachers, counselors, coaches, and, of course, police, youth, and their parents and other family members to understand the culture conflict when the two come together so that policy, programming, and practice align with research. The intersection between youth and police must be understood to deter crime, build legitimacy, and increase social bonding.

As Department Chair at the University of Houston–Clear Lake, Penn created a minor in the field, described as:

> The Youth and Police Studies minor from UHCL begins with the premise that both youth culture and police culture exist in American society. By studying topics such as Developmental Theory/Teen Brain and Implicit Bias, and by participating in experiential learning with the Teen and Police Service Academy (TAPS), students learn to bridge the social distance between American youth and law enforcement.
>
> *(University of Houston–Clear Lake, n.d.).*

The required courses for the minor include: CRIM 1301 Introduction to Criminal Justice; CRIM 4313 Juvenile Delinquency; CRIM 4338 Policing and Society; CRIM 4339 Youth, Law and Society; and PSYC 4315 Adolescent Psychology.

Included in the Youth and Police minor, there is a course titled "Youth, Law, and Society" that is offered annually, usually in the Spring. In teaching it, Penn rotates through a variety of texts, including *Policing in the 21st Century: Community Policing* (Brown, 2012); *Evidence-Based Policing: Translating Research into Practice* (Lum & Koper, 2017); *The New Guardians* (Alexander, 2016); *Community Policing: Partnerships for Problem Solving, 7th Ed.* (Miller, Hess, & Orthmann, 2014); *Race and Juvenile Justice* (Penn, Greene, & Gabbidon, 2006); *Hands Up, Don't Shoot* (Cobbina, 2019); *The New Jim Crow: Mass Incarceration in the Age of Colorblindness* (Alexander, 2012); *Human Targets: Schools, Police, and the Criminalization of Latino Youth* (Rios & Vigil, 2017); *Policing the Black Man: Arrest, Prosecution, and Imprisonment* (Davis, 2017); *Punished: Policing the Lives of Black and Latino Boys* (Rios, 2011); and publications from the International Association Chiefs of Police, the Office of Juvenile Justice and Delinquency Prevention, and the Police Executive Research Forum. The course looks at youth culture in comparison to police culture within a context of race and social class in the United States as youth and police interact. The course, taught in a service-learning format, requires students to be a part of real-world interactions between youth and police, usually through the TAPS program. The service-learning format followed is EAR: Education in the classroom, Action in the real-world, and Reflection about the learning experience (Penn, 2003).

Some review comments included: "I got to know police in a different way"; "I am glad I took this course, now I know I do not want to be a police officer"; "This course helped me know how to be a good officer."

A course and minor is not enough for this important subject; instead a discipline is needed. Clear (2001), in his Academy of Criminal Justice Sciences (ACJS) Presidential Address, presented elements needed to create a discipline. These elements are useful to answer the question about the creation of the Youth and Police Studies discipline: (1) need for the discipline; (2) scholars in the field dedicated to promoting the work of the field through teaching, training, and research; and (3) a body of literature in the field.

This text demonstrates the need for a Youth and Police Studies discipline. Youth culture and police culture are different and often interact to produce unrest, conflict, and division. From the various cases of violence and death that have occurred, it is clear there needs to be a place that combines the rigors of academia with the practice of real-world police interaction to frame solutions, build bridges, and reduce the social distance that currently exists among these two groups. This text provides a cadre of scholars in this chapter and throughout the citations found in the book whose work supports the importance of building better relationships between citizens and police—for our purposes, specifically youth and police. There is a growing body of literature in the field that will help turn problems into solutions and training for officers and youth alike. Current oases include the TAPS Center in Houston, Texas; Strategies for Youth in Cambridge Massachusetts, and the COPS Office in Washington, DC.

Now is the time for Youth and Police Studies because:

- As technology and social media evolve, so has ignoring or displacing issues that remain prominent between youth and police. Youth are asking the question: Why are injustices and acts without explanation continuing to occur?
- DARE, GREAT, PALS, Explorers, Youth Academies, and so many other youth and police programs exists in silos without true measures of performance or standards. One place is needed that combines research on all of these programs and approaches in order to allow the synergy of the whole to outperform the output of each individual program.
- Policy makers, youth, parents, and government officials need a central location providing best practices and assistance so that solutions at a national level can best respond to the needs at a local level. One size does not fit all; thus, assistance is needed to assist local leaders to make choices when developing policy and practice to improve youth and police relations.
- Research is a constant in any field of study. Thus, the scholars must be directly tied to the work of the field in order to dig deeper, go into specific issues, and find solutions that carry the field further meshing theory to practice.

- Building research comes through academic and practical training. Through combining service-learning into the classroom and academics into the training arena, the two become one, making for student, officer, youth care worker, childcare worker, or any other person in the fields of youth and police studies to be best trained to solve problems and create better understanding between the two.

The TAPS Center in Houston, Texas, is best suited to be the home for the Youth and Police Studies discipline. Founded in December 2016, on the fifth anniversary of TAPS Academy, the TAPS Academy Center has as its vision to be the international destination for research, programming, teaching, and training to reduce the social distance between youth and law enforcement. With a variety of partnerships between universities, government agencies, social groups, non-profits, and the private sector, the TAPS Academy Center ties to the University of Houston system. At present the University of Houston–Clear Lake offers the only minor in Youth and Police Studies, bringing together minds from the public, non-profit, and private sector to understand the perceptions of youth, the business of policing, and realities of society to move past rhetoric and divisiveness. It strives to provide a voice to those often unheard differences and a receptacle of ideas to be heard and interpreted to move thoughts into researched practices for teaching, training, and programming.

As we come to the end of looking at police and youth with a focus on the extraordinary time of 2012 through 2017, later events move into focus, including the murder of George Floyd, the election of Joseph Biden, and the January 6th insurrection at the United States Capitol. We offer 10 take-aways for police departments as well as 10 take-aways for citizens.

Policing Take-Aways

1. Reduce the social distance.
2. Read, train, implement, and assess using TAPS Academy, Policing by TO-TALS, the President's Task Force on 21st Century Policing, and the Community Safety Education Act.
3. Improve police legitimacy.
4. Continue to implement and assess the use of body cameras.
5. Make information available to the public through social media and other forms of communication. Get in front of an issue before it becomes a problem.
6. Strive to assess officer performance on measures other than traditional warrior practices such as Uniform Crime Reporting (UCR) data.
7. Diversify the police force.
8. Promote citizen partnerships through joint training, review boards, and assessment.

9. Create a process for citizens to complain or compliment police that is not intrusive to deter but instead is inclusive to encourage dialogue.
10. Employ the services of a resident criminologist.

Citizen Take-Aways

1. Reduce the social distance.
2. Read, train, implement, and assess using TAPS Academy, Policing by TOTALS, the President's Task Force on 21st Century Policing, and the Community Safety Education Act.
3. Strive to remove the Us (neighborhood)-vs.-Them (police) through an action process.
4. Use personal cameras and recordings to document complaints and compliments related to citizen and police interaction.
5. Be receptive listeners and communicators with police.
6. Be prepared to receive and appreciate the guardian police officer and practices.
7. Strive to assist police agencies to make their departments more diverse.
8. Volunteer and attend training sessions with police and serve and encourage others to build policy and programming with citizen input.
9. Work to create a process for compliments and complaints that is the least intrusive.
10. Constantly look for opportunities to improve police and citizen interaction and promote the process whenever possible.

Conclusion

As Americans move to a time when "we are great again," we have concerns that a spirit of nationalism, condescension, egotism, and narcissism will overpower the goodwill and works of community policing, TAPS Academy, and the President's Task Force on 21st Century Policing. An effective police force must have the cooperation of citizens through a process of mutual respect that treats all persons with dignity. Effective policing has little breadth to survive with a tone of self-promotion at the same time demoting and belittling gender, cultures, ethnicities, and races that do not fit the mold of a time in America's past when few if any minorities or women held significant policy-making positions. Elected and appointed officials set policy for the states to enact at their level. A wave of policy decisions, memos, and decrees, or the lack thereof, form a pattern of practice that local legislatures, councils, districts, and police departments follow. The concepts of legitimacy, procedural justice, responding to bias, and 21st Century policing are now becoming practice for training, policy, and implementation in police departments. Let us hope the nation does not sing a song that erases what is most effective in making policing work for police officers, citizens, and the United States of America. Let us sing a song in which all voices are heard and are a part of the process.

Perhaps a new way of looking at police and citizen relations goes beyond the Golden Rule of "treat others as you want to be treated" and expands what Penn learned while training officers in Tuscaloosa, Alabama; that is, the Platinum Rule: "Treat others as *they* want to be treated." The new tools of TAPS Academy, policing by TOTALS, 21st Century policing, and the Community Safety Education Act do just that by arming both citizens and police with voice so that they both are active parts of a fair and just criminal justice system striving to improve relations when interactions occur.

9

RESOURCES TO REDUCE THE SOCIAL DISTANCE BETWEEN POLICE AND YOUTH

First there was Criminology, then Criminal Justice; after that came Youth Studies and Juvenile Justice. Now there is a need for Youth and Police Studies. In 1988, the Office of Juvenile Justice and Delinquency changed its function from disproportionate minority confinement to disproportionate minority contact—using the same letters (DMC) but having an entirely different focus and meaning. This change from confinement to contact places focus on the commencement into the justice system rather than the final stop. It allows us to place our collective energy in research, training, and teaching to avoid placement in the system. Youth and Police Studies places academic, practitioners, policy makers, parents, and youth at the front door in order to control entry, thus making sure youth and police move toward understanding each other and reducing their social distance.

This chapter presents some of the organizations crafting the elements of Youth and Police Studies. Creating a discipline in which both are equally studied will synergize their individual contexts to create greater understanding and outcomes when the two come together.

- Center for Evidence-Based Crime Policy, George Mason University (cebcp.org/).
    The purpose of the CEBCP is to provide a resource to local, state, federal, and other groups who seek to strengthen and foster relationships between criminal justice practitioners, scholars, and students.
- College of Juvenile Justice and Psychology, Prairie View A&M University (https://www.pvamu.edu/cojjp).
    The College offers masters and doctoral degrees in focusing on juvenile justice.

DOI: 10.4324/9780429424519-10

- Community Oriented Policing Services (COPS) Office, Department of Justice (https://cops.usdoj.gov/).
  This is the component of the U.S. Department of Justice responsible for advancing the practice of community policing.
- Crime Solutions (Crime Solutions.org).
  This is a resource to help practitioners and policy makers understand what works in justice-related programs and practices.
- Police Executive Research Forum (PERF) (www.policeforum.org/).
  PERF is a police research and policy organization and a provider of management services, technical assistance, and executive-level education to support law enforcement agencies.
- President's Task Force on 21st Century Policing (www.theiacp.org/TaskForceReport).
  This Task Force and its report were designed to help agencies promote effective crime reduction while building public trust and safeguarding officer well-being.
- Teen And Police Service (TAPS) Center (www.tapsacademy.org).
  The TAPS Center is an academic and practitioner center designed to lead in teaching, training, programming, and research to reduce the social distance between at-risk youth and police officers.
- National Center for Youth Opportunity and Justice (https://ncyoj.policyresearchinc.org/about/).
  This is a program designed to improve life opportunities for youth.
- National Gang Center (https://www.nationalgangcenter.gov/).
  This Center responds to gang involvement by implementing prevention and intervention using the OJJDP's Comprehensive Gang Model.
- National Mentoring Resource Center (https://nationalmentoringresourcecenter.org/).
  This Center aims to prevent and reduce substance use and associated risk among youth.
- National School Resource Officers Association (https://www.nasro.org/main/about-nasro/).
  This association provides training for school-based law enforcement officers.
- Enhancing Law Enforcement Efforts and Engagement with Youth (https://ojjdp.ojp.gov/programs/enhancing-law-enforcement-efforts-and-engagement-youth).
  This initiative ensures that young offenders are held accountable, enhances public safety, and empowers youth to live productive, law-abiding lives.
- Gang Resistance and Education Program (http://www.great-online.org/).
  This is a school-based, law enforcement officer–instructed classroom curriculum that educates elementary and middle-school children to avoid becoming a gang member.

- Strategies for Youth (www.strategiesforyouth.org).

  This organization aims to connect cops and kids and provide strategies for youth transforming structural impediments to improving police-youth interaction.

- Policing Youth Policy Briefs: Opportunities for Positive Interaction (www. policefoundation.org/policing-youth-policy-briefs/).

  This police foundation project deals with issues surrounding the role of law enforcement in communities and specifically in schools.

- Texas Juvenile Crime Prevention Center (https://www.pvamu.edu/cojjp/ texas-juvenile-crime-prevention-center/).

  This Center offers research focusing on the reduction of juvenile crime.

APPENDIX 1

TEEN POL

TAPS Academy Theory-to-Practice Model

TEEN POL (N1130025) Course Description

The TAPS course includes specific topic areas associated with Children and Youth Safety (COPS-CPD-2011–3) such as violence, physical and sexual abuse, stalking, domestic trafficking, sexual exploitation, and bullying. The course is designed to help youth (1) change behavior, (2) learn responsible decision making, (3) participate in crime prevention projects, and (4) reduce the social distance between themselves and law enforcement.

Student Selection	Students qualify by having 1 or more of the 13 risk factors as prescribed by Texas Education Agency. Accredited course by Texas Education Agency, #N1130025, for (1) high school credit.
Learning Environment	8th grade and High School students who successfully complete this course receive one credit towards graduation. Meets like any other weekly class (2-3x/week). Pre-test administered to evaluate baseline objectives & outcomes.
Semester Logistics	15–18 week semester. Taught by TAPS Educational Specialists. Officers support and reinforce the content with teaching, personal stories, examples, and interaction. Tests administered by teacher of record (certified social studies teacher.
11-Part Core Curriculum	TEEN POL is designed with 11 core curriculum modules. 19 additional modules available to address various skill-building areas. Grading & evaluation are completed in accordance with each school district; TAPS provides syllabus and evaluation materials.
Graduation & Life After TEEN POL	Post-test administered to show progress towards objectives & outcomes. Students join TAPS Clubs: *- Student led with support from TAPS Officers.* *- Clubs host assemblies, and other activities to raise school-wide awareness of youth, policing & community safety issues, and bridge the gap between youth, police, CJ professionals, & school/community leaders.*

TAPS/TEEN POL Risk Factors:

1. Eligible for free or reduced lunch program
2. Below C average in 2 or more classes
3. Failed a grade level
4. Failed a state assessment
5. Pregnant or a parent
6. Alternative school placement
7. Expelled from school
8. Currently on conditional release
9. Former drop-out
10. Limited English proficiency
11. Currently in CPS custody
12. Identified as "homeless"
13. Institutionalized: detention/substance abuse

TAPS/TEEN POL MISSION:

Reduce the social distance between at-risk youth and police officers through:

- Positive interactions
- Learning together
- Voice, dialogue, and active-listening
- Life skill building

TAPS/TEEN POL OBJECTIVES:

Increase social bonding by creating:
  a. **New attachments** (*positive attachments to family, friends; and associations including TAPS Officers and staff*)
  b. **New involvements** (positive involvement in activities including: community organizations, school clubs, city government, community service.)
  c. **New commitments** (20 year plan for life, goal setting, life success)
  d. **New beliefs** (*"I can succeed," "I can go to college", "I do not have to sell drugs"*)

TAPS/TEEN POL OUTCOMES:

  1. Reduce social distance between at-risk youth & police
  2. Work to build community-led policing
  3. Gain (1) high school credit towards graduation
  4. Develop life skills
  5. Develop a plan for future success
  6. Create a network of social services/social capital
  7. Increase school involvement
  8. Reduce truancy
  9. Reduce negative behavioral instances in class
  10. Reduce crime/delinquency

FIGURE A1.1   TEEN POL – A Community-Led Policing Program

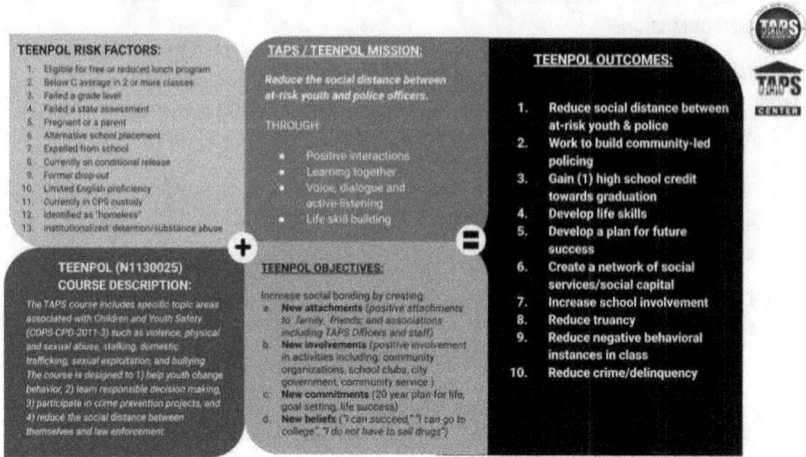

FIGURE A1.2 TAPS Programming: TeenPol Chart A

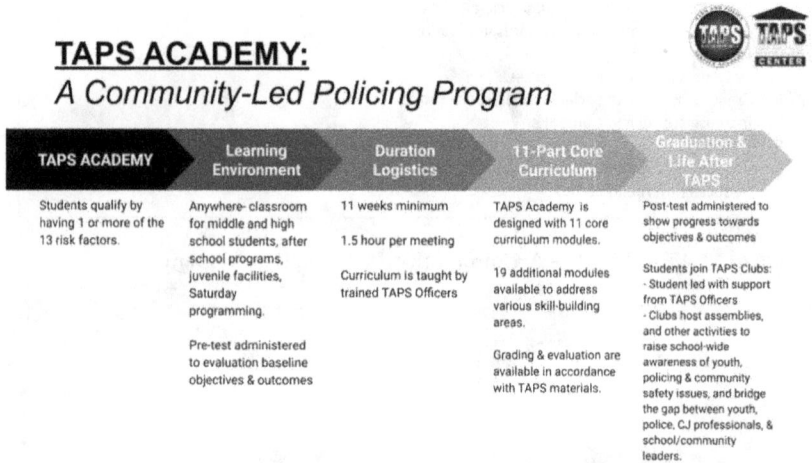

TAPS ACADEMY:
A Community-Led Policing Program

TAPS ACADEMY	Learning Environment	Duration Logistics	11-Part Core Curriculum	Graduation & Life After TAPS
Students qualify by having 1 or more of the 13 risk factors.	Anywhere- classroom for middle and high school students, after school programs, juvenile facilities, Saturday programming. Pre-test administered to evaluation baseline objectives & outcomes	11 weeks minimum 1.5 hour per meeting Curriculum is taught by trained TAPS Officers	TAPS Academy is designed with 11 core curriculum modules. 19 additional modules available to address various skill-building areas. Grading & evaluation are available in accordance with TAPS materials.	Post-test administered to show progress towards objectives & outcomes Students join TAPS Clubs: · Student led with support from TAPS Officers · Clubs host assemblies, and other activities to raise school-wide awareness of youth, policing & community safety issues, and bridge the gap between youth, police, CJ professionals, & school/community leaders.

FIGURE A1.3 TAPS Programming: TAPS Academy

TEENPOL:
A Community-Led Policing Program

TEENPOL	Classroom Learning Environment	Semester Logistics	11-Part Core Curriculum	Graduation & Life After TEEN POL
Students qualify by having 1 or more of the 13 risk factors.	8th grade and High School students who successfully complete this course receive one credit towards graduation	15-18 week semester	TEENPOL is designed with 11 core curriculum modules.	Post-test administered to show progress towards objectives & outcomes
Accredited course by Texas Education Agency, #N1130025, for (1) high school credit	Meets like any other weekly class (2-3x/week)	Taught by TAPS Educational Specialists	19 additional modules available to address various skill-building areas.	Students join TAPS Clubs: - Student led with support from TAPS Officers - Clubs host assemblies, and other activities to raise
	Pre-test administered to evaluation baseline objectives & outcomes	Officers support and reinforce the content with teaching, personal stories, examples, and interaction	Grading & evaluation are completed in accordance with each school district; TAPS provides syllabus and evaluation materials.	school-wide awareness of youth, policing & community safety issues, and bridge the gap between youth, police, CJ professionals, & school/community leaders.
		Tests administered by teacher of record (certified social studies teacher)		

FIGURE A1.4   TAPS Programming: TeenPol Chart B

APPENDIX 2

EVALUATION RESULTS

The Community Safety Education Act participant evaluation employed the Likert Scale to measure the effectiveness of both the training content and instructor delivery, with 5 indicating "strongly agree," and 1 indicating "strongly disagree." This randomized sample (n=1005) includes both youth (ages 14–24; high school- and college-aged persons), and police officers who participated in the Civilian Interaction Training Program (TCOLE course #30418) as required by the State of Texas.

	CITP	Youth SB30	TOTALS
	n=454	*n=551*	*n=1005*
TRAINING CONTENT: [Ideas presented were relevant to my job / driving]	4.67	4.59	4.58
TRAINING CONTENT: [Audio/Visual aids/Class Materials were relevant]	4.67	4.51	4.59
TRAINING CONTENT: [Class Objectives were clear]	4.72	4.67	4.70
TRAINING CONTENT: [Class met my expectations]	4.66	4.49	4.58
INSTRUCTOR: [Knowledgeable about subject]	4.78	4.68	4.73
INSTRUCTOR: [Organized & prepared]	4.75	4.62	4.69
INSTRUCTOR: [Met stated objectives]	4.77	4.62	4.70
INSTRUCTOR: [Encouraged group participation]	4.78	4.49	4.64
INSTRUCTOR: [Maintained interest (eye contact, clarity, enthusiasm)]	4.79	4.64	4.72

INSTRUCTOR: [Used examples to illustrated learning points]	4.78	4.58	4.68
INSTRUCTOR: [Was responsive to students' questions]	4.79	4.63	4.71
INSTRUCTOR: [Effective use of time]	4.76	4.56	4.66
INSTRUCTOR: [Displayed a positive attitude towards material]	4.80	4.66	4.73
Overall CONTENT Score	4.68	4.54	4.61
Overall INSTRUCTOR Score	4.78	4.61	4.69
Overall CLASS Score	**4.75**	**4.59**	**4.67**
I Intend to change my behavior during my next encounter with law enforcement [5 = Very likely; 1= not likely at all]	*Not assessed*	**4.36**	**4.36**

CITP SUMMARY:

- *Most participants enjoyed Dr. Penn's presentation style, but noted that the Officer presenter was perhaps unrelatable, too far removed from "the beat."*
- *Many appreciated the role-play exercises, but complained that it was too light-hearted and needed to be more realistic and taken more seriously.*
- *Many participants complained of technical issues and suggested preparing and troubleshooting the videos ahead of time.*
- *Participants repeatedly requested snacks.*

YOUTH SB30 SUMMARY:

- *Most students reported that they enjoyed the presentation style and level of engagement.*
- *Many students reported that they learned not only their rights, but also their behavioral responsibilities during a traffic stop.*
- *Interaction areas that could be improved according to the youth: treatment by officers, respect/one-sidedness, more communication & understanding.*

Presentation improvements: content perhaps outdated/not relevant

Source: Middleton, J. E. (2020). Community Safety Education Act Data Summary: Randomized Sample 2018–2020. TAPS Center for Research.

REFERENCES

About Black Lives Matter (2020, October 16). https://blacklivesmatter.com/about/.

About IACP (n.d.). https://www.theiacp.org/about-iacp.

Adamson, B. (2017). Reconsidering pre-indictment publicity: Racialized crime news, grand juries and Tamir Rice. *Alabama Civil Rights & Civil Liberties Law Review 8(1)*.

Adamy, J., & Overberg, P. (2019). Playing catch-up in the game of life: Millennials approach middle age in crisis. https://www.wsj.com/articles/playing-catch-up-in-the-game-of-life-millennials-approach-middle-age-in-crisis-11558290908.

Adegbile, D. P. (2017). Policing through an American prism. *Yale Law Journal 126* (7): 197–259.

African Proverbs – 300 Inspirational Proverbs and Quotes (2019, January 30). https://safarijunkie.com/culture/african-proverbs/.

Ahmed, S., & Walker, C. (2018, May 25). There has been, on average, 1 school shooting every week this year. https://www.cnn.com/2018/03/02/us/school-shootings-2018-list-trnd/index.html.

Akers, B. & Chingo, M. (2014). Is a student debt crisis on the horizon? https://www.brookings.edu/research/is-a-student-loan-crisis-on-the-horizon/.

Alcindor, Y. (2015, October 08). Walter Scott family reaches $6.5M settlement with city. https://www.usatoday.com/story/news/2015/10/08/family-of-walter-scott-reaches-65m-settlement-with-city-officials/73619624/.

Alexander, C. L. (2016). *The new guardians: Policing in America's communities for the Twenty-first Century*. CreateSpace.

Alexander, M. (2012). *The new Jim Crow: Mass incarceration in the age of colorblindness*. Revised edition. New Press.

Alexander, M. (2011). The new Jim Crow. *Ohio State Journal of Criminal Law 9(1)*: 7–26.

Amadeo, K. (2018). Hurricane Harvey facts, damage and costs. *The Balance*. https://www.thebalance.com/hurricane-harvey-facts-damage-costs-4150087.

American History USA (n.d.) The Atlantic slave trade to the United States. https://www.americanhistoryusa.com/the-atlantic-slave-trade-to-the-united-states/.

Anderson, E. (2019). Code of the street. *The Wiley Blackwell Encyclopedia of Urban and Regional Studies*, 1–3.

Anderson, E. (1999). *Code of the street: Decency, violence, and the moral life of the inner city.* W.W. Norton and Company.

Anderson, E. (1994). The code of the streets. *Atlantic Monthly 273(5)*: 80–94.

Anderson, S. A., Sabatelli, R. M., & Trachtenberg, J. (2008). A process and outcome evaluation of police working with youth programs. *Journal of Youth Development 3(2)*: 18–37.

Anderson, S. A., Sabatelli, R. M., & Trachtenberg, J. (2007). Community police and youth programs as a context for positive youth development. *Police Quarterly 10(1)*: 23–40.

Arain, M., Haque, M., Johal, L., Mathur, P., Nel, W., Rais, A., Sandhu, R. & Sharma, S. (2013). Maturation of the adolescent brain. *Neuropsychiatric Disease and Treatment 9*: 449–461.

Armour, J. (1997). *Negrophobia and reasonable racism: The hidden cost of being Black in America.* New York University Press.

Association of Public and Land-Grant Universities (n.d.). What is the typical debt load for graduates of four-year public universities? https://www.aplu.org/projects-and-initiatives/college-costs-tuition-and-financial-aid/publicuvalues/student-debt.html.

Barlow, D. E., & Barlow, M. H. (2018). *Police in a multicultural society: An American story.* Waveland Press.

Bates, J. (2020). What is "Social Distancing?" Here's how to best practice it as Coronavirus spreads. *Time.* March 11. https://time.com/5800442/social-distancing-coronavirus/.

Beehrer, L. (2007). The effects of "youth bulge" on civil conflicts. April 13. https://www.cfr.org/backgrounder/effects-youth-bulge-civil-conflicts.

Beirne, P. (1987). Adolphe Quetelet and the origins of positivist criminology. *American Journal of Sociology 92(5)*: 114–169.

Blake, A. (2016). The first Trump-Clinton presidential debate transcript, annotated. *The Washington Post.* September 26. https://www.washingtonpost.com/news/the-fix/wp/2016/09/26/the-first-trump-clinton-presidential-debate-transcript-annotated/.

Blakemore, E. (2019). How the GI Bill's promise was denied to a million Black WWII veterans. History.com. https://www.history.com/news/gi-bill-black-wwii-veterans-benefits

Blinder, A. (2016, October 30). A somber Charleston reflects on race as 2 murder trials begin. Nytimes.com. https://www.nytimes.com/2016/10/31/us/charleston-dylann-roof-walter-scott.html.

Blum, R. & Mmari, K. (2004). The health of young people in a global context. *The Journal of Adolescent Health 35*: 402–418. 10.1016/j.jadohealth.2003.10.007.

Bogardus, E. S. (1933). A social distance scale. *Sociology & Social Research 17*: 265–271.

Bogardus, E. (1925). Social distance and its origins. *Journal of Applied Sociology 9*: 21–26.

Brito, C. (2020). President Trump uses term "Chinese virus" to describe coronavirus, prompting a backlash. March 19. https://www.cbsnews.com/news/president-trump-coronavirus-chinese-virus-backlash/.

Brito, C. (2019, August 20). Colin Kaepernick talks about the police shooting that led him to protest during national anthem. https://www.cbsnews.com/news/colin-kaepernick-mario-woods-shooting-kneeling-nfl-san-francisco-49ers-nessa/.

Brokaw, T. (1998). *The greatest generation.* Random House.

Brooklyn College, City College of New York (CUNY) (n.d.). Children and youth studies. http://www.brooklyn.cuny.edu/web/academics/schools/socialsciences/interdisciplinary/undergraduate/childrens.php.

Brown, L. P. (2012). *Policing in the 21st century: Community policing.* AuthorHouse.

Brown, L. P. (1994). Clinton's drug "czar," identifies eight myths about drugs in the arguments of the drug legalizers. Ndsn.org. http://www.ndsn.org/july94/czar.html.

Brunolaw.com (n.d.). 10 differences between adult and juvenile criminal court. https://brunolaw.com/resources/general-criminal-law/10-differences-between-adult-and-juvenile-criminal-court.

Brunson, R. K., & Weitzer, R. (2009). Police relations with Black and white youths in different urban neighborhoods. *Urban Affairs Review 44(6)*: 858–885.

Brunson, R. (2007). Police don't like Black people: African-American young men's accumulated police experiences. *Criminology, and Public Policy 7(2).*

Bryant-Davis, T., Adams, T., Alejandre, A., & Gray, A. A. (2017). The trauma lens of police violence against racial and ethnic minorities. *Journal of Social Issues 73(4)*: 852–871.

Burgess, E. (1925). The growth of the city: An introduction to a research project. In *The City*, R. Park and E.W. Burgess (eds.), pp. 2–4, University of Chicago Press.

Bump, P. (2014). Here is when each generation begins and ends, according to facts. https://www.theatlantic.com/national/archive/2014/03/here-is-when-each-generation-begins-and-ends-according-to-facts/359589/.

Carroll, C. (1991). *"The Negro a beast" or "in the image of God."* American Book and Bible House.

CDC COVID Data Tracker (n.d.). https://covid.cdc.gov/covid-data-tracker/.

Christodoulou, H. (2018). Ryanair racist who called woman "Black b★★★★★d" says he just lost temper. *The Sun.* https://www.thesun.co.uk/news/7586648/ryanair-racist-gmb-rant-black-woman-stansted-apology/.

Chua, A. (2011). "Tiger mother" explains her strict parenting. https://www.today.com/parents/tiger-mother-explains-her-strict-parenting-2D80556156.

Clear, T. R. (2001). Has academic criminal justice come of age? ACJS Presidential Address Washington, DC, April. *Justice Quarterly 18(4)*: 709–726.

Chadwick, B. (2017, May 2). How police brutality shaped New York City. https://www.thehistoryreader.com/us-history/nypd_police_brutality/.

Cintron, M., Dawkins, M., Gibson, C., & Hill, M. C. (2019). "The talk" regarding minority youth interactions with police. *Journal of Ethnicity in Criminal Justice 17(4)*: 379–404.

CNN (2020). American generation fast facts. https://www.cnn.com/2013/11/06/us/baby-boomer-generation-fast-facts/index.html.

Cobbina, J. (2019). *Hands up, don't shoot.* New York Press.

Cockcroft, T. (2012). *Police culture: Themes and concepts.* Routledge.

Cohen, A. (1955). *Delinquent boys: The culture of the gang.* Free Press.

Communities In Schools (n.d.). Communities In Schools and the five basics. https://www.communitiesinschools.org/media/uploads/attachments/Communities_In_Schools_and_the_Five_Basics_5.pdf

Community Policing Dispatch (2014). *E-newsletter of the COPS Office 7(8).* https://cops.usdoj.gov/html/dispatch/01-2015/index.asp.

Cops.usdoj.gov (2020). School violence prevention program (SVPP), COPS OFFICE. https://cops.usdoj.gov/svpp.

Cops.usdoj.gov (2014). https://cops.usdoj.gov/RIC/Publications/cops-p157-pub.pdf.

Corley, C. (2017). President Johnson's Crime Commission Report, 50 years later. Npr. org. https://www.npr.org/2017/10/06/542487124/president-johnson-s-crime-commission-report-50-years-later.

Cornelius, C. V., Lynch, C. J., & Gore, R. (2017). Aging out of crime: Exploring the relationship between age and crime with agent-based modeling. In *Proceedings of the Agent-Directed Simulation Symposium*, April 2017, pp. 1–12.

Cox, S., Allen, J., Hanser, R., & Conrad, J. (2017). *Juvenile Justice: A Guide to Theory, Policy, and Practice*. SAGE.

Dabashi, H. (2012). *The Arab Spring: The end of postcolonialism*. Zed Books Ltd.

Damaske, S., Bratter, J. L., & Frech, A. (2017). Single mother families and employment, race, and poverty in changing economic times. *Social science research 62*: 120–133.

DARE (n.d.). Drug Abuse Resistance Education. https://dare.org/.

Davies, A. R. and Frink, B. D. (2014). The origins of the ideal worker: The separation of work and home in the United States from the market revolution to 1950. *Work and Occupations 41(1)*: 1–9.

Davis, A. J. (Ed.). (2017). *Policing the Black man: Arrest, prosecution, and imprisonment*. Vintage.

Deane, P. M., & Deane, P. M. (1979). *The first industrial revolution*. Cambridge University Press.

del Carmen, R. V., Parker, M., & Reddington, F. P. (1998). *Briefs of leading cases in juvenile justice*. Anderson Publishing Co.

Dimock, M. (2019, January 1). Defining generations: Where Millennials end and Generation Z begins. https://www.pewresearch.org/fact-tank/2019/01/17/where-millennials-end-and-generation-z-begins/.

Du Bois, W. E. B. (Ed.). (1903). The Negro common school: Report of a social study made under the direction of Atlanta University; together with the proceedings of the sixth conference for the study of the Negro problems. Atlanta University, May 28, 1901 (No. 1–6). Atlanta University Press.

Du Bois, W.E.B. (1899/1996). *The Philadelphia Negro: A social study*. The University of Pennsylvania Press.

DuBois, D. L., & Karcher, M. J. (Eds.). (2013). *Handbook of youth mentoring*. SAGE.

Duffin, E. (2020a). Median household income by race or ethnic group 2019. Statista. https://www.statista.com/statistics/233324/median-household-income-in-the-united-states-by-race-or-ethnic-group/.

Duffin, E. (2020b). U.S. population by age and gender 2019. Statista. https://www.statista.com/statistics/241488/population-of-the-us-by-sex-and-age/.

Duvall, T., & Costello, D. (2021). Louisville police fire 2 detectives, others disciplined, in Breonna Taylor shooting. *Louisville Courier Journal*. January 6. https://www.courier-journal.com/story/news/local/breonna-taylor/2021/01/06/two-louisville-detectives-officially-fired-in-breonna-taylor-shooting/4125160001/.

Economy Watch (n.d.). United States Economy. https://www.economywatch.com/world_economy/usa.

Eastern Kentucky University (n.d.). Police studies degree programs. https://police-studies.eku.edu/.

Elliott, M., & Merrill, F. (1934). *Social disorganization*. Harper and Brothers Publishers.

Ennett, S., Tobler, N., Ringwalt, C., & Flewelling, R. (1994). How effective is drug abuse resistance education? A meta-analysis of program DARE outcome evaluations. *American Journal of Public Health 84(9)*: 139–405.

Equal Justice Initiative (2017). Black children five times more likely than white youth to be incarcerated. https://eji.org/news/black-children-five-times-more-likely-than-whites-to-be-incarcerated/.

Erkkinen, M. (2017). The role of activists in the news coverage of the case of Philando Castile. Master's thesis. https://conservancy.umn.edu/handle/11299/191296.

Esbensen, F., Osgood, D., Taylor, T., Peterson, D., & Freng, A. (2001). How great is G.R.E.A.T.? Results from a longitudinal quasi-experimental design. *Criminology & Public Policy 1(1)*: 8–18.

Esbensen, F. A., Osgood, D. W., Peterson, D., Taylor, T. J., & Carson, D. C. (2013). Short-and long-term outcome results from a multisite evaluation of the GREAT program. *Criminology & Public Policy 12(3)*: 375–411.

Executive Office of the President of the United States (2020). Report of the President's Commission on Law Enforcement and the Administration of Justice. https://www.justice.gov/file/1347866/download.

Fausset, R. (2020). What we know about the shooting death of Ahmaud Arbery. Nytimes.com. https://www.nytimes.com/article/ahmaud-arbery-shooting-georgia.html.

Foner, P. S. (1975). *History of Black Americans: From the Compromise of 1850 to the end of the Civil War (Vol. 3)*. Greenwood.

Fox 8 (2015). Dylann Roof confesses to killing 9 people in Charleston church, wanting to start "race war." https://myfox8.com/news/charleston-shooting-suspect-dylan-roof-confesses-to-killing-9-people/.

Fox 8 (2020). Montrell Jackson, Matthew Gerald and Brad Garafola identified as officers killed in Baton Rouge. https://myfox8.com/news/montrell-jackson-matthew-gerald-and-brad-garafola-identified-as-officers-killed-in-baton-rouge/.

Gabbidon, S. (2020). *Criminological perspectives on race and crime, 4th Ed.*, Routledge.

Gabbidon, S. L., & Greene, H. T. (eds.). (2013). *Race, crime, and justice: A reader.* Routledge.

Gabbidon, S. L., Penn, E. B., Jordan, K. L., & Higgins, G. E. (2009). The influence of race/ethnicity on the perceived prevalence and support for racial profiling at airports. *Criminal Justice Policy Review 20(3)*: 344–358.

Gabbidon, S. L., Penn, E. B., & Richards, W. A. (2003). Career choices and characteristics of African-American undergraduates majoring in criminal justice at historically Black colleges and universities. *Journal of Criminal Justice Education 14(2)*: 229–244.

Gaines, C., & Yukari, D. (2017, April 27). Here's how much money players lose when they fall in the NFL draft. https://www.businessinsider.com/nfl-draft-contract-values-2017-4.

Gay, R. (2016). Alton Sterling and when Black lives stop mattering. *The New York Times*. July 6. https://www.nytimes.com/2016/07/07/opinion/alton-sterling-and-when-black-lives-stop-mattering.html.

Gimbel, V. N. (2015). Body cameras and criminal discovery. *Georgetown Law Journal 104(6)*: 1581.

Gleeson, P. (2018, July 01). The average salary without a college degree. https://work.chron.com/average-salary-college-degree-1861.html.

goarmy.com (2020). Basic pay: Active duty soldiers. https://www.goarmy.com/benefits/money/basic-pay-active-duty-soldiers.html.

Gottfredson, M. R., & Hirschi, T. (1990). *A general theory of crime.* Stanford University Press.

Graham v. Connor, 490 U.S. 386, 109 S. Ct. 1865, 104 L. Ed. 2d 433 (1989).

Graham v. Florida, 560 U.S. 48, 130 S. Ct. 2011, 176 L. Ed. 2d 825 (2010).

Grasmick, H. G., Tittle, C. R., Bursik Jr, R. J., & Arneklev, B. J. (1993). Testing the core empirical implications of Gottfredson and Hirschi's general theory of crime. *Journal of Research in Crime and Delinquency 30(1)*: 5–29.

Grauschopf, S. (2020, September 25). What age of majority is and why it's important for sweepstakes. https://www.thebalanceeveryday.com/what-age-of-majority-means-its-definition-and-usage-882666.

GREAT (n.d.). Gang Resistance Education and Training. https://www.great-online.org/GREAT-Home.

Grimshaw, D. P. (2004). Living wage and low pay campaigns in Britain. In *Living Wage Movements,* D. M. Figart (ed.) (pp. 121–141). Routledge.

Guariglia, M. (2017). Perspective. "Blue lives" do matter – that's the problem. *Washington Post.* November 30. https://www.washingtonpost.com/news/made-by-history/wp/2017/11/30/why-blue-lives-matter/.

Hadden, S. E. (2001). *Slave patrols: Law and violence in Virginia and the Carolinas (Vol. 138).* Harvard University Press.

Hagedorn, J. M. (1994) Homeboys, dope fiends, legits, and new jacks. *Criminology 32(2)*: 197–219.

Hall, A. V., Hall, E. V., & Perry, J. L. (2016). Black and blue: Exploring racial bias and law enforcement in the killings of unarmed Black male civilians. *American Psychologist 71(3)*: 175.

Harper, C. C. & McLanahan, S. S. (2004). Father absence and youth incarceration. *Journal of Research on Adolescence 14(3)*: 36–97.

Hasler, J. P. (2009). Is America's space administration over the hill? Next-gen NASA. *Popular Mechanics.* May 26. https://www.popularmechanics.com/space/a4288/4318625/.

Helsel, P. (2015, September 9). No charges for Pasco police officers who killed Antonio Zambrano-Montes, man who threw rocks. https://www.nbcnews.com/news/us-news/no-charges-pasco-police-officers-who-killed-antonio-zambrano-montes-n424571.

Herbert, S. (1998). Police subculture reconsidered. *Criminology 36(2)*: 343–370.

Hermann, P., & Weiner, R. (2014, December 2). Issues over police shooting in Ferguson lead push for officers and body cameras. https://www.washingtonpost.com/local/crime/issues-over-police-shooting-in-ferguson-lead-push-for-officers-and-body-cameras/2014/12/02/dedcb2d8-7a58-11e4-84d4-7c896b90abdc_story.html.

Hill, E., Tiefenthäler, A., Triebert, C., Jordan, D., Willis, H., & Stein, R. (2021). How George Floyd was killed in police custody. Nytimes.com. https://www.nytimes.com/2020/05/31/us/george-floyd-investigation.html.

Hirschi, T. (1998). A control theory of delinquency. In *Criminology theory: Selected classic readings,* F. P. Williams, III and M. D. McShane (eds.), pp. 289–305, Routledge.

Hirschi, T. (1969). Key idea: Hirschi's social bond/social control theory. In *Key Ideas in Criminology and Criminal Justice,* T. C. Pratt, J. M. Gau, & T. W. Franklin (eds.), pp. 55–69. SAGE.

Hirschman, C., & Mogford, E. S. (2009). Immigration and the American Industrial Revolution from 1880 to 1920. *Social Science Research 38(4)*: 897–920.

Hoffower, H. (2019, September 11). Gen Z started building wealth earlier than millennials, and an expert says 9/11 is the main event that divided the 2 generations and their views on money. https://www.businessinsider.com/millennials-vs-gen-z-divided-by-911-different-money-habits-2019-4.

Horton, S. (2019). Understanding the 2017 "me too" movement's timing. *Humanity & Society 43*(2), 217–224.

The Houston Chronicle (2020). 19-year-old man charged with shooting at helicopters responding to fatal police crash. Police1. May 12. https://www.police1.com/investigations/articles/19-year-old-man-charged-with-shooting-at-helicopters-responding-to-fatal-police-crash-EcG195SzYpASiaKI/.

Houston Police Department (2020). Mental health division training. https://www.houstoncit.org/training/.

Houston Police Explorers (n.d.). http://www.houstonpoliceexplorers.com/p/about-hpd-explorers.html.

Howe, N., & Strauss, W. (2000). *Millennials rising: The next great generation.* Vintage.

Indeed.com (n.d.). How much does a driver make at Uber in Texas? Retrieved April 20, 2021. https://www.indeed.com/cmp/Uber/salaries/Driver/Texas.

Industrial Revolution (2009, October 29). https://www.history.com/topics/industrial-revolution/industrial-revolution.

International Association of Chiefs of Police (n.d.). The effects of adolescent development on policing. https://www.theiacp.org/sites/default/files/2018-08/IACP-BriefEffectsofAdolescentDevelopmentonPolicing.pdf.

Jackman, T. (2020). Attorney general launches presidential commission on law enforcement. *The Washington Post.* January 22. https://www.washingtonpost.com/crime-law/2020/01/22/attorney-general-barr-launches-presidential-commission-law-enforcement/.

Jauregui, A. (2021). HuffPost is now a part of Verizon Media. Huffpost.com. https://www.huffpost.com/entry/nypd-officers-dead-brooklyn-shooting_n_6360434.

Jauregui, A., Goyette, B., & Hart, A. (2014). 2 NYPD officers dead in Brooklyn shooting. Huffpost.com. https://www.huffpost.com/entry/nypd-officers-dead-brooklyn-shooting_n_6360434,.

Jones, C. A., Penn, E. B., & Davenport, S. (2015). Social distance between minority youth and the police: An exploratory analysis of the TAPS Academy. *Journal of Juvenile Justice 4*(1). https://www.ojp.gov/pdffiles/251064.pdf.

Justice.gov (2015). United States Department of Justice Civil Rights Division, Investigation of the Ferguson Police Department. www.justice.gov/sites/default/files/opa/press-releases/attachments/2015/03/04/ferguson_police_department_report.pdf.

Juvenile "Waiver" (Transfer to Adult Court). (2019, January 28). https://criminal.findlaw.com/juvenile-justice/juvenile-waiver-transfer-to-adult-court.html.

Katz, Jess (1995) Corrupt cops: The big sleazy? *Los Angeles Times.* March 8.

Keating, L. M., Tomishima, M. A., Foster, S., & Alessandri, M. (2002). The effects of a mentoring program on at-risk youth. *Adolescence 37*(148): 717–734.

Keegan, P. (1996, March 31). The thinnest blue line. *New York Times Magazine*: 32–35.

Kelly, J. (2020). Why young voters are embracing Bernie Sanders and democratic socialism. *Forbes.* February 5, 2020.

Kennedy, J. (1961). Presidential Inaugural Address, January 21, 1961. https://libquotes.com/john-f-kennedy/quote/lbv2n8b.

Kerpen, C. (2016, April 21). How has social media changed us? https://www.forbes.com/sites/carriekerpen/2016/04/21/how-has-social-media-changed-us/?sh=3cc50d55dfc4.

Kersting, K. (2004, July/August). Brain research advances help elucidate teen behavior. *Monitor on Psychology 35*(7): 80. https://www.apa.org/monitor/julaug04/brain.

Khamis, S., Ang, L., & Welling, R. (2017). Self-branding, "micro-celebrity" and the rise of social media influencers. *Celebrity Studies 8(2)*: 191–208.

KHOU-TV CBS (1978). Joe Campos Torres murder trial, Fred Rose 1978. https://www.bing.com/videos/search?q=ytube+joe+campos+torres&docid=607988298862167378&mid=81A684C2ABBA34F336A081A684C2ABBA-34F336A0&view=detail&FORM=VIRE.

King, R., & Spagnola, L. J. (2012). *The riot within: My journey from rebellion to redemption.* Harper Collins.

Kirk, D. S., & Papachristos, A. V. (2011). Cultural mechanisms and the persistence of neighborhood violence. *American Journal of Sociology 116(4)*: 1190–1233.

Klein, G. C. (2018). On the death of Sandra Bland: A case of anger and indifference. *Sage Open 8(1)*: 6. https://doi.org/10.1177/2158244018754936.

Koo, D. J., Peguero, A. A., & Shekarkhar, Z. (2012). The "model minority" victim: Immigration, gender, and Asian American vulnerabilities to violence at school. *Journal of Ethnicity in Criminal Justice 10(2)*: 12–47.

LaPuertorra69 (2011, February 5). *Teen suspect, Chad Holley, gets BEAT by Houston* [Video]. YouTube. https://www.bing.com/videos/search?q=ytube+chad+holley+video+beating&docid=608054016144509161&mid=5E9DD030F0D4DB1B09F15E9DD030F0D4DB1B09F1&view=detail&FORM=VIRE.

Laub, J. H. (2014). *Understanding inequality and the justice system response: Charting a new way forward.* William T. Grant Foundation.

Law & Disorder (n.d.). https://www.pbs.org/wgbh/pages/frontline/law-disorder/etc/cron.html.

Law Enforcement Exploring (n.d.). https://www.exploring.org/law-enforcement/.

Lawrence, C. (1987). The id, the ego and equal protection: Reckoning with unconscious racism. *Stanford Law Review 39*: 31–88.

Lawson, K. (2015). Police shooting of Black men and implicit racial bias: Can't we all just get along? *University of Hawai'i Law Review 37*: 339.

Lawrence, R. (2006). *School crime and juvenile justice, 2nd Ed.* Oxford University Press.

Lentz, S. A. & Chaires, R. H. (2007). The invention of Peel's principles: A study of policing "textbook" history. *Journal of Criminal Justice 35(1)*: 6–9.

Li, S. D. (2004). The impacts of self-control and social bonds on juvenile delinquency in a national sample of midadolescents. *Deviant Behavior 25(4)*: 351–373.

Lombroso, C. (1871). *White man and colored man: Lectures on the origin and variety of the human races.* F. Sacchetto.

Long, C., & Peltz, J. (2014, December 21). AP sources: Cops' killer angry at chokehold death. https://apnews.com/article/new-york-shootings-brooklyn-crime-eric-garner-132d998fa3044e84be53d09efbdc950b.

Longshore, D., Chang, E., & Messina, N. (2005). Self-control and social bonds: A combined control perspective on juvenile offending. *Journal of Quantitative Criminology 21(4)*: 419–437.

Love, D. A. (2015). Brown Lives Matter, Muslim Lives Matter. April 27. https://www.huffpost.com/entry/brown-lives-matter-muslim_b_6757280.

Lum, C. M., & Koper, C. S. (2017). *Evidence-based policing: Translating research into practice.* Oxford University Press.

Lumpkin, B. & Penn, E. (2013). Can police officers be effective mentors for at-risk youth. *Police Chief 80(3)*: 26–29.

Ly, L., Vera, A., & Ries, B. (2020, June 05). Dog returned to white woman who called police on Black man bird-watching in Central Park. https://edition.cnn.com/2020/06/05/us/amy-cooper-dog-returned-trnd/index.html.

Mallin, A. (2018). President Trump calls travel ban ruling 'a great victory' for the Constitution. ABC News. June 26. https://abcnews.go.com/Politics/president-trump-calls-travel-ban-ruling-great-victory/story?id=56172413.

Mark, J. (2020). Officers who killed Mario Woods used 'unnecessary force' — but will face no discipline. Mission Local. https://missionlocal.org/2020/09/officers-who-killed-mario-woods-used-unnecessary-force-but-will-face-no-discipline/.

Maslow, A., & Lewis, K. J. (1987). Maslow's hierarchy of needs. *Salenger Incorporated 14*: 987.

Masnick, G. (2012). Defining the generations. http://housingperspectives.blogspot.co.id/2012/11/defining-generations.html.

Matier, P., & Ross, A. (2016). Mario Woods' last moments: "You better squeeze that... and kill me." SFGATE. https://www.sfgate.com/bayarea/article/Mario-Woods-last-moments-You-better-6778777.php.

Maurantonio, N. (2014). Remembering Rodney King: Myth, racial reconciliation, and civil rights history. *Journalism & Mass Communication Quarterly 91*(4): 740–755.

McLeod, S. A. (2020, March 20). Maslow's hierarchy of needs. *Simply Psychology*. https://www.simplypsychology.org/maslow.html.

Meares, T. L. (2016). Policing in the 21st Century: The importance of public security. *University of Chicago Legal Forum 2*: 1–11. https://digitalcommons.law.yale.edu/cgi/viewcontent.cgi?article=6180&context=fss_papers.

Meares, T. L., & Neyroud, P. (2015). *Rightful policing.* US Department of Justice, Office of Justice Programs, National Institute of Justice.

Medlin, J., Ball, R., Beeler, G., Barry, M., Beaman, J., & Shepherd, D. (2016). Hurricane Katrina – August 2005. Weather.gov. https://www.weather.gov/mob/katrina.

Merton, R. K. (1938). Social structure and anomie. *American Sociological Review 3*(5): 672–682.

Middleton, J. E. (2020). Community Safety Education Act data summary: Randomized sample 2018–2020. TAPS Center for Research. https://www.tapsacademy.org/research/.

Miller v. Alabama, 132 S. Ct. 2455, 567 U.S. 460, 183 L. Ed. 2d 407 (2012).

Miller, L. S., Hess, K. M., & Orthmann, C. M. (2013). *Community policing: Partnerships for problem solving, 7th Ed.* Cengage.

Morgan, R., & Oudekerk, B. (2019). *Criminal victimization, 2018.* U.S. Department of Justice. https://www.bjs.gov/content/pub/pdf/cv18.pdf.

Morris, W. A. (1910). *The frankpledge system (Vol. 14).* Longmans Green.

Mulligan, T. S. (1992, May 21). After the riots: L.A. insurance claims will hit $775 million: Property: The figure makes the Los Angeles disturbances the most costly civil unrest in U.S. history. https://www.latimes.com/archives/la-xpm-1992-05-21-fi-477-story.html.

Mydans, S. (1994, April 20). Rodney King is awarded $3.8 million. https://www.nytimes.com/1994/04/20/us/rodney-king-is-awarded-3.8-million.html.

Nadeau, C., & Glasmeier, D. (2018). Living wage calculator. Livingwage.mit.edu. https://livingwage.mit.edu/articles/31-bare-facts-about-the-living-wage-in-america-2017-2018.

National Organization of Black Law Enforcement Executives (n.d.). The history of NOBLE. https://noblenational.org/history/.

National Association of Police Athletic/Activities League, Inc. (n.d.). National PAL: The world's foremost leader in engaging kids, cops & community. https://www.nationalpal.org/aboutus.

National Association of School Resource Officers (n.d.). Basic SRO course. https://www.nasro.org/training/training-courses/.

Neuhauser, A. (2017). Justice Department ends COPS Office review of police. usnews.com. https://www.usnews.com/news/national-news/articles/2017-09-15/justice-department-ends-cops-office-review-of-local-police.

Nunn, K. B. (2002). Race, crime and the pool of surplus criminality: Or why the "War on Drugs" was a "War on Blacks." *The Journal of Gender, Race & Justice 381*. http://scholarship.law.ufl.edu/facultypub/107.

Office of Juvenile Justice and Delinquency Prevention (n.d.) Model Programs Guide. https://www.ojjdp.gov/mpg/.

O'Kane, J. (2020). Finally we know Covid isn't the China virus but the Taig plague. https://www.irishnews.com/lifestyle/2020/10/24/news/jake-o-kane-finally-we-know-covid-isn-t-the-china-virus-but-the-taig-plague-2107065/.

Oppel Jr., R., Taylor, D. & Bogel-Burroughs, N. (2021). What to know about Breonna Taylor's death. January 6. Nytimes.com. https://www.nytimes.com/article/breonna-taylor-police.html.

Park, R., & Burgess, E.W. (1925). *The City*. University of Chicago Press.

Park, R. E., Burgess, E. W., & McKenzie, R. D. (1925). *The city Chicago*. University of Chicago Press.

Park, R. E., & Burgess, E. W. (1924). *Introduction to the science of sociology*. University of Chicago Press.

PBS (2018, February 16). Analysis: 10 ways we can prevent school shootings right now. https://www.pbs.org/newshour/nation/analysis-10-ways-we-can-prevent-school-shootings-right-now.

Penn, E. B. (2016, October). Responding to minority youth: Policing by TOTALS. *Community Policing Dispatch Justice Education 9(10)*. https://cops.usdoj.gov/html/dispatch/10-2016/responding_to_minority_youth.asp.

Penn, E. B. (Ed.). (2013). *Homeland security and criminal justice: Five years after 9/11*. Routledge.

Penn, E. B. (2003). Service-learning: A tool to enhance criminal justice. *Journal of Criminal Justice Education 14(2)*: 371–383.

Penn, E. B., & King, V. L. (2016, December 14). Moving police officers from enforcers to protectors. https://jjie.org/2016/12/15/moving-police-officers-from-enforcers-to-protectors/.

Penn, E. B., Greene, H. T., & Gabbidon, S. L. (eds.). (2006). *Race and juvenile justice*. Carolina Academic Press.

Perlstein, M. (1994). Officer had a history of complaints. *Times-Picayune*, December 7.

Pisciotta, A. W. (1983). Race, sex, and rehabilitation: A study of differential treatment in the juvenile reformatory, 1825–1900. *Crime & Delinquency 29(2)*: 254–269.

Platt, A. M. (1969). *The child savers: The invention of juvenile delinquency*. University of Chicago Press.

Police Magazine (2014). U.S. – number of serious violent crimes by youth 2018. July 13. Teen and Police Service Academy program earns Texas high school accreditation. http://www.policemag.com/channel/patrol/news/2014/07/13/teen-and-police-service-academy-program-earns-texas-high-school-accreditation.aspx.

Police Officers Association of Michigan (n.d.). Five behavior characteristics that tend to get cops killed. https://www.poam.net/train-and-educate/train-educate/.

Pollock, J. (2017). *Crime and criminal justice in America, 3rd Ed.* Routledge.

Postrel, V. (2004). The consequences of the 1960's race riots come into view. Ny-times.com. December 30. https://www.nytimes.com/2004/12/30/business/the-consequences-of-the-1960s-race-riots-come-into-view.html.

Prairie View A&M University (n.d.). College of Juvenile Justice and Psychology, Mission statement. https://www.pvamu.edu/cojjp/mission-statement/.

President's Commission on Law Enforcement and Administration of Justice (1967). The challenge of crime in a free society. A Report by the President's Commission on Law Enforcement and Administration of Justice. https://www.ncjrs.gov/pdffiles1/nij/42.pdf.

President's Task Force on 21st Century Policing (2015). Final report of the President's Task Force on 21st Century Policing. Office of Community Oriented Policing Services. https://cops.usdoj.gov/pdf/taskforce/taskforce_finalreport.pdf.

Quetelet, A.(1883/1994). *Research on the propensity for crime at different ages*. Anderson.

Quinney, R. (1970). *The social reality of crime*. Transaction.

Rabois, D., & Haaga, D. A. (2002). Facilitating police–minority youth attitude change: The effects of cooperation within a competitive context and exposure to typical exemplars. *Journal of Community Psychology 30(2)*: 189–195.

Ratliff, J. (1999). *Parens patriae*: An overview. *Tulane Law Review 74*: 1847.

Reiss Jr, A. J. (1992). Police organization in the twentieth century. *Crime and Justice 15*: 5–7.

Rendleman, D. R. (1971). *Parens patriae*: From chancery to the juvenile court. *South Carolina Law Review 23*: 205.

Rios, V. M. (2011). *Punished: Policing the lives of Black and Latino boys*. NYU Press.

Rios, V. M., & Vigil, J. D. (2017). *Human targets: Schools, police, and the criminalization of Latino youth*. University of Chicago Press.

Roberts, K. (2020). Kim Kardashian apparently makes $1 million per Instagram post. *Marie Claire*. https://www.marieclaire.com/celebrity/a27362936/kim-kardashian-makes-1-million-per-instagram-post/.

Rogers, B. (2013). Jurors convict HPD officer charged in Holley beating: Trial marks the end of a controversial saga. *Houston Chronicle*. June 12. https://www.chron.com/news/houston-texas/houston/article/Jurors-convict-HPD-officer-charged-in-Holley-4595716.php#:~:text=A%20Harris%20County%20jury%20on%20Wednesday%2C%20June%202012%2C, the%202010%20videotaped%20beating%20of%20teenager%20Chad%20Holle.

Roper v. Simmons, 543 U.S. 551, 125 S. Ct. 1183, 161 L. Ed. 2d 1 (2005).

Rosen, J. D., & Brienen, M. W. (eds.). (2015). *New approaches to drug policies: A time for change*. Springer.

Rothenberg, P. S. (2007). *Race, class, and gender in the United States: An integrated study*. Macmillan.

Sampson, R. J., & Bartusch, D. J. (1998). Legal cynicism and (subcultural?) tolerance of deviance: The neighborhood context of racial differences. *Law and Society Review 32*: 777–804.

Schuck, A. M. (2013). A life-course perspective on adolescents' attitudes to police: DARE, delinquency, and residential segregation. *Journal of Research in Crime and Delinquency 50(4)*: 579–607.

Serow, R. C. (2004). Policy as symbol: Title II of the 1944 GI Bill. *The Review of Higher Education 27(4)*: 48–99.

Shaw, C., & McKay, H. (1942). *Juvenile delinquency in urban areas*. The University of Chicago Press.

Shaw, C. R., & McKay, H. D. (1931). *Social factors in juvenile delinquency: A study of the community, the family, and the gang in relation to delinquent behavior for the National Commission of Law Observance and Enforcement.* US Government Printing Office.

Simons, J. A., Irwin, D. B., & Drinnien, B. A. (1987). *Psychology: The search for understanding.* West.

Slattery, D., & Chia, J. (2018, April 07). Trump takes veiled shot at Kaepernick, says NFL owners should fire kneelers: "Get that son of a b--- off the field." https://www.nydailynews.com/news/politics/trump-takes-veiled-shot-son-b-kaepernick-speech-article-1.3514708.

Smith, T. A. (2017). Police brutality: The statistics behind the peaceful protests. https://www.ny-criminal-defense-lawyer.com/police-brutality-protests/.

Snyder, S. A., Rahman, S., Hamilton, J. K., & Hamdi, H. T. (2017). The Eric Garner case: Statewide survey of New York voters' response to proposed police accountability legislation. *Journal of Social Service Research 43(1)*: 1–17.

Spotrac.com (n.d.). https://www.spotrac.com/.

Statista (2020). U.S.–number of serious violent crimes by youth 2018. September 28. Statista. https://www.statista.com/statistics/477466/number-of-serious-violent-crimes-by-youth-in-the-us/.

Steinberg, L. (2007). Risk taking in adolescence: New perspectives from brain and behavioral science. *Current Directions in Psychological Science 16(2)*: 5–9.

Stites, A. (2017). Bob McNair said NFL can't have 'inmates running the prison.' SBNation.com. https://www.sbnation.com/2017/10/27/16559952/bob-mcnair-houston-texans-nfl-owners-meeting-protests.

Strategies for Youth (2013, February). If not now, when? A survey of juvenile justice training in America's police academies. https://multco.us/file/48817/download.

Sullivan, J., Thebault, R., Tate, J., & Jenkins, J. (2017). Number of fatal shootings by police is nearly identical to last year. *The Washington Post.* July 1. https://www.washingtonpost.com/investigations/number-of-fatal-shootings-by-police-is-nearly-identical-to-last-year/2017/07/01/98726cc–b5f-11e–fc6-c7ef4bc58d13_story.html.

Suzuki, B. H. (2002). Revisiting the model minority stereotype: Implications for student affairs practice and higher education. *New Directions for Student Services 2002(97)*: 21–32.

Swadener, B. B., & Lubeck, S. (Eds.). (1995). *Children and families "at promise": Deconstructing the discourse of risk.* SUNY Press.

Sweeten, G., Bushway, S. & Paternoster, R. (2009). Does dropping out of school mean dropping into delinquency? *Criminology 47(1)*: 47–91.

Tatum, B. (1994). The colonial model as a theoretical explanation of crime and delinquency. *African American Perspectives on Crime, Causation, Criminal Justice Administration, and Crime Prevention,* 33–52.

Tea.texas.gov (2021). https://tea.texas.gov/academics/learning-support-and-programs/innovative-courses.

Teigen, A. (2020, July 1). https://www.ncsl.org/research/civil-and-criminal-justice/juvenile-age-of-jurisdiction-and-transfer-to-adult-court-laws.aspx.

Teigen, A. & McInnes, K. (2020). Juvenile age of jurisdiction and transfer to adult court laws. www.ncsl.org/research/civil-and-criminal-justice/juvenile-age-of-jurisdiction-and-transfer-to-adult-court-laws.aspx.

Tennessee v. Garner, 471 U.S. 1, 105 S. Ct. 1694, 85 L. Ed. 2d 1 (1985).

Texas Education Agency (n.d.). 2007–2008 PEIMS data standards.

Text – H.R.3355–3103rd Congress (1993–1994): Violent Crime Control and Law Enforcement Act of 1994. Congress.gov. (1993). https://www.congress.gov/bill/103rd-congress/house-bill/3355/text.

The Consequences of the 1960s Race Riots Come Into View (2004). Nytimes.com. https://www.nytimes.com/2004/12/30/business/the-consequences-of-the-1960s-race-riots-come-into-view.html.

The Economist (2014a). America's police on trial. December 11. https://www.economist.com/leaders/2014/12/11/americas-police-on-trial.

The Economist (2014b). Don't shoot. December 13. http://www.economist.com/news/united-states/21636044-americas-police-kill-too-many-people-some-forces-are-showing-how-smarter-less.

The Economist (2014c). On trial: What has gone wrong with policing in America. December 13. https://www.economist.com/weeklyedition/2014-12-13.

The Guardian (2018). Colin Kaepernick honored by Amnesty International for peaceful protest. April 21. https://www.theguardian.com/sport/2018/apr/21/colin-kaepernick-awarded-by-amnesty-international-for-peaceful-protest.

The History of NOBLE (2020). https://noblenational.org/history/.

The Inauguration of President Barack Obama (2009, January 21). http://archive.boston.com/bigpicture/2009/01/the_inauguration_of_president.html.

The Sentencing Project (2017, September). Fact sheet: Black disparities in youth incarceration. https://www.sentencingproject.org/wp-content/uploads/2017/10/Racial-disparities-in-youth-incarceration-fact-sheets.pdf.

The Washington Times (2016). Hillary's "implicit bias." Op. Ed. https://www.washingtontimes.com/news/2016/oct/3/hillary-clintons-implicit-bias/.

The Weed and Seed Strategy (2004). https://www.ncjrs.gov/pdffiles1/207498.pdf.

Tilly, C., Levett, A., Lodhi, A. Q., & Munger, F. (1975). How policing affected the visibility of crime in nineteenth-century Europe and America. University of Michigan Research on Social Organization Working Paper, p. 77.

Turner, D. (2017). Crack epidemic. United States history [1980s]. Encyclopedia Britannica. https://www.britannica.com/topic/crack-epidemic.

Tyler, T. R. (2001). Public trust and confidence in legal authorities. *Behavioral Sciences and the Law 19*: 215–235.

Tyler, T. R. (1990). *Why people obey the law: Procedural justice, legitimacy, and compliance.* Yale University Press.

Tyler, T. R., & Fagan, J. (2008). Legitimacy and cooperation: Why do people help the police fight crime in their communities. *Ohio State Journal of Criminal Law 6(23)*: 1–75.

Uchida, C. D. (1993). *The development of the American police: An historical overview.* Critical Issues in Policing: Contemporary Readings, 2nd Ed., pp.16–32. Waveland Press.

Ucr.fbi.gov (2019). Victims adult and juvenile age category by offense category homicide offenses. https://ucr.fbi.gov/nibrs/2019/tables/pdfs/victims_adult_and_juvenile_age_category_by_offense_category_2019.pdf.

Ulmer, J. T., & Steffensmeier, D. J. (2014). The age and crime relationship: Social variation, social explanations. In *The nurture versus biosocial debate in criminology: On the origins of criminal behavior and criminality*, Kevin M. Beaver, J.C. Barnes, Brian B. Boutwell (eds.), pp. 377–396, SAGE.

Uniform Crime Reporting (UCR) Program, Federal Bureau of Investigation (2014). https://www.fbi.gov/services/cjis/ucr.

University of Houston–Clear Lake (n.d.). Minor in youth and police studies. https://uhcl.edu/academics/degrees/youth-police-studies-minor.

Unnever, J. D., & Gabbidon, S. L. (2011). *A theory of African American offending: Race, racism, and crime.* Routledge.

U.S. Bureau of Labor Statistics (n.d.). https://www.bls.gov/.

U.S. Census Bureau.] (2015). The U.S. Census Bureau uses different constructs for the adolescent population dependent on the specific topic including 12–17 and 15–19. https://www.census.gov/content/dam/Census/library/publications/2017/demo/p20-579.pdf.

U.S. Census Bureau (n.d.). Population and housing unit estimates data. https://www.census.gov/programs-surveys/popest/data.html.

U.S. Census Bureau (2020). What is the 2020 census? https://2020census.gov/en/what-is-2020-census.html.

U.S. Department of Justice, Federal Bureau of Investigation (September 2012). *Crime in the United States, 2011.* https://ucr.fbi.gov/crime-in-the-u.s/2011/crime-in-the-u.s.-2011.

U.S. Department of Justice, Federal Bureau of Investigation (2018). *Crime in the United States, 2017.* Table 43. https://ucr.fbi.gov/crime-in-the-u.s/2017/crime-in-the-u.s.-2017/tables/table-43.

U.S. Department of Justice (2020). *Attorney General William P. Barr announces the establishment of the Presidential Commission on Law Enforcement and the Administration of Justice.* Press release, January 22. https://www.justice.gov/opa/pr/attorney-general-william-p-barr-announces-establishment-presidential-commission-law.

Varney, J. (1994). Trust in police vanishes as horror stories unfold. *Times-Picayune,* December 14.

Vitale, A. (2018). *The end of policing.* Verso Books.

Vogels, E. (2019). Millennials stand out for their technology use, but older generations also embrace digital life. https://www.pewresearch.org/fact-tank/2019/09/09/us-generations-technology-use/.

Walker, S., & Katz, C. M. (2012). *Police in America.* McGraw-Hill.

Ward, M. (2016). Whitmire wants schools to teach kids how to act during police stops. HoustonChronicle.com. https://www.houstonchronicle.com/politics/texas/article/Whitmire-wants-schools-to-teach-kids-how-to-act-9455091.php.

Ward, G. K. (2012). *The Black child-savers: Racial democracy and juvenile justice.* University of Chicago Press.

Watson, D. (2005). *Race and the Houston Police Department: 1930–1990: A change did come.* Texas A&M University Press.

Websdale, N. (2001). *Policing the poor: From slave plantation to public housing.* Upne.

Wermund, B. (2015, July 24). Program aims to reduce 'social distance' between police, youth. http://www.houstonchronicle.com/news/houston-texas/houston/article/Program-aims-to-reduce-social-distance-between-6404273.php.

Werner, L. (1984, December 08). U.S. sues on racial bias already illegal in deeds. https://www.nytimes.com/1984/12/08/us/us-sues-on-racial-bias-already-illegal-in-deeds.html.

White, M. D. (2014). Police officer body-worn cameras: Assessing the evidence. U.S. Department of Justice: Office of Justice Programs Diagnostic Center.

White, K. (1831). *Nat Turner's rebellion.* Gilder Lehrman Institute of American History.

Wilkey, R. (2013). Police shoot and kill Andy Lopez, 13-year-old boy carrying pellet gun. *Huffington Post.* October 23. https://www.huffpost.com/entry/andy-lopez_n_4152819.

Williams III, F. P., & McShane, M. D. (2018). *Criminological Theory, 7th Ed.* Pearson.

Williams III, F. P., & McShane, M. D. (1998). *Criminology theory: Selected classic readings.* Routledge.

Williamson, S. H., & Cain, L. P. (2011). *Measuring slavery in 2011 dollars.* www.measuringworth.com/slavery.php.

Wilson, W. J. (2012). *The truly disadvantaged: The inner city, the underclass, and public policy.* University of Chicago Press.

Wilson, W. J. (1999). When work disappears: New implications for race and urban poverty in the global economy. *Ethnic and Racial Studies 22(3):* 47–99. https://www.cnbc.com/2019/02/15/colin-kaepernick-reaches-settlement-in-collusion-case-against-nfl-lawyer-says.html.

Wilson, W. J. (1996). *When work disappears: The world of the new urban poor.* Vintage Books.

Wilson, W. J. (1987). *The truly disadvantaged.* University of Chicago Press.

Wilson, J. Q., & Kelling, G. L. (1982). Broken windows. *Atlantic Monthly 249(3):* 29–38.

Winter, M. (2013). Hundreds protest police killing of Calif. teen. *USA Today.* October 29. https://www.usatoday.com/story/news/nation/2013/10/29/santa-rosa-funeral-protest-youth-killed-by-police/3306875/.

Worldometer (n.d.). https://www.worldometers.info/coronavirus/

Wyche, S. (2016). Colin Kaepernick explains why he sat during national anthem. NFL. com. https://www.nfl.com/news/colin-kaepernick-explains-why-he-sat-during-national-anthem-0ap3000000691077.

Youth Voice on Recommendations for Police Reform (2020), June, Houston, Texas.

INDEX

Note: **Bold** page numbers refer to tables and *italics* page numbers refer to illustrations.

www.ingramcontent.com/pod-product-compliance
Lightning Source LLC
Chambersburg PA
CBHW070335270326
41926CB00017B/3874